ISBN 978-1-331-48088-4
PIBN 10195994

This book is a reproduction of an important historical work. Forgotten Books uses
state-of-the-art technology to digitally reconstruct the work, preserving the original format
whilst repairing imperfections present in the aged copy. In rare cases, an imperfection in
the original, such as a blemish or missing page, may be replicated in our edition. We do,
however, repair the vast majority of imperfections successfully; any imperfections that
remain are intentionally left to preserve the state of such historical works.

1 MONTH OF
FREE
READING

at

www.ForgottenBooks.com

By purchasing this book you are eligible for one month membership to ForgottenBooks.com, giving you unlimited access to our entire collection of over 700,000 titles via our web site and mobile apps.

To claim your free month visit:

www.forgottenbooks.com/free195994

Similar Books Are Available from
www.forgottenbooks.com

THE COMPANY AND THE CROWN

BY THE

HON^{BLE} T. J. HOVELL-THURLOW

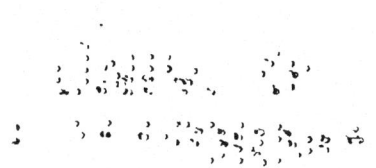

WILLIAM BLACKWOOD AND SONS

EDINBURGH AND LONDON

MDCCCLXVI

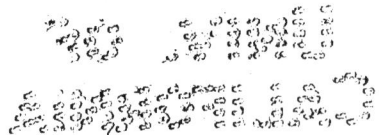

MUCH as has been written respecting what was termed in India the "Company Bahadoor," and those events in consequence of which the soil of Hindostan has now become encircled by the British Crown, it is still matter for regret that so little should be generally known of the scope and spirit of current Anglo-Indian administration. Great men of wide experience, representing every shade of human thought, have recorded volumes of opinions and decisions on each question as it has been born; while others, rich in the faculty of turning to account a rare research, have laboured at the almost hopeless task of teaching England how to know her Eastern Empire. Yet such of the results attained as are accessible to all, have rather tended to obscure than to enlighten general readers, while the opening for sensation writing, afforded by such thrilling themes as our trans-Indus wars, and the events of 1857, have too frequently been used as frames for highly-coloured pictures, drawn by able advocates of different schools and services. Thus,

512454

while in the daily intercourse of life it has become the general practice to confess an ignorance concerning India of which men would rightly blush on less important subjects, leading members of both Houses of our Legislature have frequently preferred to borrow doctrines of the hour advanced by public journals, rather than work out the sum of their own individual impressions. To endeavour to dispel the cloud of error which dulls the public eye on all regarding India has hence become a fair legitimate ambition ; and in this aim the present author ventures to submit a few remarks upon that country as it is, or rather was, when his position there enabled him to know the truth.

It may be thought by many, and the writer once thought himself, that information bearing on the individuality of public life, obtained while holding any kind of office, should remain unwritten history ; and no doubt some reticence is needed in discussing living men, while much responsibility attaches to each word so uttered. In the solution of such doubts the author was assisted by encouragement received from native friends in India ; and the following extract from a private letter, not meant originally for publication, addressed to him by one of the earliest natives chosen to take part in mixed Imperial legislation, was not without its influence on his decision :—

"Above all I have been touched by the proof, which the main subject of your letter evinces, of the high confidence reposed in my humble self by an alien in creed, in country, in manners, in race, and indeed in everything which distinguishes man from man, and my personal intercourse with whom was so suddenly cut short by the decree of Providence, and with the space of ten thousand miles between us at this moment. I only hope you may never have the slightest cause to regret this feeling. I very well approve of the idea of publishing your impressions of this country, and your observations on its politics and public characters; I always thought to myself you should do such a thing, specially remembering to what literary use another Private Secretary of Lord Elgin put his experiences with that nobleman in another part of the world. I can well appreciate your embarrassment at the manner of publication; that is a well-known puzzle with authors, and the puzzle increases to a tremendous extent when an author has to attend to the peculiarities of three different audiences, two in one country, and the third in another at the antipodes. Besides, a great deal of the success of a work depends on the manner of publication—indeed, the title of a book often leads to its popularity. I can understand your desire to bring your work well out before the Indian public, who alone can take the greatest interest in it, and who alone will heartily recognise the right which belongs to you from your antecedents to address them."

The title chosen tells its story for itself, and needs but little comment. The transition of the Government of India from all but boundless wealth, and a far larger measure of independence than is enjoyed by most members of the European family of nations, to utter bankruptcy and a struggle for existence all dependent on the mother country—this transition had come of dire necessity and not of man's selection. The life of the East India Company had died out as a tale that is told, and nought remained but debt and disaster, in which England had a deep and national share. Succeeding to the darkness of rebellion, the transition dawned upon Lord Canning with the light of breaking day, and his last years of power were spent in healing wounds of awful magnitude. This task, still incomplete, he left a legacy to Lord Elgin, whose previous life, spent as it had been in the reconciliation of conflicting creeds and races, appeared to the public of that time to offer the most solid pledges for the future.

Counting Lord Dalhousie, three college friends were called to govern India in succession. The first, who entered youngest on his duties, ruled eight—the second, six eventful years; while the reign permitted to the third but embraced the space of two. Yet, although differing in duration, these three periods resemble one another, in that each received and bore the impress of a ruling mind. The first period was characterised by almost ceaseless warfare and the wide spread of our dominion; the second, by alternate light and shade, the light occupying both foreground and far distance, the middle plane alone being bathed in shadow; the third was the calm that follows on a storm, affording time to the Indian people and their ruler to weigh the future in the balance of the past, to sink their differences in the appreciation of order and good government, and finally to meet together, the Hindoo and the Mussulman, the Christian and the Jew, to manufacture laws adapted to their general use. This last period it is, to which, in these pages, most frequent reference will be found.

CONTENTS.

THE COMPANY AND THE CROWN.

CHAPTER I.

THE GOVERNMENT OF INDIA.

MAHOMEDAN history relates that, in the year 1611, Jehangeer, Emperor of Delhi, granted a spot to some Englishmen on which to build a factory in the city of Surat; and that His Majesty introduced this company of white adventurers to his subjects by a proclamation, wherein it was announced that the English had a separate king independent of the King of Portugal, to whom they owed no allegiance, and that, on the contrary, these two nations put each other to death wheresoever they met. "At present," it was added, "owing to the good offices of Jehangeer, they are at peace with one another; though God only knows how long they will consent to have factories in the same town, and live on terms of amity and friendship."

The tale, however, of the rise of British India has been too often told to call for repetition at our hands. We

A

shall not therefore trace the gradual development of our
Eastern provinces and power, but shall at once proceed
to the consideration of some questions dictated by experience, and to the inquiry whether the existent state
of things is merely the result of progressive energy and
accident, demanding rearrangement rather than reform,
or the success and full achievement of a settled policy
pursued.   And in the course of these inquiries we shall
see first how, in early times, many of the greatest miseries
of India—miseries affecting both the rulers and the
ruled—were owing to the rapidly succeeding muster-roll
of men and policies whereby her destinies were guided, to
the full force of whose crotchets and ambition her whole
resources were exposed ; and secondly, how, in later days
of a more enlarged consciousness of the magnitude of
the work intrusted to us, everything has been too often
risked upon a vote of that great body of professional,
hereditary, and dilettanti legislators who constitute our
Parliament.   Incalculable as have been the benefits conferred upon ourselves at home by the gradual perfection
of the representative system and ministerial responsibility, there exists in the minds of few who know the
facts the shadow of a doubt, that the extension of Parliamentary control to the details of Indian administration
and finance is a measure as fraught with ill, as proved,
a hundred years ago, that similar assumption of power
to impose the taxes and impede the commerce of our
great western colonies, till then conspicuous for their
loyalty.

    Yet that was a lesson neither easily read nor likely
soon to be forgotten ; and it behoves us, if we will

not see its precepts lost, to study them by the light of our improved intelligence. Those who know India, and have had opportunities of appreciating her incomparable wealth and the industry of her people, will readily admit that conditions of government are alone required to enable her to reassert and justify her traditional position. Those to whom this confidence has become familiar will further confess that the actual policy of England toward her greatest vassal is not the one best calculated to attain such ends. The rule of the great Company was marked by much that was ignoble. Under the wings of her protection favourites sought paths to fortune unknown in other spheres of life; those whom birth or accidental causes entitled to support often embraced a career distasteful to themselves, with the certainty, not of rendering good service, but of reaping pensions and promotion. Yet this was perhaps rather the exception than the rule; and it is customary in these days to cast reflection upon the sons of competition, and to reserve praise and approbation for their more happy predecessors. Under the East India Company certain families had won and retained consideration; and although the sons and nephews might not approach in excellence or zeal to the examples set them by their uncles or their fathers, yet it often happened that a youth of twenty-two or twenty-three was sent to rule a native state, whose name alone acted as a talisman more powerful with those he had to govern, than any renewed assurances of goodwill dictated by the Government of India.

A system of administration which long withstood the

test of time, and rivalled sovereignty, could not be devoid of merit. For years and decades it was the custom to advance in argument the prosperity of India, in proof of the advantages of commercial government; and into so great security had the rich men of Leaden-hall Street suffered themselves to be lulled by Lord Dalhousie's eloquent success, that prudential measures of all kinds had been alike condemned. The result was inevitable. There had been no failure; the success had only been too manifest. In a vast peninsula, peopled by a hundred and eighty millions of inhabitants, teeming with caste prejudices and innate jealousy of white rule, it was impossible such blind confidence should pass unnoticed. Private reasons were not wanting for discontent among all classes; many harsh rulings, bad in themselves, but still more dangerous as precedent, had fanned and fed the flame. Neither Oude nor cartridges were the paramount causes of rebellion; unseen and unsuspected by us all it came, the inevitable result of too rapid a convulsion of the native mind. Our armies had advanced, and kings had quietly been swept away, their kingdoms incorporated with our possessions, barely calling for geographical remark. Then came the Crimean war and the rise in money; and the Company, ever avowedly a mercantile community, bethought itself of gain. The gain was its own, but it was of short duration. The clouds, long gathering, at length burst, and the Company, shortsighted in its unrivalled prosperity, shared the fate of those rulers it had dethroned.

"It was with strange feelings," we are told, "that

men who had served the Company from boyhood, coming home after the mutiny, fresh from scenes of war and
fire, razed forts and pillaged palaces, visited the East
India House, and wandered through the gloomy corri-
dors and deserted rooms, which they remembered to
have seen thronged with soldiers and civilians, clerks
and messengers, anxious and earnest on their several
errands. And few could help lingering in the Council
Chamber, and thinking of the men of bygone generations, who, by the sword or by the pen, had been instrumental in conquering India, and whose marble
statues stood in their lofty niches, with the dingy gilt
ceiling above, and the old-fashioned arm-chairs below,
once occupied by successive generations of potentates,
who, under the plain names of Chairman and Directors
of a London Company, had exercised a degree of authority over millions of people, to which that of the Doge
and Council of Venice in its palmy days was poor beyond comparison. Here the fate of emperors, kings,
and governors-general had been decided upon; here
the career of Clive and Warren Hastings had been
watched and criticised step by step; here the subsi-
diary system of Lord Wellesley, and the social reforms
of Lord William Bentinck, were discussed; and, lastly,
here the annexations of Lord Dalhousie were suggested
and applauded. Another turn of the wheel, and the
arm-chairs of the Directors were left as vacant as the
peacock throne of Delhi, and scores of other ivory
thrones or jewelled cushions, the lumber of extinct
power."

Such was that Company, whose greatness proved its

ruin. The first blow at its independence had, indeed, been struck by Pitt in the days of our fathers; but since then it had gathered more than former wealth, and girt itself around with conquests. Magnificent at all times as a monument of English energy, it was still grand in its misfortunes, and grander in its fall; and not until its doom was sealed did the country become cognisant of the responsibilities incurred. Yet, impossible though it be now to call in question the justice and necessity of this change, it is equally impossible to contemplate it without much mingled feeling of regret.

Of the revolt to which that Company's fall is due, we will not here repeat the oft-told history. Its horrors rank, in their intensity, second to few of bygone times; and thus, while Englishmen are found to fully justify all other risings of a creed or people against oppression, the peculiar cruelties of the Sepoy War have trampled under foot all sympathy and pity. So much, indeed, is this the case, that not only writers bidding for the public ear, but even some historians, have lost sight of the national character of the rebellion, and only treated it as mutiny. The struggle, though short, was long enough to prove the futility of all attempts to wrest our Indian dominion from us by force of native arms, and to show the stuff our men are made of. Some classes were, however, convulsed with fear — foremost among them the merchants of Calcutta. And so remarkable was this phenomenon of Englishmen trembling in inaction, as to call from the lips of Lord Elgin, who, at the time of India's need, came steaming up the Hoogly, the well-known words, " that all around stood blanched with fear save one, Lord Canning," whose fate it was to govern India during six long years, memorable of themselves, yet rendered more so by the calm deliberation and high courage by which so much has been averted.

The touching story of the personal attachment between those three successive rulers has been recorded in ' A British Friendship;' and we shall only seek to cast a clearer light on the part that each has played in Indian history. The antecedents of Lord Dalhousie had rather been commercial than political. Equally sound and brilliant in debate, his splendid talents had previously found scope in railway schemes and home administration. Yet, strange to say, once transplanted to Calcutta, his whole soul embraced by preference the paths of war and foreign policy. With Lord Canning the opposite was true. Bearer of an illustrious name, with associations specially belonging to the period when England's foreign influence stood highest, he himself chose peace and commerce, and, when permitted, devoted the entire energies of his nature to the material progress of the land he ruled. Men more opposite in all respects could hardly have been found, though some delight to look for traces of resemblance. Both were young, and both had giant powers, which both bestowed ungrudgingly wherever duty called; both had wives who fell sacrifices to their country's cause not less truly than had they died on fields of battle; both worked in the same vineyard, pursuing each his path of honour, each ending in an early grave ;—but here resemblance ceases. The outlines are the same—the lights and

shades contrasting strangely. Lord Dalhousie carved
an empire with the sword for Lord Canning to cement
with clemency.

Few reigns have dawned more brightly than Lord
Elgin's. The sun, so long obscured, shone lovingly
again on all throughout that broad peninsula. The
theory of our sword-rule had been reduced to bloody
practice, and the last years of Lord Canning's government had served to heal, though not to hide, the scars
the sword had made. A feeling not unlike contrition
had replaced fierce hatred. The last demand for vengeance on the Indian people for the crimes of 1857, had
been hushed by the cry of famine that rose up from
the North-West in 1860. To that appeal Great Britain
and her colonies had responded by a million of rupees ;
and Colonel Baird Smith, to whose unflinching zeal
the stupendous task of distribution had been intrusted,
had fallen a noble sacrifice in a noble cause. Finally,
with railways, seventy thousand British troops, and
unmatched artillery in European hands, we could at
length afford to adopt a less crushing policy towards
the natives. This opportunity had been not only
seized, but made the most of. Shaking off his early
bad advisers, Lord Canning had selected men of far
different stamp, who, less prejudiced, soon became the
skilful tools of a still more skilful master. To the disposal of accumulations Lord Canning's last year's toil
had been devoted, and to Lord Elgin was confided, one
March morning, a machine of government more perfect and harmonious than Asia yet had seen. But the
echoes of Lord Canning's last salute had hardly died

away when difficulties arose. Sir Bartle Frere became
Governor of Bombay; Mr Ritchie died; Mr Laing fell
ill; Mr Grey promoted to the Council, Colonel H. M.
Durand showed some slight symptoms of dissatisfaction; while the Home Department, intrusted to Mr
E. C. Bayley, was overridden by Bengal. In a word,
the reins of Indian government are so numerous, and
each horse becomes so well acquainted with the driver's
will, that any change of hand is fraught at first with
danger. The transfer to Lord Elgin had been accompanied by every favourable combination. The former
policy, a proved success, fell to one to whom it had
been specially indebted; and the author of our colonial
constitutions was a fitting instrument to carry out the
Queen's command, and call in native rulers to the
administration of her Eastern empire. The basis of
good government consists in insight into human hearts,
and tact in dealing with human weaknesses. Both
these qualities Lord Elgin possessed to an extent by
few surpassed; and with the knowledge that India
would not take his character for granted, he sought
the readiest mode of becoming familiar with its people.
In this spirit was undertaken that brilliant progress
so fatal to himself. At Cawnpore, Agra, Meerut,
Simla, he had addressed assembled chiefs in words of
easy comprehension, and after that his voice was heard
no more. Then in virtue of the Indian Council's Act,
Sir William Denison, the senior Governor, assumed the
Viceroyalty. His rule was short, and mainly remarkable for studied inaction; and if we except a cricket
match, to fight which a Madras eleven was ordered

up post haste, no measure of importance marks this period. Then came Sir John Lawrence ; the selection hardly calls for observation. The first civilian Viceroy inherited his office by an accident, and whether the experiment will merit repetition must depend entirely on the measure of its success.

Any attempt to describe the nature and the attributes of the society over which Sir John Lawrence was thus called to reign, must almost of necessity fail to render to the general reader a fair conception of the reality. More than twenty different and distinct classes enter into its elementary composition, and each of these is so varied and intensified by the peculiar circumstances attending any change in persons and in things, as to baffle every effort at an ordered classification. There are officials, and the crowd of non-officials. The former are divided into members of the covenanted and uncovenanted civil, military, naval, clerical, and legal services ; the latter counts within its ranks bankers, merchants, planters, missionaries, travellers, and adventurers, and all these put together form but one tint in the social rainbow of Calcutta ; for, in addition, high-capped Parsees, turbaned representatives of both prevailing native creeds, mixed Eurasians of every shade, deposed dynasties, whose object seems to be to sink the little that remains to them of Oriental noble blood in the vices of our importation—these almost countless particles meet together each day on the Maidan of Fort-William. The Viceroy of the hour is the axis on which they all revolve, and by the precedent which he establishes are decided the claims of this or that colour or religion to intimacy in their dealings with ourselves. The deposed royal family of Mysore, being in practice renegades from their ancestral faith, accept of European dinners. Their royal brethren from Oude, who pollute with their numerous presence the fair retreat of Garden Reach, now vainly strive to attain to a like pre-eminence in degradation. The young King of Oude indeed, and his wily ex-Wuzeer, Ali Nucki Khan, are seen at times at evening parties in Calcutta, and sometimes condescend to ride or drive in Eden Gardens with a white acquaintance; but the memory of their family crimes is still too recent to admit of much good-fellowship. The question of the admission of natives into English drawing-rooms is surrounded with much that is difficult and much that is obscure. In the eyes of Eastern princes, our dances, our dresses, our conversation, and all that constitutes the intercourse between the sexes, is so strangely at variance with their own notions of propriety, as to render it impossible to present to them a picture of European life at which they would not cavil. From the time of Lord William Bentinck it has been attempted to educate them in our ideas, and the mutiny with its sorrows did not obliterate this practice. No doubt the system received a rude shock by the conduct of the favoured Azimoolah and of his brutal master of Bithoor; but the ladies of Burdwan did not on that account absent themselves from the picnics and parties on the lake to which they were invited by the Croesus Maharaja of the place; neither did Lord Canning thenceforth on that account with-

hold his invitations from those entitled by imme-
morial usage to attendance at the Viceroy's balls; and,
strange to say, it remained for one of Indian antecedents and of known philanthropy, of cast-iron faith
in native virtue and the deepest sympathy with missionary enterprise—in a word, to Sir John Lawrence
—to trace a line and say, Thus far shall the native
come in contact with ourselves, and no farther.

The step thus taken by Sir John Lawrence at the
outset of his viceroyalty, whether right or wrong, was
retrograde, and as such affords cause for great regret.
It was a blow struck at the native social character, in
such a manner as to go home to those most intimate
with Europeans, and most partial to the aspect of a
white man's court.   And in every eye it assumed the
more significance as coming from a friendly quarter,
from one whom natives deemed allied to them by every
instinct engendered by the daily commerce of more
than thirty years.   Though the pride of the dominant
race might be flattered by watching the shadows as
they formed on the downcast heads of highborn natives,
excluded from their presence, and turned away from
Government House, somewhat roughly perchance, by
a white policeman, who took a coarse pleasure in his
ungrateful task; yet the reflecting element could but
regard with sorrow as an evil omen society thus
officially divided, and recast according to its primitive
colours, by the fiat of a former servant of the Company.

Thus such is the condition of Indian affairs that, in
great things as in small, all depends upon the nature
of the men in power.   The present system of subser-

vience to Westminster that clogs each wheel of ponderous Government machinery with reference and delay, has only tended to enhance this truism. A Governor-General, to do aught to-day, must have a taste for opposition, and an almost total disregard of what they say at home. Yet the manly and consistent attitude maintained by Sir Charles Wood throughout the course of the last few years, in meeting Parliamentary clamour for Indian Reform, has not received sufficient recognition. Power must remain with some, and perhaps, pending the complete development of the Indian Council's system, it was in good keeping in his hands. However this may be, one can but admire the firmness and ability with which he has succeeded, against the determined opposition of the services and Parliament, in constituting himself, as Secretary of State, sole exponent of the Royal pleasure where India is concerned. The history of the world affords but few examples of such mass of power being given to one man. For years the map of Hindostan lay prostrate at his feet; and though, in the interest of truth, one must confess that kicks, when wanting, have not been spared, it is equally incumbent on us to record our fixed belief, that, at least in Native questions, his policy ever has been such as to sow the priceless seed of restored confidence in England's loyalty, and this alone is a service of no common order. The vast powers thus centred in a single human will, cause the question of who may, or who may not, be Sir Charles Wood's successors, to be fraught with anxiety to millions of our fellow-subjects. Will they cancel certain military measures—will they permit to the so-called Supreme and Local Goverments under them any independent action, and if so, how much? These are indeed weighty considerations, the true importance of which can only be appreciated by those possessed of personal acquaintance with the interests at stake.

The fact is, that Sir Charles Wood's measures have been of three classes totally distinct, and the success of two has been so signal as to stifle criticism of the third. An English member of the House of Commons, rich indeed in home experience, but wanting in all local knowledge, had undertaken to dictate the laws, restore the finances, and gather up the fragments of the army, of our Indian empire. The result we deem a wonder of our days. The laws prescribed are daily gathering strength and popularity. The finances have acquired an elasticity unrivalled in our times, and the fragments, to all appearance neatly swept together, have so deceived the eyes of Parliament, as to pass for a construction perfect in proportion and design. Yet to those who know the truth in military matters, the melancholy patchwork is self-evident, and it but remains for time to scatter broadcast, and remodel on a sound and healthy footing, those martial institutions whose best interests have been so rashly dealt with.

In India the so-called legal question had always been one of unusually difficult decision. Under the Company, might too often took the place of right, and the doctrine that the country had been got, and must continue to be held, by the sword, never lacked supporters. In the opinion of those indeed who knew the country best, there was much truth in this assertion. The native mind is strangely fitted to evade our justice. The weapon of false witness is especially its own. Each Vakeel or native pleader has at his beck and call a well - trained phalanx of professional perjurers. In native cases of importance the mass of oral and spurious documentary evidence adduced in court, would utterly bewilder an English judge and jury; and the relative value of the oath of men of different shades of creed and colour has ever been much canvassed. The Company went no doubt too far in favour of white evidence; and in those days an Englishman could practically ill-treat natives with impunity. Now, if we err, it is on the other side, and the white are often at the mercy of their native plunderers. Hindoos and Mahomedans, possessing their own social codes and notions of what is right or wrong, care little for our forms of swearing witnesses; and though in remote Mofussil districts, where natives and white men dispense the laws and justice of the land upon an equal footing, one meets with more regard for truth than in the Presidency towns, yet even there corruption thrives to an extent incredible.

Many Indian statesmen have devoted great talents and research to the framing of one law for British India; and all attemps as yet have failed. The most successful efforts are unquestionably those of Sir Charles Wood's reign. The establishment of the High Court, and the introduction of the circuit system, are great experiments, both of which seem likely to succeed. These measures found an earnest advocate and zealous executor in Mr Henry Sumner Maine, who was appointed Legal Member of Council after the death of the lamented Mr Ritchie.   Mr Maine was a man of feeble constitution, but most refined and cultivated intellect. His home career had been more occupied with literary labours than the active branches of his profession.   His contributions to the 'Saturday Review' and other critical papers, were always masterpieces of taste and style, and his well-known work on ancient law had finally secured to him an honourable and lasting place in the literature of his country.   Mr Ritchie had risen gradually to the summit of his aspirations, through the long and crooked, though profitable, paths of the Indian bar, while Mr Maine's first experience of the East dated from his appointment to the Council.   He lost not a moment, however, in mastering the intricacies of native law, and at Lord Elgin's instigation became associated with Mr H. B. Harington in the revision of our Indian Penal Code—a colossal undertaking, well worthy of the energies of two such untiring jurists.   Moreover, at that time the conditions of Hindoo polygamy, and the establishment of a Divorce Court in India, were eagerly discussed, and, in addition to his other labours, the consideration of these subjects devolved on Mr Maine.   To the solution of such problems he brought great talents, with zeal of no common order ; and in all confidence the Indian public watched these complicated tasks intrusted to his care.

The new High Court was constituted under principles most calculated to render it a popular institution. Its ranks absorbed civilians like Messrs Seton Karr and Campbell, of tried and eminent ability, for whom executive appointments equal to their claims could not at the time be found. Its doors were also open to barristers from home, and on its bench two new and startling precedents had been adopted. Natives were to be appointed to this high tribunal, with power to judge our countrymen in criminal as well as civil cases; and, for the first time, natives of high rank became entitled to the same emoluments as their English colleagues. The effect of this was quite electrical, and throughout Bengal the native public prints teemed with praise at the happy omen. It was clear, however, that as regards the native question, the chances of success or failure depended on the men selected. The statutes of the court had been thus liberally framed, bearing in view a man of proved integrity and parts. Ramapersad Roy was a name, at the very sound of which corrupt vakeels or pleaders quitted court. He was without price, and the office had been made for him; but ere the letters patent had reached Calcutta he had died. Sumbhoonath Pundit Roy Bahadoor indeed was found to reap the honours invented for another; but the new High Court went forth shorn of its greatest ornament.

Thus strictly following in the track prescribed to him, Sir Charles Wood's best endeavours have been directed towards reconciliation. The wounds were so deep and recent that all his skill was needed; but the result has been that Indians, great and small, regard the " Maharaja Wood of Westminster " as a certain cure for all political disorders. Yet this triumph, incomparable as it is, has been dearly bought—bought at the cost of much native prestige in our local institutions, previously regarded with the respect due to tribunals from whose decision there practically existed no appeal.

His conduct of finance was not less bold or happy. Not sharing in the ill-timed fear of humiliating our Anglo-Indian services, a special man was found for a very special duty, and Mr Wilson went to India. What has since happened is well known. Mr Wilson lived just long enough to invent machinery for other hands to work. Those then at Calcutta will not have forgotten the feeling of despair that took possession of their minds, when, one evening of unusual heat and dust, the enfeebled society of that capital, issuing from their air-tight houses to take their short hour's drive, learnt the worst they long had feared. Never strong, and always overworked, Mr Wilson had gone forth, at an advancing age, to act a part whose grandeur he alone could properly appreciate. He soon broke down, and shortly after died—a fresh instalment of that mortality so fatal to the interests of India in England.

Mr Samuel Laing was his successor; and though neither the equal nor the prototype of Mr Wilson, this is a name Indian history should not utter without praise. Vast abilities, and home-bred fundamental knowledge of finance, enabled him to hold his own against all comers, and his short term of office was singularly prosperous. Cautious in manner, distinguished for readiness in argument and writing, much was his that an Indian statesman needs. One great quality he lacked—forgetfulness of self; and as successor to a man like Mr Wilson this want was the more conspicuous. Mr Laing was a man whom all commercial undertakings do wisely to employ. He could speak, defeat adversaries, record minutes of unusual length and force, and challenge opposition with unvarying success. To him it mattered little whether chemistry or his Aryan brothers formed the subject of an evening lecture; his powers were flexible, and, equally at home in finance or poetry, he never failed to please. Whether such versatility of thought, and, we may add, of action, fitted him to the same extent for the performance of State offices, may remain question for remark. All we know is, that during his tenure of his post he gave at least local satisfaction. The circumstances under which he quitted India never to return have been long and largely discussed, and of that controversy more than enough has seen the light. Faults there were on both sides; Sir Charles Wood and Mr Laing both forgot that each had pride; neither made concessions, and the weaker fell. By submission Mr Laing might have served his adopted country longer, but by independence he really served it most.

And then it was that even Sir Charles Wood hesitated. The powers in part given, part assumed, by the Financial Department had grown so rapidly, that an autocrat in England might well begin to deem the sacrifice too great. In his council there were, however, many who, though Bengal civilians, fully recognised the value of outsiders; and to others, who were loth blindly to admit this principle, public opinion had found means to whisper the well-known name, Trevelyan. Smarting,

perhaps, still under the lash of his recall, official idleness had become intolerable to him; the place was
offered and accepted; and one of the greatest Secretaries
our Treasury has seen, one whose familiarity with India
dated from his childhood's first ambitions, was duly
named Financial Member of the Viceroy's Council.
His experience of Madras, no doubt, enabled him to
avoid more readily the rocks on which his predecessor
split; and the spirit in which his duties were undertaken
left nothing to be desired so far as Westminster was
concerned. With the Government of India, properly
so called, the case was different; and all the tact and
wisdom of his local master were needed to restrain his
accumulated zeal. Tall and worn, but of iron frame,
he landed in Calcutta to replace Mr Laing's shadow of
his former self. Such was his energy, that barely had
Fort-William's guns announced his advent, ere he
sought and found an opportunity to lay before his colleagues schemes for all kinds of radical improvements.
With each branch of home and foreign administration
he was all familiar: some hobbies were indeed his own,
and those he rode to the death. Such was the immediate removal of the seat of Government to some
unknown region situate in Central India, watered by
some as yet unnavigable river, on whose banks, according to Lord Canning, all grew that white men want, and
beneath whose soil both coal and marble should abound
to an extent unknown. His arguments and eloquence
were such that the Council, fully acquainted with the
evils of Calcutta, remained dumbfounded, all save its
President, Lord Elgin, who, at all times eager to arrive

at knowledge, naturally solicited more accurate details before consenting to transplant to a mythical land the whole machinery of Government. Such an exodus for a site but vaguely dreamt of could only have embarrassed all, and most of all Sir Charles Trevelyan, the very existence of whose department was dependent on Bengal.. Neither were schemes for education wanting; and here, again, Madras experience came into play. In short, his energy and reputation, always great, and certainly the former greater since his fall, rendered him singularly calculated to embarrass a superior. The scope of his labours could not be confined even within the pliant limits of Finance: no passing mention of his measures can form an outline of his aims, and we can only deal with the most prominent as they may occur.

While touching on finance, it may not be amiss to contemplate a moment the class of local men in trusted with it. In the Company's days its special character had not been ignored, but rather the reverse; and the conservative nature of directors' patronage had almost gone so far as to constitute the conduct of accounts an office for which hereditary claims were deemed the fittest qualification. Thus it was that when a vacancy occurred, a member of the house of Lushington was sought; and if one could be found of decent antecedents he was generally pitchforked into power. At the demise of the Company many Lushingtons were thus bequeathed to us, and with them their supposed facility for figures; and though it is true that upon the departure, superannuated, of one member of this happy family, justice was done by Lord Elgin to a singularly able, zealous public servant, who for long years had played an up-hill game in this exclusive walk; yet shortly after, strange to say, the old tradition re-asserted its prerogative, and upon Mr Drummond's appointment to the Lieutenant-Governorship of the North-West Provinces, a Lushington was his successor as Financial Secretary to the Government of India.

Sir Charles Trevelyan, among his Treasury predilections, appears to have harboured a pet project for a system of exchanges between India and Whitehall; and no doubt the plan possesses many merits. Yet the rules of the Civil Service proper retain so much of their exclusive character, that a so-called "uncovenanted officer" of junior grade still occupies a place well-educated Englishmen object to. An instance of this recently occurred, when a well-bred scholar, after trial, finding all doors to advancement shut against him, and he himself condemned to the work, and much of the society, of a class of writers known as "native Christians," neither remarkable for talent nor morality, reluctantly exchanged his Indian prospects for such work as he could get at home, with smaller pay, but the position of a gentleman.

The third class of Sir Charles Wood's measures demands more careful scrutiny. His military policy has failed to an extent the more apparent when compared with his successes in other branches of the public service. The misfortunes of our Indian army, during the years it has been helpless in the hands of home authorities and Horse Guards prejudice, have attained to a pitch only rendered possible by a fatal war resulting in the utter bankruptcy of India's proper share of independence. Thenceforth all not personally interested welcomed any change, however fraught with wrong, that promised to relieve the land we live in from enhanced financial burdens, without neglecting the integrity, or, we might more truly say, recovery, of our Eastern rule.

The night of mutiny was long and pitifully dark. During its continuance it had been barely possible to watch the fortunes of the few on whom we all depended; and when morning dimly broke—the storm yet raging with increasing fury, the waves of war still lashing our frail bark, and the rollers of rebellion surging past to melt in foam upon the rugged Punjab strand, that, acting as a breakwater, was at once our greatest danger and sole chance of safety, and beyond which the waters, thick and turbid still, were calm enough to allow of rest to the exhausted and diminished crew who had fought with death and conquered,—then, indeed, all who could appreciate the past did dread the future. Cadres of British officers were all remaining of our native army. So long as actual fighting lasted their value had been priceless; with the energy of despair they had formed themselves in bands of heroes, against whose prowess all attacks proved vain; outnumbered many times, they had cut their bloody way through countless hosts of enemies; and now that all was over, England felt they had done well their country's work, and honours and rewards were freely showered on them. It was not long, however, before all became aware of their anomalous position. The army-list showed rolls of names to whom death had dealt promotion, and who for a time found occupation in stamping out in far-off districts the last embers of revolt. Then suddenly arose the cry of bankruptcy, and each rupee was watched in circulation and grudged to our defenders : yet a little, and was born that word " amalgamation :" offspring of economy and wrongs, it proved the parent of embarrassments untold, a fruitful source of misery to many, of jealousy to all.

In those days India was in everybody's mouth, and two men's names were paramount. Both were abused, each in the country of his residence, and both, abroad, were prophets. Lord Canning, who at the earliest moment had stayed the hand of butchery, had reaped the reward of those who interpose between soldiers and success ; the very merchants, recovering their colour, now clamoured for revenge ; and the natives, crushed in their turn by our heavy heel, not unnaturally regarded the head of Government as the source of their misfortunes. With Sir Charles Wood the case was different : not strictly popular at home, enough had happened to heap odium upon one so singularly well placed to prove the scapegoat of a nation's crimes ; whilst in India, his consistent care of native interests had placed him on the pinnacle of their hopes for future favours. The demand for amalgamation had been very general. Having fought and died together, there arose between the Queen's and Company's armies a feeling that each was not unworthy of the other : neither was this feeling purely sentimental ; each saw, or thought he saw, a positive advantage in such union. To English officers who had devoted time and opportunities to the study of native languages and character, the broad preserves of Indian administration should at length be opened; and Indian officers were not loth to serve the Queen and wear her lace, with the prospect of improved position when circumstances should call them home; neither were they blind to the advantages implied in changes and exchanges from India's dusty camps to Aldershot or Chobham. Thus, in a way and for a time, the scheme was positively popular, and only more inquiring minds read the mutual sacrifices such a measure must entail. Among the endless difficulties besetting its consideration, ranked primarily pensions, funds, and local service claims., Then there was the fact of the commission money, by means of which our English pay could only be compared to interest on capital invested; and the purchase system, though indeed existing in both armies, was conducted in so different a manner as practically to preclude comparison. With the special arms, or branches of our services, the question appeared to offer more ready promise of solution. Original gratuitous cadetships might be held of equal value, whether received from Queen or Company; and conditions as to special training for an Indian or a home career might easily have been dictated. However this may be, the means employed seemed such as to baffle opposition; and, armed with a royal warrant, Sir Charles Wood went forth, ostensibly to deal out royal favours with a lavish hand upon distinguished men, himself most ignorant of what lay before him. The position was one really forced upon him, and not of his selection. It was a task which fell to him as an item of his daily labours : great as it was, to have hesitated might have displayed cowardice or want of confidence in the powers that God had given him. Neither of these feelings was likely to deter Sir Charles Wood; and he commenced with characteristic energy to call together men, and establish data for his guidance.

Among the men so called together was one whose name can hardly be too prominently recorded. As adjutant of his regiment, not many years before, young Norman had become remarkable for bearing, zeal, and knowledge of his work. Selected by Lord Clyde, he had served in offices never previously committed to one so young in years. Called by the rapidly-succeeding deaths of three superiors to act as Adjutant-General to our army before Delhi, General Nicholson and he together had grappled with and overcome the greatness of that crisis. Although his honours had been reaped on others' graves, both pen and sword were ever in his hand; and to those who knew him then and fought beside him, his name will be inseparably connected with Metcalfe's ruined house, and that intrenched position on the heights commanding Delhi where Hindoo Rao once dwelt.

Indeed, all who could shed light on the obscure questions to be dealt with were earnestly addressed, and all responded by reports embodying their private hopes and fears, and breathing opposite advice. Sir James Outram and Sir William Mansfield, with junior officers like Colonel Baker, each had his say, and all the doctors differed. Commission sat upon Commission, and the work advanced but little. The patience of the Horse Guards had been sorely tried—action of some kind had become essential; and at length in despair some ready pens put certain figures down on paper which, aiming at a compromise with all, eventually pleased none. A basis thus established, much was hurried over, and still more omitted altogether. Then came the Staff Corps, which, with its painful changes and uncertainty, has wrought more wrong and deceived more minds than aught else we know of. The establishment of a Staff Corps originated in a known necessity—the only question was the mode of execution. The knot was so entangled, and had been tied by such countless hands, that cutting seemed the only remedy. Time pressed, moreover, so the sharpest sword was sought. That sword was Colonel Norman's. The blow was bold, and dealt with skill; the tangled skein parted at its centre, and for a time all hoped a conjuror had done it, and that the threads, proving of equal length, might all be worked up without waste. This hope, like many others, was doomed to bitter disappointment. The immediate pressure was, indeed, removed—amid whispered approbation the expectant crowds had vanished—but the real difficulties of the situation had practically increased tenfold.

It happened that most of the heads of the Indian army had profited in some measure by amalgamation, and that rewards for recent service had reached the higher grades of officers and won their silence for a time at least; hence the junior captains and subalterns were those who really suffered most, and it was exactly they who naturally were least consulted, and whose opinions, when expressed, received least consideration. Thus it is, also, that as these grew from boys to men they awoke to a consciousness of wrongs that now are uttered and repeated each year with increasing force. Neither can it be lost sight of, that in practically endeavouring to obliterate all former service claims and regimental pride, the Government has been guilty of a policy as unwise, and calculated to estrange the army, as those measures of the Restoration, when the tricolor, with the names and numbers of distinguished corps, gave place to the Bourbon flag, and to a series, perfect, indeed, in arithmetical progression, but wanting in those grand associations upon whose wings the eagles had been borne to Moscow and Madrid.

Thus it was with the " Bengal Engineers," who had ever been conspicuous for talent and distinction. Thrice weeded, those who withstood the test of such a crucible might well boast of merit. The merit was theirs, and they were duly proud of it. No service had produced a greater number of brilliant representatives. In peace and war her sons had sought and found a field of action worthy of themselves. Equally great in practice and in theory, many of the highest administrative offices of India had almost become hereditary to them. They possessed a powerful identity not easy to erase ; they were ripe, at least, in glory ; so their doom was sealed : the scythe went forth, they were gathered into the royal ranks, and since have been forgotten.

Of military measures two more only call for immediate remark. First, the oft-quoted breach of faith in the want of observation by the Indian Government of the gracious terms of the amalgamation warrant; and, secondly, the establishment of the Military Finance Department, to whose tender care was handed over all that remained of our former Indian army. The first has been so much discussed and fully proved, that few lines will serve to record our deep conviction that the royal word has not been kept. Quite recently, and with perhaps the best intentions, a Parliamentary Committee sat on this inquiry; some evidence was taken, and the matter was dismissed with certain unimportant observations. In such questions all depends upon the composition of the Committee, and the one to which reference is made was singularly calculated to defeat the objects aimed at by its authors.

The Military Finance Department had its origin in economy. Its childhood had been passed in those days when, as has been said, each rupee was watched in circulation; and even later, when fortune smiled again, its object was not so much to check excess in some departments as to reduce the estimates of all without reference to obligation or utility. For the sole control of this machine, under the personal authority of Lord Canning, a man of obstinate ability had been selected and armed to the teeth, with power and promise of support. Colonel Balfour appeared upon the stage of past extravagance. For some two years he conducted the work of pruning with a knowledge of detail only exceeded by his zeal in execution. To him succeeded Major Mallison. The writer of 'The Red Pamphlet' was not likely to shut his eyes to facts, and his conduct of military finance proved worthy of his name and reputation.   Lord Elgin wrote, on Colonel Balfour's resignation, that " a man who, right or wrong, saved his country several millions, well merited some reward." And thus it was with Major Mallison, who, in the discharge of duties specially unpopular, ever sought to reconcile the support of the finances with the interests at stake.

CHAPTER II.

THE MINOR PRESIDENCIES.

THE relations between the Government of India and the Minor Presidencies of Madras and Bombay have never been very clearly traced. Many efforts have indeed been made to obtain from home a definition of their respective authority and independence; but the wisdom of leaving each separate question to be decided upon its own merits, and of maintaining the general responsibility of every one concerned, is so apparent that such demands have been ever met with silence or evasion. In matters of prerogative, a person whose position is uncertain is naturally most susceptible; and thus, though this system has no doubt produced great public benefits, it has also been the cause of much personal hostility. In former days, when Indian mails went round the Cape, the fact of a Hastings or Cornwallis watching, for aught he knew, an early opportunity of meddling, might often tend to keep a sleepy Governor awake; and it must at all times be a comfort for a Governor-General to have it in his power to turn his weary eyes from the contemplation of his own measures to the more pleasant occupation of criticising others. Again, whenever it so occurred that a really happy understanding existed between supreme and local governors, each did his work the better for a little constitutional encouragement. Fortunately this was the case when Lord Harris ruled Madras and Lord Canning was in India. Their friendship dated from their school-days; each occupied the place for which his talents fitted him; both had a modest unspoken consciousness of this, and all went well. The antecedents of Lord Harris were colonial, and in Madras he found a field more ready for the seed he had been used to sow than would have been the case in any other part of India. The people of his kingdom were more industrious and agricultural than Hindoostanees properly so called, and not even the events of 1857 could rouse them from their apathy in things political. Moreover, many causes had conduced to render the Madras troops the most stanch in their allegiance. Not only were they of lower caste and less open to religious impulse than the Sepoys of the other Presidencies—not only had they known us longest and watched with envy our successive conquests over the warlike races of more northern India, to whose hard terms they had so often bent—but they, and they alone, had, owing to their maritime position, full opportunities of judging of our vast resources. Yet the fact that the nature of this people is not prone to mutiny, does not detract from the credit due to Lord Harris, who, knowing them as a ruler should his subjects, turned his knowledge to the best account, and, by dismantling his own Presidency of both guns and men, enabled

Lord Canning and Lord Clyde to reconquer Northern India.

Lord Harris was succeeded by Sir Charles Trevelyan. Much has been already said of him, but more remains to tell. Bred to the Indian Civil Service, he had mastered young the elements of native thought, and to the perfection of this study he had since devoted such leisure as belongs to London office life. Education was a subject on which, in England, he had bestowed much labour, and its Eastern branches were those he specially delighted in. It was therefore natural that he should turn his earliest attention to these considerations, and the result was such that during his year's local government he paved the way to most of our subsequent Indian educational reforms. One thing, however, he could not brook—interference; and least of all in matters of finance. Hence arose that well-known opposition which Mr Wilson's measures met with at his hands; and when the local sway over income and expenditure became, by a stroke of Mr Wilson's pen, reduced to a simple question of account, Sir Charles Trevelyan could no longer hold himself, and solemnly recorded his insubordination. In the struggle that ensued, as usual the weak went to the wall, and Sir Charles returned to England, in disgrace indeed with his employers, but not without the consciousness that, short as was his tenure of Madras, it had yet proved long enough to stamp his name indelibly on the history of India.

Sir Charles Trevelyan was a man not easy to replace. His appointment had been viewed as the reward of

genius. In boldness of design and energy of execution
no one was his superior ; and, added to these qualities,
he possessed an earnestness of manner, and a thirst for
learning, singularly pleasing to those he had to teach.
In conversation he appeared ever to take for granted
that all were equal to himself. With attainments most
remarkable, and thoughts most varied, that seldom failed
to find the happiest expression, he combined a practical
philanthropy, which made him love his fellows. In
those social attributes which tend to make the stranger
feel at home, the partner of his household almost rivalled him, and the union of the two was almost calculated
to take popularity by storm. By natives, soldiers, merchants, and civilians in Madras, he was equally beloved.
He was, in short, a type of what a governor should be ;
and local enthusiasm reached its highest pitch when all
within that jealous presidency learnt how resistance to
Calcutta had proved his ruin. From that moment he
became to the eyes of millions a martyr in a people's
cause, and he left their surf-bound shores amid more
tears and honest expressions of regret than we have
ever known bestowed upon a presidency ruler.

His recall thus caused a gap not easily filled up.
Yet some one was required who, while possessing such
abilities as might command respect, and not pave the
way to unnecessary comparisons, should yet be ready
to act in all things in conformity with the prescriptions
of his masters. Such a man was the late Sir Henry
Ward ; and, moreover, he was almost on the spot. As
Governor of Ceylon he had but to cross the Paumben
Channel to land within the limits of Madras. Besides,

his term of service in Ceylon was drawing to a close, and he had established claims to future confidence not easy to ignore. In him, therefore, centred all requirements, and to Madras he went—alas, to die! His reign was counted but by weeks; for scarcely had he trod the promised land of India, and embraced her mighty interests, than he paid with death his life's promotion. After him came Sir William Denison. Born of a family whose widespread branches have furnished pillars to both Church and State, Sir William first entered on a soldier's life. Later called to civil government, his last laurels had been reaped in practical Australia; and though his Young-England notions were not exactly those most fitted to find favour in Conservative Madras, yet knowledge of detail and fixity of purpose soon gained for him, if not the hearts of all, at least the fear of many.

In point of climate, Madras, though more southerly, is superior to Bengal, and, many say, even to Bombay. To the English traveller the first sight of the low dark outline of its land, fringed with a foaming belt, is not indeed inviting; but to an Anglo-Indian its never-failing evening sea-breezes are invaluable. Of these sea-breezes Madras reaps full benefit, while the same fresh air, before it can reach the exhausted inhabitants of Calcutta, must cross some hundred miles of swampy sunderbund, thence gathering most noxious exhalations. None who have ever known Calcutta can forget how anxiously all watch soon after sundown for the coming of that fatal wind. During the warmest months it hardly ever fails—it comes, and the temptation is not to be withstood. Doors and windows, hermetically sealed since daybreak, are thrown open, and the white man's bed is placed within the range of the cool though deadly air. At Madras the case is altogether different. The salt wind blows each night upon you untainted by the strip of sand it has to traverse, and you wake refreshed, without having inhaled with your dose of daily life the seeds of those disorders so fatal to humanity. In another point of view the comparison has hitherto been drawn in favour of Calcutta. Both presidency cities have native suburbs or bazaars ; both partially surround our dwellings ; and both are death's preserves. To the so-called "black town" of Madras the palm of dirt has been awarded. Native cleanliness is purely a matter of religion, and Bengalis are equally straitlaced in ablution and theology. On the other hand, science has done much within the precincts of the black town, while the rich municipality of Calcutta has as yet effected little. In the interest of truth, however, it must not be omitted that while Calcutta lies on the low banks of the hideous Hoogly, whose successive tides defeat the aims of drainage, Madras is so situated as to render problems of this nature comparatively easy of solution.

Thus Fort St George, with all her failings, has ever been a favoured presidency ; and, landing there, Sir William Denison found all ready to his hand; for, thanks to the ability and zeal displayed by Mr Morehead, who during repeated interregnums had administered the government, its springs had not worn rusty. Distance from England, the character of her people, and her secondary commercial weight, have contributed to render Madras more independent of home direction than either of her sister presidencies ; and within those limits which financial pressure first prescribed, her governors were practically absolute. Bengal claimed the precedence of wealth, and was rightly termed the Company's "milch cow." Politically speaking, from the time she had become a British appanage, Bombay perhaps had been most prized. The possession of Madras was an accident secured to us by other accidents, and as such we held it firmly, but cared little how. She paid her way, though not much more ; but her troops, not dreading the salt-water, soon became a valuable auxiliary in the execution of our Eastern destiny. In Burma, China, and the Andamans their value has been fully tried, their courage never failing, and they have thus become essential to our national defence.

The jealousy prevailing in the so-called benighted Presidency has been chiefly caused by the mode pursued in conducting her political relations. Mysore has been a constant source of discord. Literally surrounded on all sides by the influence of Fort St George, her Commissioners have received their nomination and instructions from Bengal ; thus greatly tending to disparage the proper weight of all advice to other native neighbours dictated by Madras. But the peaceful nature of the different tribes upon the Malabar and Coromandel coasts is now happily so marked, that all those races, whether speaking Canarese or Tamil, have embraced our rule and governance as the best security to undisturbed possession of the produce of their fields. In this policy of confidence in British honesty a

noble example has been set them by the learned
Raja of Travancore, who, furthest from the seat of
power, has been the first to recognise the benefits our
sway confers. Unfortunately for us, the geographical
position of his State is such as to restrict the sphere
of his utility within the narrowest compass. Half-sur-
rounded by the ocean, his north-eastern frontier was
his only source of foreign wars and friendships. His
wisdom has prompted him to choose the latter; and,
devoting all his energies to development at home, and
his hours of leisure to the study of our language and the
Eastern classics, he has lived a life " sans peur et sans
reproche." His great attainments and domestic virtues
have more than once suggested him for the Viceroy's
Council, as a fitting member for Madras; but circumstances, proverbially impatient of control, have built up
difficulties in the stronger claims of others from more
northern India; and Travancore, though raised to the
rank of Knight of the Star of India, has not as yet
achieved the aim of his ambition.

It was the good fortune of Sir William Denison to
be associated with Sir Hope Grant as his Chief Commander, and the association was of mutual advantage;
for while Sir William in civil matters learnt to count
for firm support upon his military adviser, Sir Hope,
in those measures of professional reform which are his
soul's delight, found his surest advocate in the Governor himself. Thus, with exceptions to be counted on
one's fingers, they worked unjealously together, and the
result of such harmonious action in both branches of
the executive has proved of good incalculable. The at-

mosphere of Colonial Government is singularly prone, however, to awaken strong opinions with class and service prejudices. Of these it would be false to say Sir William Denison had none; and to say that such a man had lived long years and bred no home convictions, would indeed be damning with faint praise. Yet his prejudices were comparatively innocent, and especially confined to things he ought to know with reference to his own professional education. Thus works of public utility or improvement never failed to stir up in him a longing for personal activity. But, as ill-luck would have it, the Public Works Department, involving large expenditure, had become dependent on Imperial finance, and all schemes of any magnitude required the Viceroy's sanction. At the other end of this constitutional checkstring sat, once, Colonel Yule, and later, Colonel Strachey; they were Lord Canning's choice, and had fully justified selection. During the administration of the former, things worked tolerably well for Colonel Yule was a man of large ambitions, and left the mode of execution more in local hands than his successor chose to do; but after his departure, the Madras Public Works Department, fretting under Colonel Strachey's somewhat heavy hand, more than once displayed symptoms of impatience. In such affairs as these it is that a Viceroy's tact has fullest scope and value, and that a few conciliatory words, spoken or conveyed in private letters, suffice to cool down local wrath, and thus avoid the necessity of reference to England, with entailed delays, and scandal generally proportionate to the measure of publicity acquired.

Horseflesh, again, was a subject on which Sir William Denison held strong opinions of his own; and here he was at issue with his general. The mounting of our Indian army has been a much-debated ground, and the rival merits of Arab and Australian blood have never lacked supporters. To rulers fond of riding, the question of the stud is sure to recommend itself, and Sir William Denison was no exception to the rule. In some degree it might appear that antecedent causes had swayed his judgment; for, conscious of his Walers' points, he seemed to shun a closer intimacy with Arabs. Thus landing in Madras with his horses and his preconceived opinions, he at once engaged in equine controversies, and with all his natural energy espoused Australian interests; while Sir Hope, with equal force and more experience of fact, upheld the Arab cause. The problem, however, was too involved for any definite solution. Each race possesses its own qualities, and both are fully prized; but, thanks to this amicable variance, the general question of the mounting of our Indian army has at length received due prominence and consideration.

Amid such practical issues as these, Sir William Denison spent his five years' tenure of Madras; and it is not too much to say, that under him advance was made in every branch of human industry known to a singularly domestic and peace-loving people. Of this people we shall now take leave, and, quitting the pleasant shades of Guindy Park, we shall proceed to Bombay Castle by what is termed the Beypore route. Were it not that Bombay at this hour can well afford

to hold her own as a half-way house between London
and Calcutta, it might be necessary to enter at some
length into the demerits of a scheme which once received some share of public favour. But train and rail
and cotton roads have lately made such rapid strides,
that a project of communication between England and
Bengal which should add to other perils of the deep
the danger of additional discharge of cargo upon an
iron-bound coast, with a second embarkation in an open
roadstead where the Peninsular and Oriental Company's
steamers do not always guarantee the landing of the
mails, may well afford to pass uncriticised.

A Governor of Bombay ought to be a happy man.
Nearest to England of all our Indian rulers, he gets
his letters and his papers at earlier dates with greater
regularity. The climate is quite tolerable, and with
average ability he must have it in his power to render
the long tropical days too short for his requirements.
Custom has awarded to him a constant change of
residence, more recognised and varied than the Governor-General himself enjoys ; and, regarding Bombay
as his axis, he pleasantly revolves between Matheran,
Parell, Mahableshwar, and Dapoorie, according to the
exigencies of the seasons, and as his health demands
sea-breezes or the Hills. Surrounded by Mahrattas
and Beloochees, his political reports usually forestall in
interest the perhaps more careful letters of the Government of India. Until the other day he had besides
at his absolute control a navy whose proportions and
equipment rank second to none afloat in Eastern
waters. This arm of power, however, has not escaped

the policy of extermination applied to local services whom special fitness for a special duty disqualified for absorption and amalgamation; and with few exceptions, —such as the "Ferooz,"now become the Viceroy's yacht —those teak-built men-of-war are now reduced to guard-ship and to transport duty. Their service mostly lay in the Red Sea and Persian Gulf, and Mohammerah and Bate have proved that they were equal to per-form it. Extravagance, not incompetence, was the crime imputed to them, and the Admiralty offered to do the work for less. The bait was too tempting to be refused at a time of general embarrassment, and par-tial and imperfect schemes of compensation to those deprived of lucrative and honourable employ were hurriedly sketched out. Here, as with the shore services, the elders had the best of it, and many got pensions on more favourable terms than they could otherwise have expected. Neither had the very junior officers much to cavil at. They, many of them, got, at the age of twenty, retirements of some sixty pounds a-year, with permission and facilities to serve their Queen in other walks of life. Those hardest dealt with were the non-commissioned officers and men of ten years' service ; for, if we except inadequate gratui-ties, the only consolation they received was the un-welcome information that, in all measures for the general weal, experience has taught that some at least must suffer.

Thus died Her Majesty's Indian Navy, and with it passed away much of the influence of a Bombay Governor over the lawless tribes that fringe the neigh-

bouring coasts. Prominent amongst the reasons why
such influence should have been most jealously preserved, ranks the fact that in it lay the surest means
of securing adequate defence along the line of our
Gulf Telegraph, which, after years of labour, the energy
of Colonel Patrick Stewart succeeded in perfecting,
only just in time to flash as its first message the
sudden news of his own death in the moment of the
most complete success. For many hundred miles this
wire is laid upon the wildest coast, inhabited by mur-
derous races whom fear of consequences alone has
taught to tolerate our friendly intercourse. The landing, sinking, and hard work attaching to the construction of this line, were mainly left to Indian naval
officers, as most conversant with those shores; and
when, at cost of life and treasure, their task at last
was done, its future was intrusted to the fleeting influence of a visit now and then from some Royal
Navy ship, whose captain might neither be acquainted
with the character and language of the people dwelling on those burning sands, nor feel himself bound
up professionally with the credit of the interests ac-
cidentally confided to his care.

A Royal Navy vessel goes on a given station with
general orders to oppose or afford protection to certain
stated objects. To the exercise of this power her captain brings experience of perhaps every other quarter
of the globe to that in which he may be called to act.
In war and navigation this is perhaps a matter of less
consequence; but when the nature of the duties ap-
proaches nearer to, or at least combines, political with

other work, special qualifications, such as knowledge
of locality, would appear of some importance. This
we deem essentially the case in Gulf and Red Sea
service; and, pending proof, we must acknowledge
hesitation in accepting as a gain the trifling saving
introduced by the abolition of a system which always
did thoroughly and well whatever task fell to it by
reason of the force of special circumstances.

Before permanently dismissing the subject of our
Indian Navy, some mention should be made of two
men deserving record. The name of the last Commo-
dore who hoisted the broad pennant of the Company was
Wellesley, and Rennie was his last flag-captain. This
latter calls for most remark. In younger days, upon
those seas wherever danger most abounded his hard
face was seen. He was remarkable for those qualities
and failings so often common to great mariners. With
an oath on his sunburnt lips he had led his sailors to
success in expeditions whose title to temerity would
inevitably have been proved under weaker guidance.
He loved desperate attempts, and seemed to lookers-
on to breathe with greatest ease the atmosphere of
war. In proportion as smoke thickened, and the din
of battle drowned all other sounds, his clear voice rang
more cheerily with words of bold command. In time
of peace his temper was not always equal to the
monotonous confinement of a ship, and his talents had
procured for him the charge of the Marine Department
in Calcutta. There his energy of character found
ample scope for outlet. Earliest in attendance at his
office, he was last to leave the whist-tables of Chow-

ringhee, and seldom failed at daybreak on the course to watch his racers take their morning's exercise. But in Bengal even Captain Rennie's cast-iron constitution could not stand this life for long, and from time to time he took sick leave to England, at last returning to Calcutta only to retire on the abolition of his office.

The history of late Bombay Governors hardly affords such salient points for observation as that of Bengal or Madras; they have come and gone more quietly, and in more regular succession, most serving their full time. Lord Elphinstone's career has been ably sketched in two telling lines by Mr Kaye. In mind and manners he was the very essence of personal distinction; and though his early youth was more remarkable for social than political success, yet, rapidly promoted to a government, he proved himself a ruler of uncommon wisdom. Sir George Clerk next demands attention. Lord Elphinstone had been essentially a governor by birth; Sir George was one by education. His earliest honours had been won among the rank and file of the Bengal Civil Service, and, gradually rising to the surface, he had constant opportunities of judging of those classes whom later he was called to rule. He twice was Governor of Bombay—before and since Lord Elphinstone—and between those reigns, and after their completion, his time was passed in counselling at home. In 1861, ill-health a second time compelled his resignation, and then it was Sir Charles Wood made perhaps his happiest appointment. To fill the vacant throne a man was chosen known to all in India as a pattern of vigorous intelligent refinement. A civilian of Bombay extraction, whose ideas had been enlarged by experience in Bengal, he had become Lord Elgin's senior councillor. Throughout the trying times of 1857 he had displayed a courage only exceeded by his modesty, and tempered by his chivalry to natives of all creeds and classes. Sir Henry Bartle Frere belonged to a race of men wellnigh extinct in modern days. To courtly bearing, and all that fascinates the eye, he added a facility of thought clothed in simplest language that seldom failed to bring conviction. But beneath his smooth and silky touch and style there lurked a firmness of decision and tenacity of will which natives seemed to learn by intuition. Arriving at his post, he found a practised Council, well composed, and in Sir William Mansfield, the Commander-in-Chief, he had a colleague who, with management, was priceless. All know Sir William Mansfield who are acquainted with the times they live in, and few words will serve to introduce him. In both Sikh wars of 1846 and 1848 he had played a conspicuous part, and when the Russian war broke out, his merits claimed for him high political employment. In the Crimea and at Constantinople his reputation was thus tested and enhanced, and on the Peace of Paris in 1856 he was sent as Consul-General to Warsaw. Although civil, and specially financial, matters were his delight, yet he knew that war was his profession, and in 1857 he again returned to India. A grateful country has not been slow in recognising the services he then rendered as Chief of Lord Clyde's Staff, and shortly after their conclusion he was appointed Chief Commander in Bombay. It has been said above that he, with management, was priceless; with Sir Bartle Frere as Governor this condition was secured; and Sir William's constant craving to dive beyond a constitutional depth in finance and policy, was steadily met with courteous tact, and forced to find legitimate vent in lengthy minutes of singular ability.

The great political influence that Bombay wields in Cabul, Central India, and Rajpootana, owes its steady increase and development to many different causes; the principal of which are geographical position, and the gradual diffusion among natives of the knowledge that the so-called Supreme Government is not supreme at all, but, like local governments, the faithful mouthpiece of a man in Westminster. Commercial interests have also greatly tended to augment her wealth and weight; and the cotton crisis, with its attendant consequences, has at length opened the eyes of all to the real value of Bombay. We say of all—but there are still exceptions, in whose foremost rank are found the old school of prejudiced Bengal civilians; and these it is who really coin the obstacles to a change of seat of Government, which could but have as one of its effects the conversion of the rich preserves of Bengal patronage into outlying provinces, only prized for their production of indigo and opium.

This change in the seat of Government has been most seriously discussed, but seldom with sobriety. Sir Charles Trevelyan's hurried manner, and somewhat crude suggestions, only served to create unnecessary alarm, while others of the school of Messrs Grey and Beadon have hedged the scheme around with fictitious difficulties and dangers. The truth, as usual, lies between the two extremes of treatment. The change must come, but should not be rashly undertaken till all details are well matured. Suggestions have not been wanting with reference to selection of a site; some have urged Simla or the Neilgherries; and while some have advocated the necessity of a maritime situation, others, with Lord Canning, have recorded preference for a central capital equidistant from our coasts. No doubt that all, more or less, are warped in their opinions by the circumstance of their position, and the wise are those who best conceal the prejudices inherent to their office. Thus it is to dictates of common sense rather than elaborate arguments that we prefer to look for guidance on this point, and we hold that these lean conclusively towards Bombay.

In the execution of this change it would be necessary to transfer the prestige of a separate presidency from Bombay to Bengal Proper, the former being retained under the immediate supervision of the Viceroy. We deem that this solution of the difficulty would afford a prospect of reconciling honestly, and at least expense, more of the opposed interests at stake than any other scheme which has hitherto been broached. In Calcutta a Governor would find wide choice of machinery and accommodation awaiting his selection, the superfluous being sold at profit to the State. The Colonial Office might perhaps at last be made to undertake the charge of Singapore; and Bombay, retaining Aden, Burma, and the Andamans, might rest subject to Calcutta. On Bombay buildings might be spent the profits of Calcutta sales, and if done judiciously, this would produce an ample total of requirements. Sea-carriage would be open to all that needs removal, and much of doubtful matter might be temporarily left until its want was felt. A special train or two might convey those councillors and secretariats whose labours could not brook the interruption of a voyage, and the move might thus be carried out with great facility, and none of the embarrassments accompanying a transfer to an unmade place.

CHAPTER III.

THE LIEUTENANT-GOVERNMENT OF BENGAL, SUBORDINATE TO
THE GOVERNOR-GENERAL IN THE HOME DEPARTMENT.

To Lord Dalhousie's annexations and protracted absences from Calcutta was owing the establishment of
a separate Bengal Government; his object being to
provide for the administration of the Lower Provinces
without reference to himself, that he might devote his
energies to perfecting the non-regulation system in the
Punjab and other recent acquisitions. The result was,
that an excessive measure of responsibility and power
was dealt out to Bengal, and it has been said that Lord
Dalhousie himself regretted later the extent of independence granted.   In the framing of the Bengal
statutes, however, a careful clause had been inserted, by
which the Governor-General should have the power at
any time of redefining the position of that Government and reassuming patronage as experience might
dictate.   Now patronage is power, and from the moment that Bengal acquired control over all the members
of her civil service, the Governor-General became
throughout those provinces an institution to which
men no longer looked for honours and promotion.

Although Lord Dalhousie and his successors fully felt the mischief of this system, it has happened that circumstances have hitherto prevented any practical advantage being taken of the saving clause above referred to. Lord Dalhousie, doubtless, did not like so soon to cancel or revise a measure of his own. Lord Canning cared, personally, little for dispensing patronage, and without previous experience in government it took a Governor-General some time before he awoke to the consciousness that his customs duties were collected by another, and that even his 'Gazette' was printed in a Bengal office, over which he exercised no direct control. Then came years of struggling for bare existence, when Lord Canning's hands were full, and then a time when men were willing to be satisfied with life and peace at almost any price; and shortly after came Lord Elgin with rumours of a change of seat of government, which embarrassed him still more than other causes had his predecessors.

The correspondence between England and the Indian Government is carried on as follows : The Secretary of State consults his so-called councillors or colleagues, among whom the routine of office is partitioned according to their special antecedents. Thus, military affairs would be referred to soldiers, and political to others—though in theory all remain alike responsible. Such advice the Secretary of State by Act of Parliament is compelled to seek; the extent to which he follows it depends upon himself and the confidence reposed in him. Despatches to the several Presidency Governors-in-Council are signed by him alone—these despatches, on receipt, are circulated by a Governor for perusal of his Council, each ordinary member usually affixing his initials. The conduct of departments is here, again, practically intrusted to professional members — the theory of a general responsibility being preserved; and by them replies and letters reporting progress are drawn up, the more important being circulated for approval in draft form. These letters, when finally prepared, are signed by the Governor-General or Governor, and by each ordinary councillor in the order of his seniority. They are then made up in the several secretariats to which subjectively they may belong, and despatched to the Secretary of State, by whom the spirit of the Indian Councils Act requires they should be handed to his constitutional advisers.

A knowledge of the difference between ordinary and extraordinary councillors should not, perhaps, be presupposed. It consists in the permission given under the Indian Councils Act to the Viceroy and Presidency Governors to call to their aid, when sitting for purposes of legislation, a certain number of non-official members selected from all classes of native and European society. Unlike ordinary councillors, such members draw no salary in virtue of their office, but serve for personal distinction like members of our House of Commons—the prefix Honourable being awarded them. Their term of office is limited by law, but, this term expired, they are eligible for reappointment. In other words, the ordinary members of our Indian Councils alone are charged with the executive, while extraordinary or additional members attend only meetings held for legislative purposes.

Legislation is conducted in the Home Department. Native members have the privilege of speaking in their own language, official translators being present. The public have access to the deliberations, and accommodation is provided for reporters of the press. Such Parliaments exist in Bombay and Madras, while Calcutta boasts of two—those of Bengal and the Government of India; and the Councils Act provides for more, as the Punjab, or North-West, may ripen into constitutional activity. A great difficulty is sometimes felt in defining what is matter for local or supreme legislation. In questions like finance, which have become Imperial departments, this difficulty exists no longer; but in such questions as waste lands or education, it once or twice has happened that the Councils of India and Bengal have legislated simultaneously in opposition to each other, thereby creating great embarrassment. A remedy for this has now been found in a provision, by which the Viceroy's sanction is essential to all bills discussed in local Councils; and this system, though requisite no · doubt, has much enhanced the labours of a Governor-General and the inherent jealousies of minor Governments.

The ordinary or Executive Council of a Presidency, of which the Commander-in-Chief is *ex officio* a member, usually meets its Governor once a-week for the despatch of business, when secretaries attend in turn to take their orders. Legislative meetings are convened twice a-year or more, as necessity requires, and usually sit until accumulations are disposed of.

Such are Indian Councils in their ordinary and extraordinary character. They are forcing-beds for the imported seed of representative government. In Asia this has been a plant of most uncertain growth, and constant watching is required to remove the weeds that tend to choke its natural development. The Indian Councils Act was a supplement to the Legislation "for the better government of India" of 1858, and became law in 1861. Its aims were gradually to acquire a real knowledge of the country's wants, and to educate natives of high standing and acquirements to a sense of our desire that they, like other subjects of our vast dependencies, should learn to rule themselves. The struggle through which India had passed had so unstrung society, that few loyal natives who could be deemed representative men were left in any class of life. Some time thus elapsed ere the measure could be carried out. Those were days of punishments and rewards, and Lord Canning was the only arbitrator competent to judge which chief had trimmed his sails so as to merit slight or favour. In very many cases the claims were nicely balanced, though the merits of one or two were happily so conspicuous as to banish hesitation. Thus the Puttialla Maharaja had been the ready instrument of reducing Delhi; he had kept our camps supplied when our friends were counted on our fingers and our enemies untold; under his enlightened sway his state, moreover, had attained to a condition of prosperity unrivalled in the Punjab. He was of the highest caste, and yet least bigoted; and to these claims he added an imposing stature and a truly kingly bearing. To him, then, Lord Canning made one of his earliest offers of a seat in Council, and the offer was accepted, though not without expressed objections to visiting Calcutta. The Puttialla Maharaja was her Majesty's first Punjab member, and overcoming, to please us, his strong prejudice against Bengal, he twice visited Calcutta to attend the Viceroy's Council. On both occasions he was treated with every mark of favour and consideration, and throughout the sittings of that period he punctually appeared to aid in the work of legislation. The Council Chamber of the Government of India occupies a portion of that palace whose four wings extend cunningly in each direction to decoy each breath of air into the presence of the Viceroy; and every Wednesday at eleven, the Maharaja Puttialla was met at the bottom of the great flight of steps that stretch towards the native city by two aides-de-camp, who literally handed him to a seat, slightly raised, above which frowned the mouldy portraits of Clive and Warren Hastings. So everything was done to make this business palatable to a proud man's pride. Many thought it was beneath the dignity of a chief like Puttialla to attend in person, and it was necessary at first to gild with dignity the pill of legislation. Once within the walls of Government House, the Maharaja's tongue seemed tied; he seldom spoke, and never at great length. Outwardly, however, his conduct was attentive, and he clearly watched with interest proceedings in which he abstained from taking prominent part; but as time passed on, and the period approached expiry for which he had been appointed, he gave symptoms of a desire to connect his name with some measure bearing on his national religion, and, after much reflection, asked for leave to introduce a bill partially prohibiting oxen-slaughter and the use of beef as food. But religion is a subject purposely excluded from the Council Board; and when this had been explained, his Highness of Puttialla at once withdrew his notice, and soon after left Calcutta never to return. Within six months the Maharajas Puttialla, Jheend, and Nabha, three Cis-Sutlej chiefs of first importance, and honest friends to England, were gathered to their fathers in the prime of life, under circumstances so sudden as to give rise to rumours of treasonable designs, which the removal of such stanch allies might well have helped to further. However this may be, these three tall men have followed one another into early graves, and with them lies buried for a time much promise of reform.

Next on the list of Lord Canning's early nominations comes Raja Dinkur Rao, the far-famed minister of Scindia, to whose sound advice it was mainly due that the Mahratta country remained faithful in 1857. His genius was devoted to the prosecution of well-laid schemes, having for their object the re-establishment of a strong Mahratta empire ruled by the Maharaja Scindia; and his intellect had taught him that this end could only be attained through British influence. In Gwalior his enemies pretended that his counsels were dictated by a selfish policy, and the mutiny of 1857

still further tended to estrange from him his master's
confidence.   His best efforts in an honest cause were
thus misinterpreted and frustrated; and, somewhat summarily dismissed from office and the Gwalior court, he
threw himself on our protection, and it became a sort of
duty to look after him.   Raja Dinkur Rao was a man
whose sharp Mahratta face, once seen, could never be
forgotten.   Slender for a native of his age, and of middle height, his figure, though full of dignity, was not
striking ; but the acute intelligence of his features shone
singularly conspicuous by the side of mild Bengal
Hindoos.   The close-fitting turban of his country was
well adapted to display to best advantage the beauties
of a manly head ; and though not altogether free from
the odious effects of betel-nut so common to his race,
his lips and their expression had, strange to say, not
suffered ; and while his eye was cold and keen as ever,
the outline of his mouth reflected energy and intellect
of the very highest order.

Two more native councillors of the Government of
India call for some remark ; the first, a third Hindoo
appointed by Lord Canning—the second, a Mahomedan
appointed by Lord Elgin.   Raja Deo Narain Singh was
the first, a native of Benares.   Remarkable for common
sense and blind devotion to our rule, his position, as one
of the wealthy high-caste pillars of his faith, rendered
him an almost priceless acquisition.   His utility in
council was moreover real, and only to compare with
that of Raja Dinkur Rao ; the difference being, that
while Central Indian affairs, until the cotton famine,
have mainly been political, Bengal has ever been famil-

iar with the interests of commerce. Thus, while Raja
Dinkur Rao devoted his brilliant parts to the achievement of a life-long patriotic dream, his colleague of
Benares bestowed his careful powers on questions of a
more material nature, and especially on such legislation
as was needed, by the great increase of real property-
holders, to confirm the strength of their position in the
eyes of European planters. The Rampore Nawab owed
his elevation to other and far different causes. Mahomedans are proverbially fond of learning — he was
everything that is most Mahomedan without bigotry,
and perfect as a representative of his creed. Possessed
of a singularly fertile country, his hereditary policy had
taught him to dread the incursions of his jealous native
neighbours, whilst the English he regarded as his natural
protectors. More than once, when danger threatened,
he has cast in his lot with ours, and never have we had
occasion to regret the confidence we placed in him.

Though we have here seen that natives of the highest
rank are now admitted to partake in legislation, and
that in many instances posts of great responsibility and
trust are confided to them, yet the doctrine of exclusion
still possesses a sufficient number of adherents to warrant the quotation of some passages, penned many years
ago, proving that even the more enlightened administrators of bygone times pleaded the claims of the native
to a greater share in the affairs of government, and were
quite alive to the mischief of exclusion. One of these,
Mr John Sullivan, a member of the Council of Madras,
wrote as follows : " If we put on one side of the account
what the natives have gained by the few offices that

have been lately opened to them, with what they have
lost by the extermination of the various native states,
we shall find the net loss to be immense; and what
the native loses the Englishman gains. Upon the
extermination of a native state the Englishman takes
the place of the sovereign, under the name of Commissioner; three or four of his associates displace as many
dozen of the native official aristocracy, while some hun
dreds of our troops take the place of the many thousands that every native chief supports. The little court
disappears—trade languishes—the capital decays—the
people are impoverished—the Englishman flourishes
and acts like a sponge, drawing up riches from the
banks of the Ganges, and squeezing them down upon
the banks of the Thames." In this view many of
the most sagacious Anglo-Indian rulers have since con-
curred, and Lord William Bentinck did not scruple to
confess that "in many respects the Mahomedans surpassed our rule; they settled in the countries they conquered; the interests and sympathies of the conquerors
and conquered became identified. Our policy, on the
contrary, has been the reverse of this—cold, selfish, and
unfeeling; the iron hand of power on the one side,
monopoly and exclusion on the other."

But all these things are passed, and have been replaced
by happier times; and from the native members of the
Viceroy's Council, who have been taken first as being
the more important, we must now turn to dwell a
moment on the class of Europeans whose services are
available for Indian legislation. In India, as elsewhere,
society is composed of the two great classes of officials

and non-officials ; and each of these is capable of further
subdivision—the first comprising as it does the military
and civil services, the second merchants and producers.
With the second class we have now exclusively to deal.
The immediate object of the merchants who congregate
in presidency towns, rapidly to acquire wealth, is best
served by a screwing policy, regardless of the country's
good, and directed only to securing the most favourable
conditions as to sale and purchase markets.   With
manufacturers and producers of raw material, such as
indigo and jute, the case is altogether different ; their
interests are of a more permanent character than those
of mere retailers, being identical and inseparably connected with the improvement of the soil they cultivate
and its inhabitants.   No one appreciated this more fully
than Lord Canning, and his ripest hours of government
were spent in publishing the "Waste Lands Sales"
measures.   Though productive of some temporary embarrassment to his successor, and the source of much
inevitable gain to a class of small capitalists known as
land-jobbers, these measures have opened up the richest
districts of our Eastern empire under circumstances
most favourable to European buyers, and have thereby
assured the best approach to the much-neglected field
of Indian colonisation.   Unfortunately, however, the
agricultural and local occupations of these settlers,
standing in the way of their attendance during legislation, practically exclude them from Council, and restrict
the Viceroy's choice to merchants of Calcutta.   Among
the ranks of these latter it was, and no doubt still is,
possible to find men like Mr David Cowie, acquainted

with and inclined to further general interests ; but, more commonly, representatives are sought among the agents of long-established firms, such as the house of Messrs Jardine Skinner ; and of these monopolists, Mr Claude Brown will be remembered as a very favourable specimen. In this respect much advantage would be reaped from the Migratory Council system, when alternate meetings at Lahore and other places might enable men like Mr Cope, whose name will be familiar to all who know the Punjab, to accept a share in legislation.

One class of Indian lawgivers remains to be discussed —those who, chosen from the paths of office life, still rank as unofficial or extraordinary members. This half-breed has grown out of the evident necessity that the minor Presidencies, and a wide tract of country like the Punjab, should be represented in a council that prescribes laws and regulations for all India, by persons competent to protect their local interests from serious official wrong. Among those earliest selected for this duty three names occur deserving of some mention. The first in seniority of years was Mr Claudius James Erskine, of the Bombay branch of the Indian Civil Service, whom literary distinction and a critical intellect well qualified for his work of picking holes in bills framed in a spirit of one-sided legislation. Mr Robert Staunton Ellis is the second to whom reference is made ; and though, from having served the Government supreme in former days, he was less of a local representative man than his colleague of Bombay, he yet proved a faithful guardian of the interests of Madras. The last of the three in date of nomination was Mr Austin

Roberts, whose substantive appointment, as it is termed in Anglo-Indian office phraseology, was that of Judicial Commissioner, Punjab; and if, in breadth of view and facile diction, he was hardly equal to the other two, in his case a long experience of the ins and outs of legal formulæ offered a sufficient guarantee for the detection of aught likely to affect the welfare of the land beyond the Sutlej.

"Officiating" and "substantive appointments"—terms that so perplex a new arrival in Calcutta, where the majority of public servants draw pay for the nominal performance of duties virtually intrusted to another— have their origin in the frequent and repeated absences of officers from their post in search of health, or while engaged on special duty. True to this principle, Mr Ellis likewise held a "substantive appointment" in Madras to which he might revert during the recess; and while engaged in sessional legislation, he and his representative colleagues from Bombay and the Punjab drew certain moneys known as "deputation allowances," calculated on a modest scale, and intended to defray the actual expenses incident to absence from their homes.

Of Lieutenant-Governments, Bengal alone as yet possesses its own Parliament; and this machine being purely local in effect, it is but just that the interests of Bengal trade should have a powerful voice in its deliberations. A fitter member, therefore, than Mr John Nutt Bullen, President of the Calcutta Commerce Chamber, could not have been selected. In this Council natives have been chosen with almost equal wisdom, and among them one must here be mentioned. Moolvie Abdool Luteef Khan Bahadoor, a Mahomedan, as his name denotes, had won distinction as a classic jurist and supporter of British institutions in Bengal, and Lord Elgin had availed himself of an early opportunity to appoint him to the Senate of the Calcutta University in the Faculty of Law. Of each successive honour his past conduct has well proved him worthy. Somewhat young in years and younger still in looks, he never lacked detractors, covert and avowed; but in corrupt Bengal this can hardly be considered as matter for surprise: and all admitted to his intimacy must acknowledge that this keen Mussulman formed a valuable element in the Bengal Council, not only as a fluent native counterpoise to special Hindoo interests, so largely represented in that province, but further as a zealous advocate of well-considered legislation.

The first President of the Bengal Council was her Lieutenant-Governor, Sir John Peter Grant, a man of powerful frame, whom strong opinions, firm courage, and extended understanding well fitted to control presumption in a newly-constituted body. He had been appointed by Lord Canning, after Mr Halliday, Lord Dalhousie's first Lieutenant-Governor. His knowledge of Bengal and the requirements of her people was comprehensive and exact. He was, in every way save one, the man best suited for the office; and the exception to which reference is made was perhaps that most necessary to prove the truth of this assertion. This exception was inherent obstinacy of character, a quality that never failed to stand him in good stead in the conduct of those controversial questions which the varied interests of Bengal inevitably engender. The growth of indigo, for instance, has given rise to constant conflicts between the paramount and subject races—the former represented by greedy zemindars and European planters, bent on getting the greatest quantity of labour for the smallest possible remuneration; the latter by the miserable ryot, to whom oppression is hereditary as a condition of existence. There is, however, a certain point beyond which neither starvation nor the lash can drive despairing human creatures to work for hated masters; and more than once this point has been attained in India. Then we have had discussions in our councils how to strengthen planters' hands, so as to avert their ruin and compel the healthy labour of the masses, without placing the bulk of the population beneath the yoke of bondage, and unduly sacrificing the liberties of the many to the moneyed interests of the few. In the consideration of this and similar questions, Sir John Peter Grant was aided by Mr Seton Karr, then Secretary to the Government of Bengal, whose commanding mind could ill brook the trammels incident to office. Zealous, able, Scotch, and honest, Mr Seton Karr was an ornament to the Indian Civil Service even in its palmy days. His eloquence was so remarkable, that if his path had led beneath St Stephen's roof it must have claimed him place beside our greatest orators. These natural gifts had been heightened by unremitting studied cultivation; and the whole was set in a frame of large proportions, crowned by a well-shaped head, whose powerfully strict lines were lit by eyes of restless energy. Such was Mr Seton Karr; and yet, with all these attributes, he lacked one element essential to executive success. This want was not ambition; neither was it knowledge of mankind in general: what he lacked was knowledge of himself, and of the way to turn his talents to the advantage of the State he shared in governing; and so little did he possess this branch of human wisdom, that, like Fox in former times, forgetful of the impartiality due to office, he threw his generous soul into the scale of oppressed mankind, and, by franking through the country the then celebrated Bengal drama, entitled 'Nil Durpan,' in which European planters were held up to general execration, aroused in ryots' breasts vague hopes of aid against their taskmasters. These hopes, however, were destined to cruel disappointment on Mr Seton Karr's compelled and speedy resignation—a disappointment that has since found vent in deeds of violence and retributive justice enacted on the lives and property of the landowning few.

Consequent on Sir John Peter Grant's own resignation in 1862, Mr Cecil Beadon was promoted by Lord Elgin, from a seat in the Executive Council, to the Lieutenant-Government of Bengal. Sir John Peter Grant was a man of strong and sound opinions, from which he seldom swerved; while Mr Beadon's greatest merit was tact and power of conciliation, to which he often sacrificed such convictions as he had. Personally, however, Mr Beadon was the more ambitious; his aim seemed to be to stretch his own authority to its utmost limits, rendering Bengal not only independent of the

Viceroy, but practically paramount in its decisions. The fact is, that lieutenant-governors enjoy more unchecked power than either governors or viceroys; the theory being, that the interests confided to them are purely local, not imperial, and that their personal responsibility is sufficient guarantee for the proper exercise of patronage and influence. Consequently, their action is not hampered by many constitutional restrictions imposed upon their betters. They have no executive or ordinary councillors to share their labours, and even the members of the Bengal Legislative Chamber are nominated by the Local Government, subject only to the approval of the Viceroy. Again, instead of several departmental secretariats, composed of men selected from amongst the most conspicuous and able in every branch of Indian administration, having a certain reputation to maintain, the Bengal Office is conducted by one secretary, a junior member of the Civil Service, chosen by the Lieutenant-Governor, too frequently from private motives, who sometimes is an instrument, harmless in himself, for working out his master's ends, but more often bends his every effort to developing his own career and acquiring some repute. As fair specimens of each class we would name Mr Edward Lushington and Mr Ashley Eden—the former always willing to do his governor's bidding without a thought of self-responsibility; the latter, clever to a fault, ever striving to attain personal pre-eminence.

Ashley Eden has become a name in India which should not be too lightly dealt with. The part he has of late years played, though one of tertiary rank, has been continuous and prominent. His facility of writing, added to the personal consideration his somewhat domineering manner has inspired, combined to render him, if not a very formidable adversary, at least a valuable colleague. Mr Beadon had one great merit, that of knowing men and how to use them. In the exercise of this knowledge he selected Mr Ashley Eden, first as secretary, and later for a legislative councillor; and a choice more calculated to augment his chances of success in governing Bengal could hardly have been made. But neither Mr Ashley Eden nor his ambition could be contained within the limits of a province; and, following in the track of that encroaching policy which had, independently of the Government of India, conducted to protracted though successful issues the Sonthal and Jyntia-Cossyah rebellions, he backed with all his logic the proposal of his master for the appointment of a mission to Bhotan for the purpose of procuring a final settlement of long-standing frontier questions, and establishing a system of commercial intercourse with that rude people more advantageous to Bengal industry and commerce than the exclusive regulations previously in force. For some time he and Mr Beadon tried to argue that this mission was of purely local interest, and did not concern the Government of India. Such arguments, however, were easy to disprove, and were finally cut short by reference to the ruling, that external policy in all its branches is specially reserved to the Government Supreme. To smooth, however, his ruffled feathers, Mr Beadon was permitted to suggest the

composition of the mission, and Mr Ashley Eden not
unnaturally named himself. How this ardent spirit
roughly penetrated to the presence of the Deb and
Dhurma Rajas of Bhotan, and narrowly escaped with
life, after having compromised his Government and
himself by the signature of a formal act of cession,
only to be cancelled by costly military measures, has
now been given to the world in a careful narrative by
Surgeon Rennie of the 20th Hussars. But as regards
the manner of the man employed, a comparison might
not seem very much out of place with Mr Kinglake's
picture of an Emperor, whose ambitious and uneasy
soul ever led him into desperate situations to which
some unfortunate peculiarities precluded his doing
justice, and proved him courageous in design, but
lacking some element essential to successful execution.

Whatever faults and failings a somewhat harsh
criticism of Mr Beadon's reign may discover, it is
impossible to deny that it has been most favourable
to the progress of Bengal. As Foreign Secretary, some
say that he committed errors of all kinds, and often
led Lord Canning into fatal blunders; as Lieutenant-
Governor of Bengal, he occupied the place calculated
for displaying to the best advantage his very varied
qualities; and since it has been above imputed to him
that his aim was independence of all supremacy, it
is only just to add that no material interest ever
suffered in his hands. He was eminently suited for
the conduct of a government of radical improvement,
and under him nothing seemed to slumber or decay.
Justice, education, docks, and drainage, public build-

ings, roads, and even theatres, all bore speedy witness
to his elevation. Under him it was, moreover, that a
practical advance was made in the execution of a
long-cherished scheme for substituting the Mutlah
river for the Hoogly, and constituting Canning-Town
the port of entry for Calcutta; thereby avoiding the
rapid tides and tortuous navigation caused by shifting
sands, and the dreaded "James and Mary" shoal,
where some hundred lives are lost each year, and on
whose account alone insurance companies augment
their rate of charge by one per cent on all vessels
destined to Calcutta. Such real services as these we
may well accept as striking a balance much in Mr
Beadon's favour, when compared with general constitutional objeetions as to the personal ambition of his
government and the rash ability of Mr Ashley Eden,
who never lost an opportunity of rushing in where
" angels fear to tread."

The proceedings of the Government of Bengal are
chronicled for communication to the Secretary of
State in the Home Department of the Government of
India. Besides the conduct of this and other corre
spondence, police, the telegraph, and post-office, and,
since the abolition of the Indian Navy, marine affairs,
are confided to its care. The post of secretary was
not long since ably filled by Mr William Grey, to
whom succeeded Mr E. C. Bayley, both civil servants
of Bengal. The character of the former was of a die
well cast for prompt despatch of business; his brain
was of a legal order, somewhat warped perhaps by
" Bengal Regulations," but accurately just in its deci-

sions. He was tall and slender, and his thin lips, hard compressed, were surmounted by the outlines of a face naturally severe, and whose severity of expression was enhanced by the furrows caused by one-and-twenty years in India. The nature of the duties of the Home Department more resembles that of work in London Public Offices than any other branch of Eastern Government; and legislation is the most exciting subject with which it has to deal. It may be said to exercise little direct administrative power, and its functions are usually confined to criticising measures introduced by others. For this work Mr William Grey was admirably qualified; but the great industry which characterised Mr Bayley, his successor, more fitted him for the compilation of blue-books of an ordinary character, or recording the proceedings of the Asiatic Society of Bengal, than to control the actions of ambitious men. So long, however, as Mr William Grey, though promoted to the Council, retained the supervision of the Home Department, little harm was done; but when the force of circumstances called him home to England his place was temporarily occupied by Mr H. B. Harrington, a North-West civilian of great ability and activity of mind, but whose turn for legislation practically impaired his executive utility; and during this short interregnum Mr Beadon's power and independence acquired a greater measure of development than was perhaps consistent with the dignity of the Government of India.

CHAPTER IV.

THE LIEUTENANT-GOVERNMENT OF THE NORTH-WEST PROV-
INCES, SUBORDINATE TO THE GOVERNOR-GENERAL IN THE
HOME DEPARTMENT.

THE North-West Provinces are bounded on the south by Bengal Proper, and, stretching upwards from Benares, occupy the neck of land between Oude and Bundelcund ; whence, extending west and north, they skirt the frontiers of Rajpootana and the Punjab, being walled in to the east by the mighty Himalayas. This tract of country is watered by the Ganges and the Jumna, and embraces every variety of climate and circumstance of life. From the dusty cities of the plains exhausted Europeans may rapidly ascend to Nynee Tal and other stations in the Hills, beyond which towers again a snowy range of twenty thousand feet.

Each Indian Government breeds its special class of civil servants ; and those of the North-West have become conspicuous for a happy combination of the efficient zeal that characterises the administration of the Punjab, with the hardy love of sport and out-door life that tended so much formerly to identify

Bengal civilians with the native population. Consequent upon the great numerical increase of Europeans in Bengal, young civilians nowadays mix much less with the children of the soil than their predecessors were wont to do. Each race has now its own pursuits. Deprived of the pecuniary advantages incident to domestic strife and foreign war, Bengalees have turned their thoughts into more commercial channels; while commissioners and magistrates, prohibited by the Regulations from entering on agricultural or trading speculations, have little left in common with the men they rule, and unbend their minds in social intercourse and the pleasures of the chase. Moreover, the smallest Bengal station now boasts of some half-dozen English ladies, who form a barrier more impassable between the different shades of colour than the want of sympathy produced by habits of existence and interests diametrically opposed. The Punjab school is of a far different stamp. Farther from headquarters, a wider measure of responsibility attaches to its governors, and has gradually diffused itself among the junior overworked civilians, thinly scattered over the vast fields of enterprise which lie enclosed between the five grand rivers whence that country takes its name. Situated midway between the Punjab and Bengal, all seems to have combined to make the North-West Provinces a government of energy and moderation. Benares, in the south, is a centre of Hindooism; while at Delhi, in the north, Mussulmans preponderate   To the east lies Oude, hitherto a hotbed of revolt, peopled by a martial race whose sons supplied the Company with soldiers, and who had but to traverse the narrow strip of land above referred to, to find among the native states of Bundelcund and Central India ample scope for political intrigue and those deeds of daring so suited to their instincts.

When, therefore, its geographical position has been examined, it cannot be a subject for surprise that the full tide of mutiny swept down upon its plains in 1857, that, for a time at least, the North-West became a term synonymous with bloodshed and revenge, and that its name will ever stand recorded as associated with one of the darkest pages in the history of British India. But that page has been so often written, and has become so painfully familiar to us all, that we shall not here attempt even the bare outline of a tragedy which reddened with the blood of England's sons and daughters a tract of country larger than Great Britain.

Yet the traces of rebellion are still too recent to render possible any faithful picture of those provinces without dealing boldly with their painful memories. There are few cities or military stations throughout the North-West Provinces but bear the mark of fire and sword. In some towns, indeed, such as Allahabad, a rapid growth of population and new buildings has done much to hide the ravages of war; but in Cawnpore the traveller is still brought face to face with General Wheeler's burnt intrenchments, and streets of blood-stained ruins.

To understand the true horrors of the Sepoy war, a knowledge is necessary of the miseries incident to Anglo-Indian life, even under the most favourable cir-

cumstances. Few subjects have been more often dealt
with to less purpose ; and to this day a European, be
he a high official or a plain English gentleman travelling for self-improvement or for pleasure, lands in India
ignorant of almost all that constitutes the sum of the
existence of his exiled countrymen, and of the real
character of their relation to the coloured races by whom
they are surrounded. So long, however, as his experience is confined to the society of Calcutta, his mind
will hardly rise to an appreciation of the truth. If his
mornings are occupied by office-work or paying visits,
and he takes his evening rides round Eden Gardens,
listening to a European band, surrounded by white faces,
even whiter than he sees at home, he at first will feel
inclined to contradict the statement that the atmosphere
he breathes is impregnated with thoughts, and hopes,
and fears, widely differing from anything he was acquainted with in England. But wait some months :
let that man, whatever his position in society, quit Calcutta, travelling north. On that railway journey he
will have to traverse a country strangely fertile and
pleasant-looking, even beautiful in places. He will
have a passing glimpse of the pretty station of Burdwan, perhaps of its wealthy Raja, whose palaces lie
scattered in rich profusion on the shores of artificial
lakes, enclosed in grounds where the last improvements
known in landscape-gardening have been introduced,
with splendid disregard for money. He will skirt the
woody hills of Rajmahal, and pass through the Sonthal
districts, not long since in rebellion. The lattice-bridge
across the treacherous Sone, one of the largest tribu-

taries of the Ganges, will teach him some, at least, of
the enormous difficulties by which nature has seen fit
to check too sudden a development of the resources of
our Indian Empire. But let our traveller proceed still
further; let him cross the Bengal frontier, and enter
those arid provinces which suffered most during the late
famine;—let him push on further still. No fields of
rice or indigo clothe that country in a fruitful green, no
undulations break the dull monotony of that clear horizon; all around is coloured by the fine white dust peculiar to the North-West Provinces, which, borne by the
hot wind, forms itself in clouds, and sweeps across the
dreary plains. Then ask that man if the light of Indian
life begins to dawn upon him, and if he sees its shadows; then ask him whether Upper India resembles
the fairy tales of modern writers, or if he does not think
success in life of almost any kind dear at such a price?

But, like sailors, the members of the Civil Service are
caught young; and once committed to a career, they,
being Englishmen, make the best of it. Their pay at
first is good, and it gradually assumes magnificent proportions as they rise in seniority. In our days they
mostly marry early, and settle temporarily as magistrate and collector at some native city, unknown perhaps to European fame. The life the new arrivals lead
is one almost beyond description. The society of the
place is probably composed of some two or more families
besides themselves, soldiers and civilians, whom professional prejudice or private jealousy render insupportable
to each other. The young people, if wise, endeavour
to steer clear of both hostile factions; but more often

espouse warmly, for want of better interest, the cause of one or other. Thus months wear on in dull monotony, only broken and relieved by successive rains and hot or so-called cold weather. Each evening a drive is taken, or a ride of small dimensions, and at sunset all return to eat their meals in discontent. This kind of life is only varied by occasional sickness, or the visit of a chance, and not always welcome, guest. The man has most occupation, and sometimes keeps his health in consequence; the woman generally breaks down with the birth of her first child, and then returns to England, or spends at least her future summers in the Hills.

The above, though a somewhat sad, is not an altogether untrue, picture of the early married life of young civilians of the present generation. With those who are single the case differs much to their advantage. Great exceptions exist, however, and many small green spots there are amid those North-West wastes, where all branches of the public service live peacefully and happily together.

In the diction of recent legislation, the North-West is styled the Government of Agra,—the original intention being to establish a fourth Presidency. The execution of this scheme, however, has been long delayed, if not abandoned; and these provinces have latterly been ruled by Lieutenant-Governors appointed by the Viceroy. The designation adopted by the English House of Commons may be deemed sufficient proof of the existence of a general feeling, based on a knowledge of the past, which pointed then, and still points now, to Agra for a capital. Agra is something more than a splendid name in Indian history,—something more even than a simple landmark, strongly fortified, by which to trace the limits of a nation's power. Her red sandstone walls surround a strong position, immediately above the Jumna, and are relieved at every angle by lofty towers and battlements. The place is one of extraordinary strength, and capable of defence against most fearful odds. To scale the citadel, if held by Europeans, would be a task from which natives would recoil. In 1857, Europeans far and near flocked to its welcome shelter ; and, well provisioned and tolerably armed, it only needed investment to prove its giant strength. Among the men within its walls were bold civilians who had held their districts till the very latest hour at which escape was possible. In the early days of mutiny, some reached its gates sick and fever-stricken, bringing in a country cart their wives and household gods. Later, others from a greater distance staggered on towards a common goal, through jungle and the enemy ; and of these some few alone were saved to tell a tale of suffering and endurance unsurpassed in history or fiction. At last those heavy gates swung to, and were no more opened to admit starving, homeless wanderers. Then followed weeks of breathless expectation, when nothing reached that unbeleaguered motley garrison from the world without but rumours, rendered doubly awful by their vague conflicting nature, and whose truth was only to be tested by reports of native spies, and such information as could be gathered by sortie-parties seeking food or forage. Upon Mr Colvin, the Lieutenant-Governor, devolved the labours of command in the absence of professional men, and while the crisis lasted he commanded well. It is true his measures taken for defence were really never tried, for the rebel army was dispersed by General Greathead while advancing to attack. But when a man does well whatever duties fall to him, and dies in their discharge, he merits honourable mention in proportion to the import of the deeds with which his name is linked.

Although Agra has been termed the key of Hindostan, it has been twice her fate to be abandoned by a government in search of a strategic capital; and as, in 1658, Aurungzebe removed his court from thence to Delhi, so, after the lapse of just two centuries, the British have again exchanged it for a slightly elevated site between the Ganges and the Jumna known as Allahabad. This tongue of land owes its selection entirely to military reasons, and the supposed necessity for river communication with Calcutta. In former times, such arguments might well have been allowed; but, in these days of Indian rail development, their value, when compared with others, such as prestige in the native mind and the enormous expenditure incurred, can hardly be permitted to hold good. It was not without regret that Lord Canning eventually sanctioned this costly transfer of a government from what many think the most striking place in Northern Hindostan to a triangle of sand clothed by scanty crops of Indian corn, and hitherto known only as the first station of importance beyond Benares on the grand trunk road. But still Lord Canning did it; and in these days Agra's greatness can only be occasional, when circumstances suggest her as a place of meeting for a Viceroy's camp or council.

Such an opportunity occurred when Lord Elgin selected Agra as the spot at which he should embark upon his northern progress, and hold his first durbar in Upper India; and those who saw her decked in the glory of the mighty chiefs who flocked to do honour to the Viceroy of the Queen, will readily confess that she then did justice to herself and the occasion. Coming from Cawnpore, Lord Elgin entered Agra by a railway that traverses a thirsty country cleft in all directions by dried-up watercourses, and bearing lasting trace of war, famine, and the locust, all which three scourges have lashed those plains in quick succession since 1857. For very many miles no inhabitants are seen; but here and there a solitary buck is startled from his lair, apparently the only animal capable of supporting life upon the burnt-up soil. While still at a considerable distance, and swiftly passing through a country that seems specially designed to bear the curse of God, the traveller observes towards the north a white speck on the horizon glittering brightly in the sun, and relieving the painful sense of desolation caused by all around. That speck as you approach assumes a dome-like form, and gradually dissolves itself in three, of which the largest is the centre. As the train draws nearer, at a distance of perhaps ten miles, a liquid silver thread is drawn across the view, and winds between the traveller and those domes. Then, with each minute, rich groves and marble minarets take shape, and seem to pierce the brazen sky above; and while the traveller strains his

eye across the scorching waste to catch each rapidly
succeeding phase of colour and development, he instinctively rises to the knowledge that he is being
brought within the presence of the Taj.

Arriving at the railway station, Lord Elgin met with
a reception worthy of the East. The road, thickly
lined with native troops, crossed the Jumna by a bridge
of boats, and wound along the river's bank beneath
those lofty sandstone walls; then, mounting a steep hill
and leaving the main entry into Agra Fort upon the
right, the Taj remaining to the left, it led, through miles
of garden-ground thickly studded with suburban villas,
to the Viceroy's camp, that occupied the centre of an
extensive plain, where tents were pitched for the accommodation of the Government of India and an escort of
ten thousand men. Beyond these were ranked, according to priority of arrival, the far-spreading noisy camps
of those rajas the number of whose followers was within
some bounds; and beyond them again stretched miles
and miles of tents containing thousands upon thousands
of ill-conditioned-looking men from Central India and
the wildest parts of Rajpootana, the followers of such
maharajas as Jeypoor, who marched to meet the Viceroy with an army thirty thousand strong, found in
horse and foot and guns, ready for the field.

No circumstance that could enhance the possible
effect was forgotten or neglected. The Mooltanee Horse
were present; and the native body-guard, commanded by
Major George Delane, wore for the first time their new
and costly uniforms. The European force comprised some
horse-artillery picked for smartness, and a battalion of

the Rifles. The road the Viceroy had to follow was long and densely thronged with dusky crowds ; and ere his tents were reached the sun had wellnigh set. After one short hour of twilight that broad expanse was lit by watchfires reflecting forms massed in every variety of attitude and colour; and later, as night wore on, revelry and native song resounded through the camps. Then came a busy hum, and then a silence broken by occasional salutes and evening guns, for which natives deem all hours appropriate. Yet a little, and a truly Eastern moon had risen, casting tall shadows strange to European eyes ; and, save the dull moaning of uneasy camels or the jackal's melancholy cry, all was wrapt in slumber for some few short midnight hours, until the early Indian sun should rise once more upon the stern realities of life.

Some ten days Lord Elgin stayed at Agra receiving native homage and visiting the many monuments of Indian history which enrich that neighbourhood. Then one morning at early dawn his mighty camp broke up, and the course it took was clearly marked by endless strings of baggage animals, and a heavy column of North-West dust ascending high to heaven.

When Mr Colvin died, Lord Canning selected Mr Edmonstone, formerly Foreign Secretary, to succeed him as Lieutenant-Governor. To him it therefore fell to convert the jungle site, selected for military reasons, into the capital of a province. At this work Mr Edmonstone laboured full four years, and on the expiration of that time Allahabad assumed an aspect, if not imposing, at any rate respectable. Like Mr Beadon,

F

Mr Edmonstone succeeded better as Lieutenant-Governor than in offices of a more subordinate character. Not only was he unacquainted with the meaning of such words as fear or danger, but his heart seemed even steeled against anxiety. He worked unremittingly, and with less thought of self than most Anglo-Indian civilians. In revenue matters he was assisted by Messrs Muir and Money, both of whom possessed considerable executive ability. The former was a man of spare habit and quick perception, who, in conversation, seemed to see a thing at once from every point of view; and the latter, though less brilliant in society, was justly popular with those with whom he came in contact.

In Bengal and the North-West Provinces, the Board of Revenue is an office of great importance and emolument. It is composed of members chosen from among the seniors of the Civil Service, and their special duty is to superintend the working of machinery by which the revenue is raised. They are nominally subordinate to Lieutenant-Governors, but really take their orders from the Financial Councillor of the Government of India. One member of the Bengal Board was so long conspicuous for ability and success in all he undertook, that in treating of his North-Western colleagues some mention may perhaps be made of him. Mr Grote, a brother of the historian, had gradually ascended the successive steps of Calcutta office life. Much of his time had been devoted to literary and scientific labours, and it had perhaps been owing to his apparent preference for comparative retirement among his books and rich collections of animal and vegetable life, that the doors to the highest civil posts remained closed against him. But Mr Grote cared little; he enjoyed good health; his days were given to finance administration; and towards evening he returned to Allipore, the St John's Wood of Calcutta, where, in a pretty house well planted out by trees, he spent his hours in the society of such men as Drs Archer or Macrae, and other congenial companions who loved the same pursuits.

The Indian career of Mr Edmonstone was one of continuous and well-merited success. He belonged to the old school of Civil servants who adopted for their own the country where their labours lay. As a boy he had gone to India in search of personal distinction; and having put his hand upon the plough, he never once looked back. He appeared indifferent to climate, and seldom visited the Hills; and having filled with honour high offices of difficulty and danger, he returned to England, after thirty years of exile, unbroken by the illness or the absence of a day, with fair prospect of much future usefulness in the Council of the Secretary of State; but in reality to receive the collar of the Bath, and within six months to sink into an obscure churchyard, apparently from want of an object for existence.

It is in such manner that Indian rulers of the second class pass away and are forgotten. A man who for years has governed thirty millions of his fellow-subjects —governed, not in the mild mode of Western civilisation by delicate contrivances known as ministers more or less responsible, but by force of individuality and the strength of his own right arm—this man quits the land of his adoption, and returns worn out to find his very name unknown in England. At first perhaps he lives in London, having business now and then to transact with the India Office; but gradually and by degrees even this resource is seen to fail him; he buys a little place in some southern county, to which he retires with books for his companions, and the tolling of a village bell soon makes known that one more weary public servant has found a home at last.

When Mr Edmonstone requested the permission to resign, it became imperative to look out for a successor. Lord Elgin was then traversing the North-West Provinces, seeing for himself how much had been done towards healing that distempered country, and how much still remained to do, in order that he might select the man best fitted for the task. Throughout that tour Lord Elgin saw enough to make him know that severity had stamped out the embers of revolt, that all classes longed for peace, and were willing to obey the laws if carried out with firmness; and that the man required was not one too ready with suspicion and harsh retributive measures, but of a calm, judicial, and administrative mind. Upon such occasions, when a viceroy has to name a new lieutenant-governor, he first passes in review the members of his Executive Council; and at the time we write of Lord Elgin's Council was composed as follows:—First in seniority came Sir Robert Napier; after him ranked Messrs· Harington and Grey, Sir Charles Trevelyan, and Mr Henry Sumner Maine. Of these Sir Robert Napier was a soldier; and whatever advantages might be derived from military domination in countries like the Punjab, the North-West Government eminently required the supervision of a civilian qualified to work out settlement details. Mr Maine and Sir Charles Trevelyan were specialties practically ineligible for routine promotion, and thus Mr Harington and Mr Grey alone remained. The service of the former dated from 1827; the latter was some thirteen years his junior. Moreover, Mr Harington's career had principally been run in North-Western India, while Mr Grey had seldom stepped beyond the limits of Bengal, and was hence regarded by the unofficial eye as Mr Beadon's heir-apparent. Within the Council Chamber, therefore, the claims were not conflicting; but beyond its walls public favour had become enlisted in the cause of candidates possessed of local confidence. Foremost among these were Mr Muir, who was on the spot, with Messrs Yule and Wingfield, both known for able government of Oude. The choice fell on Mr Harington, but the offer was only made to him to be refused on public grounds; for, though possessed of every qualification, he modestly expressed a fear that his health was too shattered to permit him to cope with work of such proportions. A second choice was thus required, and the small field for selection now necessarily became somewhat enlarged. This time the choice fell on Mr Drummond, who, as financial secretary, had won the goodwill and appreciation of every member of the Government of India. Senior to Mr Muir, Mr Grey, and Mr Wingfield, his appointment passed unquestioned, except by certain newspapers, who, balked of the fulfilment each of its own pet prophecy, made for a time a common and a harmless cause against an accomplished fact received with general approbation.

As Mr Drummond had been named just upon the eve of the Indian financial year, when his controlling presence was most necessary at Calcutta, the North-West Government was conducted for a time by the Board of Revenue. But so soon as he had rendered to Sir Charles Trevelyan the full benefit of his rich experience, and a Budget had been presented, of which the sanguine expectations have not been yet fulfilled, he set out for Allahabad, and undertook the task committed to him. In this manner was it that, owing to the accident of Mr Harington's exceeding modesty, Mr Drummond found at last a fitting sphere of action. Continued residence in Calcutta had impaired his health, but not his understanding; and he knew that if good service were expected of him, he must be permitted to spend the hottest period of the year among his mountain stations, descending to the plains to work double time throughout the cooler months. This permission was sought in writing, and the reply it met with from Lord Elgin best shows the perfect confidence he placed in his lieutenant. "Upon the propriety of such proceeding you must judge yourself. You alone can speak from day to day of the requirements of your administration; and, for my part, I possess the firm conviction that your decisions will ever be in harmony with what you deem conducive to the welfare of the interests at stake." Such was the tenor, if not the actual wording, of the letter that left Mr Drummond his own master; and, shortly after its receipt, he removed to a cool and shady spot, deep buried in the hills of Nynee Tal, upon the borders of a lake of all-surpassing beauty.

Those are really the most enviable hours of Indian government, when, on a fine spring mountain morning, the mist clears off, and the dew is rapidly drunk up by a sun just warm enough to render fires indoors essential to the comfort of a breakfast-table. At nine the daily dâk arrives, with nothing of importance demanding immediate attention. Some two hours later, guns are slung across the shoulders, and throughout the day the baying of the dogs resounds from hill to hill, relieved at intervals by the echoes of an English rifle. But in those deep valleys the sun sets early, and darkness grows apace; and our ruler, guided by the waning light, nears his temporary home, to find, perchance, upon arrival, a telegram, whose true importance time alone can test. Sufficient is, however, clear to show him that clouds have risen, gathered, and are now prepared to break upon some spot within his jurisdiction which that morning's post reported tranquil and content. But of the actual extent of the mischief vaguely hinted at in electrotype, his personal examination can alone assure him; and that night, instead of going to well-earned rest, he is seen slowly winding down some tortuous pass, leaving all that is fair and fresh behind him. As morning dawns, he exchanges with a native servant a dusty shooting-cap for a solar topee, and some hours later reaches the indifferent shelter of a postal bungalow, at which he halts awhile. There a mitigated form reaches him of the rumour of the day before; but his duty lies in personal examination of at least the causes

of excitement, and after two more days and nights of
travelling, he reaches the centre of ill-will, simultaneously, it may be, with a wing of European troops
brought from Delhi by forced marches.   The raising of
the revenue is proved, upon inquiry, to be the origin of
discontent, and some weeks are spent in adjusting dis-
agreements.   The back taxes are paid up, and the
English soldiers retrace their dusty steps ; but the Hills
see the lieutenant-governor no more that year.   He
proceeds to Allahabad, and deems it incumbent on him
to report at length to the Government of India the
origin and end of this fiscal failure.   Next he relates
how purely local it has been in all its bearings, winding
up, perhaps, by a series of elaborate arguments, all bent
to prove how utterly impossible it is that such tempo
rary confusion should ever re-occur.

It has been said that English statesmen speak beyond
their powers of reasoning, and that Anglo-Indians write
above their natural ability ; and nothing is more true.
What is known as " duftur" is the curse of India.   Each
councillor has many secretaries of some kind or other,
and each of these has countless clerks.   All draw pay,
as a rule, in inverse proportion to the measure of their
utility ; and it is the lower members of this scale of
official life who contribute to our Anglo-Indian and
Mofussil press those articles and letters from "special
correspondents" whose depreciation of our aims and
ends tends even more to degrade us in the native mind
than our arrogant affectation of superiority, and inborn
contempt for all except ourselves.

The real men who bring our rule in India into disrepute are such as the late Mr John Lang, formerly proprietory editor of the 'Mofussilite,' a daily journal of the North-West Provinces, who unhappily was possessed of talents just sufficient to secure the widest circulation for the coarsest wit. The low-bred personalities to which Anglo-Indian newspapers descend, with too few exceptions, render them completely valueless for purposes of history; and the efforts of Sir Herbert Edwardes, and of other able writers, to raise their tone to something more approaching the level of European journalism, have not yet been sufficiently respected; for few know at home the difficulties these men have to fight against in the thankless nature of their labours and the jealousies incurred.

In India the influence of one man, be it for good or evil, attains perhaps its widest sway. Of this a striking instance may be cited in the case of Mr Allen Hume, the magistrate of Etawah, who, by force of will and mild obstinacy of purpose, has become remarkable for meeting natives with measures of resistance all their own. A place more desert-looking and hopeless for the growth of any European seed than the stony field in which Mr Allen Hume has toiled at schools and Christianity, and all that elevates the human heart, could hardly be selected; and the following description, taken from the soundest Anglo-Indian book of reference, may serve to illustrate the truth of the assertion: "In no part of India do hot winds blow with greater fury; they commence in March, and rage throughout the whole of April and of May. The wind usually rises about eight A.M., and subsides at sunset; though it sometimes blows

at night as well. Every article of furniture is burning
to the touch; the hardest wood, if not well covered with
damp blankets, will split with a report like that of a
pistol; and linen taken from a press is as if just removed from the kitchen-fire. But terrible as are the
days, the nights are infinitely worse,—each apartment
becomes heated to excess, and can only be compared to
an oven. The hot winds are succeeded by the monsoon,
or periodical rains, the transition being marked by a
furious tornado. At mid-day, darkness, as of night, sets
in, caused by the dense clouds of dust; and so loud is
the roar of the storm, that incessant peals of thunder
are heard only at rare intervals, whilst the flashes of
forked lightning seldom pierce the gloom. At last the
rain descends in torrents, floods the country, and re-
freshes, for a while, the animal and vegetable world."
Yet this one pale Englishman, of slender frame and
ascetic habit, has developed upon that fiery soil a caste
of natives unsurpassed in firm allegiance and educational distinction.

Now, this tract of country, stretching down from
Delhi to Cawnpore, is known as The Doab, and lies between the sacred banks of the Jumna and the Ganges.
Here was literally the neck of Indian mutiny, which
English fugitives had to traverse, in the spring of 1857,
in order to escape the awful fate reserved for those
unable, by reason of their health or other circumstance,
to fly from that accursed plain in time. But monuments
enough still greet the eye at almost every turn of what
befell both those who fled and those who stayed behind; and, quitting the remembrance of the days when

the land above described was clothed in rapine and revenge, we shall introduce our readers to a pretty little fort, whose strategic value has of late years happily not been tried. Around it winds a road, which later makes its way between well-thatched farm-like buildings planted here and there on little rising-grounds, with pleasant streams of cool clear water flowing at their feet through grassy meadows backed with tamarind and the cactus tree. Such is the approach to a North-West oasis of celebrity for health and beauty. It lies below the outer ranges which form the Dehra Doon, and is well watered both by nature and by art. Saharanpoor affords resources of an uncommon order for the happy few who bask in its delights. The gentler members of that small community may roam for miles through shady gardens, maintained by Government at great expense as' nurseries for Himalayan plants, and as embracing the most favourable conditions for purposes of acclimatisation. The men may shoot and hunt a more extensive field of game than in almost any part of India, and the special duty which attaches to their well-favoured and well-paid office consists in looking after the birth, parentage, and education of thousands of young colts of mostly Arab blood. In other words, Saharanpoor, like Haupur and Buxar, is a stud depot, where corn and all required is grown upon the spot; and the work intrusted to the happy superintendents of that justly popular department really more resembles the employment of wealthy country gentlemen, who can afford to stay at home and nurse their own estates, than that of any class of public servants with which we are acquainted.

Five pleasant marches through a lovely country, much intersected by the drainage of the Himalayas, divide Saharanpoor from the ardent furnaces of the Roorkee workshops. These lie upon the straight, well-cultivated banks of the Ganges Canal, whose commencement, for purposes of irrigation, is here marked by two colossal lions, pointing the moral of the jealous watch maintained by the British Government over the waves of liquid treasure, which science has known how to pour upon a land by nature thirsty, but by art become one of the most fertile tracts of India.

Above Roorkee this artificial tide extends some twenty miles towards Hurdwar, where it taps the mighty Ganges just as it breaks cover from the Sawalik ranges of the Himalayas; and during that short span of twenty miles the eye is caught by three successive works of engineering skill, each of which in Europe would justly be regarded with the admiration due to mastery of mankind over matter. The ride from Roorkee to Hurdwar, rightly called the Ganges' Gate, taken on a bright spring morning, can never be forgotten. Turning your back upon those lions, your horses' heads would point to neighbouring hills, and distant mountains capped with snow. The road lies along the bank of the canal, which ends in several locks and dams abutting on the shallow rapids of the Ganges, here a full mile broad, filling a wide chasm or rather narrow valley borne between two wood-clad mountains. Where the highroad ends a narrow stony street begins, leading to the holy Ghât, or stairs of Vishnu, where two million pilgrims on an average bathe each year, and then return, comforted at heart, to homes unnumbered and unknown.

And now that we have traced the North-West Provinces from Benares to Hurdwar, and witnessed beneath one administration the most opposite effects, we shall direct our steps towards the former confines of our rule; and taking Muttra as our starting-point—that city where sainted monkeys govern most despotically—and rising with the Jumna towards its source, we reach the rocky range on which lies Delhi. The city of to-day, built by Shah Jehan, is actually subject to the North-West Government; but in character and associations it leans so strongly towards the Punjab, to which geographically it belongs, that we prefer postponing to some account of that administration a mention more detailed. So far back as 1829, Colonel Tod concluded an elaborate treatise on the Pandua dynasty, which ruled there from 1120 B.C. to 610 B.C., and counted, during that period, thirty-one generations of direct descent, by the following statement, since endorsed by actual fact : " Great Britain has become heir to the monuments of Indraprestha, raised by the descendants of Boodha and Ella ; to the iron pillar of Pandus, whose pedestal is fixed in hell— and in which some forms of Mahomedan belief are content to recognise the axis of the universe ; to the columns reared to Victory, inscribed with characters yet unread ; to the massive ruins of its ancient continuous cities, encompassing a space still larger than the largest city in the world, whose mouldering domes and sites of fortresses, the very names of which are lost, present a noble field for speculation on the ephemeral nature of power and glory." . With titles to our veneration such as these, Delhi surely forms a subject that should not be lightly touched upon towards the end of a somewhat hurried reference ; and we close the page before us with the expression of an earnest hope that, as years wear on, and England's Eastern Empire fulfils the expectations of the present generation, both courtly Agra and the imperial city of the Padshahs may again resume a precedence that the history of Asia still jealously reserves for them.

CHAPTER V.

THE LIEUTENANT-GOVERNMENT OF THE PUNJAB SUBORDINATE
TO THE GOVERNOR-GENERAL IN THE FOREIGN DEPARTMENT.

THE Foreign Department of the Government of India
is the mouthpiece of those decisions of the Crown, by
which so many Eastern kingdoms, principalities, and
powers, have ceased to throb with independent life,
and taken rank among the visions of the past. Hence
the high importance which in native minds instinctively
attaches to aught that serves to indicate the nature of
the thoughts that cloud the brows of Foreign Secretaries. In quiet times, when the Government of India
is reposing normally upon the putrid shores of the
Hoogly river, a Foreign Secretary's sense of personal
importance is reduced to something like a minimum;
but should any stirring question arise to unsettle native
thought in Oude or Rajpootana, or the succession be
disputed to some estates in Central India with which a
title and a taste of power still lurks, on such occasions
the antechambers of the Foreign Office are thronged
with subtle natives seeking access to the presence, and
bold aspirants with heavy purses girt around their
loins, whose golden burden is still brought half in

hope, though half perhaps in fear of failure, or still more in fear of the perils attendant on success: for those men of wild appearance, though born perhaps beyond our furthest frontier of Peshawur, know full well what deserts are dealt out to corruption by the British Government. Still the force of habits rife among themselves, enhanced by such education as they have enjoyed, and to which they owe a scanty knowledge of our early Anglo-Indian crimes,—these have taught them to consider that, though gold may be refused, and though no fitting opportunity of offering it may occur, yet to come empty-handed would render them a laughing-stock among their fellows, and might appear to signify indifference to success, or even want of due respect towards their rulers.

The coins they bring are indeed of no small use to them even in display. The lower class of native doorkeepers are open to such convincing proofs of wealth, if not respectability, and make cringing way to let their bearers pass upstairs: eventually they gain, after hours of parley and delay, the threshold of the first room occupied by Englishmen; but beyond that, few penetrate without good cause, for the presence of the Secretary himself is closely guarded by ambitious younger men, able to dispose of current cases with a perfect knowledge of the views of their superior.

A glance around the lofty spacious rooms where these picked men of action sit, will serve to illustrate the extent of country they administer. On all sides hang maps entitled Oude, Mysore, Punjab, and Rajpootana; while around lie fireproof safes bearing letters whence the intelligent may gather that the contents relate to Nagpore administration, or to that network of foreign policy in whose complicated meshes the abilities even of statesmen like Lord Ellenborough and Lord Dalhousie at last became so hopelessly entangled as to leave but one possible-escape—in war.

One of these maps has evidently been recently referred to, and still extends its length and breadth to view. It represents a tract of country whose right hand rests upon Thibet, while with its left it holds in check the hordes that would fain emerge in dark columns of destruction from the passes of Cabul, and descend like locusts on the harvest-bearing plains of Hindostan. This land is divided into nearly equal parts by six noble rivers, five of which have long since become historical, and lent to it a name now known as an emblem of well-directed energy and vigorous adminis tration.

The history of the Punjab for the last thirty years has been so pregnant with results as to render some short account requisite for the due appreciation of the conditions under which we first assumed its governance. The people, though brave, and turbulent among themselves, are quite content to be ruled by an iron hand, provided always the administration be powerful enough to inspire respect among neighbours even more turbulent and warlike than themselves. The population, which exceeds ten millions, consists of Jâts, Gugurs, Rajpoots, and Patans, of whom the second category alone are devoted to agricultural pursuits, the remaining three being wedded to the sword. Of Mussulmans recent computation has numbered seven millions, and these lie thickest as the Indus is approached. Towards the east Hindoos preponderate, but even there Mahomedans abound. Punjabees are finer-limbed and more stalwart in appearance than their brethren of Southern India. The men hold themselves erect, and have a martial bearing and bright eye unknown among Bengalees; while the women of Loodhiana and Umritsur, some of them fair as Europeans, are a type of rounded Eastern beauty. These are Hindostanees properly so called, and proud they are of the distinctive features of their race.

Such a country, so inhabited, surely was a worthy object of ambition for a man who seemed to have adopted as a rule of guidance the elementary doctrine of the fifteenth century, " that the heathen nations of the world were lawful spoil and prey, and that the right of native Indians was subordinate to that of the first Christian conqueror, whose paramount claim excluded that of every other civilised nation, and gradually extinguished that of the natives." Yet the Punjab's fall from independence was not purely the fruit of Lord Dalhousie's vast ambition, but the necessary consequence of dissensions of the Sikhs among themselves.

In 1838 the Maharaja Runjeet Singh entered into a tripartite treaty of alliance with the British and the Ameer Shah Shooja. The " Lion of the Punjab " died in the following year, and in 1840 his succeeding son and grandson both met with deaths of violence. A bloody competition followed between the widow of the son and Shere Singh, a brother upon whom was cast the stigma of an illegitimate birth. The latter gained the object of contention; but upon his assassination in 1843, a widespread anarchy prevailed, which, after desolating years, terminated in joint invasion, by all the hostile factions, of the Company's dominions. Two wars ensued, each of one year's duration, and in both victory was given to us; but in 1848 it had become apparent to the meanest comprehension that the only real guarantee for future peace lay in military occupation. It was, however, not less in the nature of things than the interest of humanity that this military occupation should become exchanged for annexation; and on the 29th of March 1849 annexation was solemnly proclaimed at Lahore, in the presence of assembled chiefs collected to receive the yoke of foreign subjugation. The yoke, however, has lain lightly on that land. Dhuleep Singh, the hereditary Maharaja, received an English education that fitted him to take his place as an Eastern prince of great accomplishments upon the steps of Queen Victoria's throne; and, liberally provided for by the bounty of the Company, he has led a happier, and probably a longer, life than he could have aspired to as ruler of a nation where assassination had become wellnigh the price of primogeniture.

Of the men selected by Lord Dalhousie to govern his greatest acquisition we shall later speak in more detail. The first form of government was a mixed military and civil board, presided over by Sir Henry Lawrence and his brother John; and in three short years the success that characterised its labours had been such as to call forth from the East India Company's Directors the following well-merited acknowledgment :—" In the short period which has elapsed since the Punjab became a part of the British dominions, results have been attained such as could scarcely have been hoped for as the reward of many years of well-directed exertion. The formidable army which it had required so many battles to subdue has been quietly disbanded, and the turbulent soldiery have settled to industrious pursuits. Peace and security reign throughout the country ; justice has been made accessible, without costly formalities, to the whole population ; industry and commerce have been set free ; and a great mass of oppressive taxation has been removed. Results like these reflect the highest honour on Indian administration. It is a source of just pride to us that our services, civil and military, should have afforded men capable, in so short a time, of carrying into full effect such a series of enlightened and beneficent measures. The executive functionaries in the subordinate ranks have proved themselves worthy of the honourable career which lies before them ; and the members of the Board of Administration, Sir Henry Lawrence, Mr John Lawrence, Mr Mansell, and Mr Montgomery, have entitled themselves to be placed in the very foremost rank of Indian administrators."

The history of the brothers Lawrence has long passed in the form of household words into English homes; and though the casual world is still in ignorance of many circumstances attending their divergence of opinion in the execution of their work, and of the reasons that forced Lord Dalhousie to change the character of Punjab administration by creating a Lieutenant-Government, conferred upon Sir John, and sending Sir Henry into prouder exile at Mount-Aboo, yet we prefer leaving to a special pen the explanation of such measures; and turning to Montgomery, later called Sir Robert, we have before us the outline of a man whose deeds are not yet written.

Sir Robert Montgomery was appointed by Lord Can ning, in a minute read by a privileged few, in which the claims of this administrator were summed up in a manner worthy of the author and his object. He assumed his office in 1859, having, as has been seen, previously enjoyed the fullest opportunities of acquaintance with his subjects. He ruled the Punjab until the other day, and has left among its martial races a name not soon to be forgotten. Still, notwithstanding his unquestioned ability and good-nature, he was not a general favourite. His detractors have accused him of endeavouring to introduce in India the system of bestowing patronage brought at home to such perfection ; and it is a fact that Anarkullee, the civil station of Lahore, has of late years become best known to the initiated by the familiar name of " Cozengunge." It is, however, far too easy to find fault ; and the narrow limit of these pages may better be employed in chronicling results than in barren criticism. The administration of Sir Robert was marked by measures of improvement, steady and progressive. Finance, specially detailed to the supervision of Mr Donald Friell M'Leod, remained in a manner subject to the general control of the Lieutenant-Governor, and has amply proved the justice of the sanguine statements advanced during the early years succeeding Punjab annexation. Education has become not only an essential qualification for those in search of place, but, more perhaps than anywhere in India, the distinctive mark of gentle blood. Some few years ago, Punjab chiefs made wellnigh boast of ignorance, pointing proudly, from the height of their descent, to native pundits and well-paid librarians, as those intrusted with the keeping of their rusty minds. But now all this has changed, and the better classes rival one another in munificent donations to scholastic institutions of all kinds. Neither have the material interests of the native population been neglected in this whirl of intellectual advancement. The progress of canal and road construction, introduced by Sir Henry Lawrence and Sir John, has not suffered interruption even of a day, and the several Doabs formed by the mighty rivers which collect the drainage of the Himalayas have steadily increased in the measure of their crops.

Under Providence all this has been effected by a pleasant-looking man of middle height, whose benign appearance militates against the known severity of his decisions. In him, regular attendance at divine service, audible repetition of the responses, and large participation in all missionary works, did not prove incompatible with, displace, or even mitigate, the readiness with which he had resort to capital punishment, or applauded a liberal use of rope by the junior members of his administration. This peculiar feature in a man so gifted as Sir Robert Montgomery has not escaped the keen observation of some previous writers; and Mr Martin quotes, in his 'Progress and Present State of British India,' a letter dated "Lahore, Sunday, 9 A.M.," wherein

the Lieutenant-Governor congratulates Mr Frederick
Cooper, one of his so-called hanging commissioners, in
the warmest terms, on the manner in which the 20th
Regiment of Native Infantry had been by him blotted
out of the book of life for some imagined signs of disaffection, adding, "Three other regiments here were very
shaky yesterday, but I hardly think they will go now. I
wish they would, as they are a nuisance, and not a man
would escape if they do." Mr Martin holds that this
rejoicing over the extermination of a thousand men, and
eagerness to find a pretext for the destruction of three
thousand more, reads strangely from the pen of one of the
most prominent advocates for the propagation of Christianity in India, but it explains in his eyes why " our
success as subjugators has been attended by failure as
evangelists." The fact is, that Sir Robert ruled in virtue of power received from others, ever stretched by
him to its utmost limits, not by the suffrage of mankind
at large ; and could at any moment the third Napoleon's
invention of the plebiscite have been introduced throughout the land of the five rivers, at that moment Sir
Robert would have ceased to reign. He governed rather
by reason of the machinery at his command than by
his personal ascendancy ; and it may be questioned
whether attributes like his would have shone with equal
lustre in the piping times of peace as in the years of
mutiny and reconquest that little short of his prosperity
could have adorned.

The Punjab is the country which has derived perhaps the largest, and certainly the most rapid, advantages from British rule, and it has become the custom

to consider these results as simple consequences of the
special vigour of its administration.   But we prefer
to trace them rather to the difference between its
people and those of other parts of India ; and without
wishing to detract from the meed of praise so well
bestowed on Mr Richard Temple, and on others of the
Punjab school, we may be allowed to question both
the justice and the wisdom of building up so high a
reputational edifice in favour of one class of public
servants, solely on the basis of the presumed inferiority
of others.   Those who rule the Punjab have great
advantages in climate over their colleagues in more
southern provinces ; for while, in Bengal, Darjeeling is
almost the solitary hill-station tolerably accessible and
worthy of the name, and the North-West Provinces
are not much better off, the sanitaria of the Punjab
are numerous, and lie unrivalled in their beauty,
thickly scattered on its north and eastern frontiers.
The principle of giving most to him that hath already,
has been clearly followed in the circumstances attending Punjab life ; and Nature has been as prodigal in
clothing her Himalayan slopes with rhododendron and
the ilex, as the Administration has been active in turning these advantages to account.

Everything thus tends to render labour in the Punjab far preferable to Bengal and North-Western service.
Moreover, the former is practically enhanced by all
the benefits military prestige can bestow, when compared with a purely civil and commercial past ; and
hence it was a heavy blow to ambitious souls like Mr
Frederick Cooper when Delhi passed into North-West

hands. Many of these men had become conspicuous in the conduct of the non-regulation system, and had thereby rather incurred the jealousy than the admiration of the milder and perhaps more strictly constitutional government of Agra. The motives for the transfer must be sought in a desire for symmetry, such as draws France towards the Rhine in search of a natural barrier, and also may be in the wish to mark the high estate from which a capital may fall by becoming a focus of revolt. Thus, for her sins, Delhi was bound hand and foot, and made over to the tender care of a once subordinate administration, thereby disconnecting the Sikh people from all supposed participation in disloyalty. Such are the only explanations of this measure; and had its details been carried out with more regard for the personal interests and position of the officials left dependent on a government not over-well disposed towards them, it might have passed uncriticised as an act of policy well conceived to flatter native vanity on both the Jumna's banks.

But this was not the case. It was indeed far otherwise; and those who have known the Delhi of more recent years have also known how Mr Frederick Cooper as Deputy-Commissioner, aided by his military colleague, Lord Mark Kerr, has worked to clear away the visible remains of mutiny; and how, by carefully remodelling what remained of native society, he has forced his former Punjab masters into a recognition, tardy and compelled, of services, which, to the last, the North-West Government seemed systematically to ignore. Of the old city, with its gates opening

on the roads to Agra and Cashmere which Lieutenants
Home and Salkeld immortalised in death, it is not
our intention now to speak; but rather of those
practical municipal reforms which have converted a
den of thieves into a pattern of propriety. Before
and after daylight two figures might be seen tracing
with their hands the lines that boulevards, streets, and
drains should follow so as to combine strategic purposes with beauty. For years this work went on, unheeded from without, except when now and then
discouraged by financial pressure, until, to each in-
habitant of that crowded city, the eager faces of those
men became familiar. On foot and unattended they
dived down cut-throat alleys, whose vicious depths
no European save drunken troops in search of plunder had previously penetrated. From these abodes
of pestilential crime they might, as the sun set with
Eastern splendour behind the sea of tombs and desolation surrounding Delhi, be often seen emerging,
and, recognised from afar, be followed home by ragged
crowds of hungry bearers of petitions. In the examination of these papers and in dispensing justice Mr
Cooper's noontide hours were spent, Lord Mark Kerr
being occupied the while with garrison affairs. To
these two men nothing appeared trivial that concerned
the welfare of that city; and while no civic work to
benefit the natives seemed too great for them to
undertake, they devoted equal thought and care to
the construction and endowment of tennis-courts and
circulating libraries, and all that tended to increase
the welfare of the white inhabitants.

When claims are so nearly balanced as between these two reformers, comparison becomes even more than usually odious. Mr Cooper was a civilian of the Punjab school, whose former life had been devoted to what may be termed the pleasures of his office. To him health and other stern realities of life were ever subordinate to the ambition of bringing credit on the administration in which he took a prominent share. Lord Mark Kerr was a keen Scotch soldier, who had passed some years on Lord Elgin's staff in Canada, and whose spurs, well earned in the Crimean War, had been worn worthily throughout the Indian Mutiny. Of his cool daring on occasions calculated to try even courage of no common cast, many anecdotes are still told by his comrades of those days, when he and they received together their baptism of fire. His was a nature that in private life made every child his friend, and in his public character no man could be his enemy. Foremost among the most prominent of bold horsemen, his spare form was always to be seen in search of danger and distinction; but, the battle won, and the sword of victory sheathed, Lord Mark Kerr became essentially a man of peace, devoted to the practical improvement of his conquests. Thus Mr Cooper and Lord Mark Kerr were men of a rare mould, such as India requires. In time of war the former could display a heroism and martial ardour only to be rivalled by the ease with which the latter, at a moment's notice, could lay aside his armour and embrace the arts of peace.

Leaving Delhi, and turning our attention beyond

the massive fort of Selimghur and the marble screens of the Dewani-Khas, we find two monuments, at some miles' distance, emblematic of the civilisation of the East and West. The first stands conspicuous among the ruins whence it towers its fluted height, and, dipping, though but slightly, towards the sun, like Pisa's leaning tower, is known throughout the world as the Column of the Kutub. The second is the remnant of a shady residence by the water-side, in whose halls Canova's models and the works of Sir William Jones once dwelt in harmony; but when the tide of mutiny swept across the land, all that owned a European origin was laid low; and Metcalfe's house, plate, pictures, and priceless manuscript collections, were plundered and destroyed by uncultivated rebels, to whom their value was unknown. All that now remains to the representative of perhaps the greatest of our Anglo-Indian families—the only family we know of that loved its adopted country well enough to settle in it, blindly trusting for protection to native gratitude—is an insufficient sum of money, with difficulty obtained from Government as compensation at a time of need, and the satisfaction of knowing that a broken limb of an historic statue is shown to every traveller who visits Delhi as wellnigh all now left of Metcalfe's property.

Leaving Delhi to the south, and travelling by the Grand Trunk Road through Kurnal, Umballa, Loodhiana, and Jullundhar, one enters the country of the Kuppoorthulla Raja, a chief whose outward signs of loyalty far exceed the studied demonstrations of his fellows. No path to English favour does he indeed appear to have left untrodden. The Christianity taught him by the proselytising members of Punjab administration he embraced with fervour; and, having made himself master of the English language, he put a finishing-stroke to the adoption of our customs by taking to himself an English wife. This distinctive conduct has marked him out to history as an early pattern of a class probably destined to become a real source of union between the Sikh races and ourselves, and for the present has secured to him a lion's share of honours and rewards, to which neither his rank nor power alone could have entitled him.

Proceeding further still, the same road strikes the Beas river, ascending which, and leaving severally to the right and left the Mundi and the Chumba Raja's territories, the traveller, turning shortly to the north, enters on a highland glen of grand peculiar beauty. Yet a little and the river, here become a mountain torrent fed by the melting snows that form a fitting frame for the granite peaks of Spiti and Lahoul, surges past the ancient walls of Sultanpore. Across that background winds amid rare loveliness the Rotung Pass of 13,000 feet, from whence can be descried the Chandra river and the mountains of Cashmere. A distant glimpse of those rugged Pinjal ranges, by which a jealous nature has hedged in the vale enclosing Sirinagur, "the City of the Sun," is sufficient to convince the most casual observer of the rich fertility of Runbeer Singh's dominions. But a closer and more careful examination cannot fail to raise within the breasts of Englishmen a deep and unavailing grief that this paradise on earth,

where Bernier has placed the site of our first parents'
happiness, should after conquest have been permitted
to pass into foreign hands, by the treaty of Umritsur
in 1846, in consideration of the payment of three-quar-
ters of a million sterling.   In those days, however,
India seemed a boundless field for gain, and the circumstances of the hour were farmed with little thought for
future generations of administrators, who, succeeding
one another with a rapidity unknown in Europe, have
landed us to-day upon the brink of bankruptcy.

After three years' government of the Punjab by the
board appointed by Lord Dalhousie, Sir Henry Lawrence estimated that, deducting ample funds for works
of general improvement, a surplus revenue would remain
of half a million sterling.   This flourishing condition
continued to improve throughout the years that followed ; and amid the ruins of Lord Dalhousie's Indian
policy, the fabric built up by Punjab annexation has
raised its monumental head in proof of at least the part
fulfilment of that statesman's prophecies.   The sweep-
ing centralisation of finance introduced by Mr Wilson,
has done, however, much to cast the bright outline of
success surrounding Northern Hindostan into the shade
of more general failure ; and thus, amidst the general
want of money, the services of special men who for
years represented the credit columns of our Indian
accounts, have almost passed unnoticed by the outer
world.   Two of these long conducted in the Punjab the
Departments of Justice and Finance.   Of Mr M'Leod,
the Finance Commissioner, a laborious lover of hard
work, it might be thought perhaps by some that he was

little more than an accountant ought to be. But those who judged him thus best proved their ignorance; for those who knew him better have expressed a blind belief in the wisdom of his scrupulous decisions; and since the claims of military candidates like Sir Herbert Edwardes, Sir Robert Napier, Colonel Lake, or Colonel H. M. Durand, to govern the Punjab, were not destined to receive a favourable consideration from Sir John Lawrence, a civilian Viceroy, no choice perhaps could have been made of a successor to Sir Robert Montgomery combining equal qualifications and requirements. The picture of his colleague, the officiating Punjab Minister of Justice, deserves more studied painting; for without sufficient care in treatment, it might appear that the character of Mr Robert Nedham Cust lacked courage. His talents were of the very highest order, and his eloquence on paper was only to be equalled by the soundness of his law. Yet, in spite of these attainments, he counted among his co-administrators many who sought to dull his fame by anecdotes in which the hero played a part remarkable for the absence of heroic qualities. Great men must take, however, the pains as well as the pleasures of high place, and may well rest contented when the balance left upon the public mind is even slightly in their favour. In this respect the man we speak of has shone conspicuous for good sense; for, leaving his repute to be judged of by professional success, he has consistently avoided seeking honours in the path of needless danger.

Among these zealous Punjab servants the name of

Sir Herbert Edwardes stands out prominently as an illustration of a class happily now numerous, whose origin is traceable to the liberal introduction by Lord Dalhousie of the military element into civil administration. The advantage of this system has been so fully proved by time, that it has become almost unnecessary to repeat the arguments brought forward in support of its efficiency and economy. In time of peace a large reserve of officers is kept employed in civil work, whose local experience thus gained cannot but conduce in time of war to the more successful conduct of campaigns, and the State, when subject to the enhanced burthens inseparable from a condition of hostility, is relieved at least from the necessity of maintaining supernumerary civilians. To impartial observers of to-day, the only question is the true proportion the elements in question should bear to one another in different parts of India. To the consideration of this point Lord Dalhousie brought his rich experience, and he has left behind him records of his views, whence it may be fairly gathered that the covenanted India Civil Service, recruited as it now is from home in its legal and financial branches by men of riper years, is still capable of safe reduction. We must not, however, permit the general question to take the place here found for a brief allusion to Sir Herbert Edwardes, whose bright career, commencing with the capture of Mooltan in January 1849, has run a course consistent with the character of a Christian, soldier and civilian.

The proselytising spirit that has become one of the marked characteristics of Punjab administration has been traced by some to the practical application of the fact that imitation is the most sincere of flattery; and this has often of late years been cast in the teeth of those who followed in the footsteps of Sir Henry Lawrence. It is not, therefore, singular that the bold position occupied by Sir Herbert Edwardes, whose purse and pen have ever been devoted to the cause of Christianity, should have become a target for the arrows of the covenanted Civil Service. The duties with which we now desire, however, to associate his name are other than those that he imposed upon himself, and though perhaps less brilliant than the exploits partially recorded in 'A Year on the Punjab Frontier,' are not without their interest, as typical of Anglo-Indian non-regulation government.

The river Sutlej separates two families of native rulers of the second class, whose broad lands and almost sovereign rights have mostly been conferred upon them by the Government of India in reward for signal service at a time of need. They are termed the Cis and Trans Sutlej States, and are ruled by officers styled Commissioners of the Jullunder and Umballa divisions, who, appointed by the Lieutenant-Governor of the Punjab, are further clothed with certain political or diplomatic powers by the Government Supreme, as accredited agents to the native courts within their jurisdiction. At the time we speak of these envied posts were occupied by Sir Herbert Edwardes and Colonel Edward Lake, to whom custom and the nature of their duties, including as they did the supervision of many mountain Rajas, had awarded two residences apiece, whereat to

H

pass in turn the cold and summer solstice. Thus with the approach of April, there known for scorching winds and the necessity for tatties, in place of the fragrant and refreshing showers with which that month is most associated in English minds, Sir Herbert Edwardes was wont to break up from his winter residence at Umballa, and retire to an elevation of some 7000 feet on the Simla road, known as the Kussowlie Heights, and there, more free from interruption, he could devote at least some portion of his time and thoughts to those literary tasks that he delighted in, and that in early days first brought him into notice as the author of a series of most able letters from " A Brahminee Bull to his Cousin John in England." In such pursuits he spent the little leisure falling to the lot of an overworked administrator; and thence at times he raised his weary eyes from the crabbed characters of ancient Persian manuscripts to gaze upon the burnt-up plains below him, stretching from the furthest Himalayan spur far beyond Umballa into dusty space, seamed only by the winding Sutlej as it bursts from its mountain home and takes its rapid course towards the west. Still this hilly solitude and the benefit of cool breezes once a-year were not enough to reinvigorate a constitution sapped by ceaseless work beneath a broiling sun; and at length Sir Herbert found himself reluctantly compelled to follow the advice of his physician, and abandon a field of action wherein lay deep imbedded the serious interests of his life.

But our readers must now turn their backs upon the Punjab and its rulers. Other opportunities will present themselves for studying the characters of men like Mr

Richard Temple and Mr Lewin Bowring, both of whom acquired the art of government in the Punjab school, and now reign over extensive provinces of South and Central Hindostan. A comparison between these two last is alike tempting to the writer and the artist; but as the picture may be introduced hereafter with greater historical precision, we shall return at once to the busy Foreign Office at Calcutta, and, rolling up the Punjab map, direct our observation first to the non-regulation provinces of Oude, Mysore, Nagpore; and, secondly, to the political department of the Government of India, through which relations are maintained with semi-sovereign and protected states, and our other Eastern neighbours.

CHAPTER VI.

THE NON-REGULATION PROVINCES OF OUDE, MYSORE, NAGPORE, SUBORDINATE TO THE GOVERNOR-GENERAL IN THE FOREIGN DEPARTMENT.

SOME writers have attempted, in a passing pleasant manner, to convey to those who stay at home some faint idea of Anglo-Indian service, and the attempt has failed, for none who have not known how the official zealot turns under India's scorching sun in despair and almost self-defence to every occupation tending to create new and local interests, can understand the frame of mind in which a civil servant day after day fastens his attention on dull conflicts of Mahomedan and Hindoo law, until to him the only life worth living seems one depending as for food on reams of foolscap paper and crowds of copying clerks.

That, however, labour of a most practical character awaits all of every grade employed in Indian office life will appear from a bare enumeration of the broad dependencies whose orders reach them through the correspondence of the Foreign Office. This Calcutta Foreign Office, though but one of the five departments to which the executive Government of India is intrusted, dictates conditions of existence to the thirty-three million human beings who live and die beneath the so-called non-regulation system. Last of the states so ruled in date of acquisition, and least in area, stands Oude, a kingdom, up to 1856, of which Sir James Outram and Sir Henry Lawrence would fain have saved the independence, had not its inhabitants and court been sunk too deep in infamy to understand the virtue of their remedies. Second in size and prestige rank the Mysore Raja's territories, which, since the days of Sir Mark Cubbon, have steadily increased both in commercial and political importance. Next come the Central Provinces, vast and ill-defined, now for the first time ruled by a man capable of doing justice to their pent-up resources. Then there is the whole of British Burma, and the Strait Settlements of Penang and Singapore; and if to these we add the Punjab, and the entire political control of the Rajpootana States, and such Central India chiefs as Scindia and Holkar, it will be readily admitted that this small world contains few offices of responsibility and power equal to that of Foreign Secretary to the Government of India.

. Oude, Mysore, Nagpore, are three great names in Indian history, each one of which, not very many years ago, represented to the eye of European imagination long lines of princes deriving their titles and estates from the most remote of ages known to even Eastern garter kings-at-arms. To each of them, mighty revenues, densely-peopled districts, and martial pride seemed to promise a long and favoured national life. In past times they had made peace and war with one another, and, when united, had more than once successfully

defied the Affghan and the Lion of Lahore. To-day
these three sovereign states are blended harmoniously
together beneath one giant administration, and minister to one another's commercial and financial wants
with all the touching tenderness of sisters long estranged.
But though they seem to form one picture, wherein each
rock and tree and blade of grass is quarried, felled, or
mown to the mutual advantage of the soil and its pro-
prietors, they are still divided into three by boundaries
which Nature has prescribed, and which neither Company nor Crown has been able to obliterate. The reins
of government centre in the hands of the Foreign
Secretary, as the constitutional repository of the Viceroy's conscience, at least with reference to non-regulation
provinces; and at the time we write of, circumstances
had placed this trust within the keeping of Colonel
Henry Marion Durand.

It is said that Lord Ellenborough selected young
Durand, then a junior officer of engineers, to accompany
him to India in the capacity of aide-de-camp; that the
quick eye of that rash statesman speedily detected
talents in his *protégé* of no common order; and that,
on arrival in Calcutta, he appointed him his private
secretary. The experience thus gained at an early age
ripened later into precious fruit beneath the burning
sun of Cabul and Indore. Throughout the Indian
Mutiny Colonel Durand's position gave him opportunities of inspiring confidence both as a soldier and
diplomatist; and shortly after its suppression he obtained a seat in Sir Charles Wood's Council, where his
restless pen found ample occupation in recording his

convictions on every Eastern question. Urged, however, by Lord Canning, he did not long enjoy the ease,
combined with dignity, of the Council Board at home,
but, returning to Calcutta, entered on the labours of
the Foreign Office. The reasons that induced Lord
Canning to desire to place a military man in charge of
the political relations of the Government of India—an
office hitherto conducted by civilians—must be sought
for, partially no doubt, in the very special fitness of
Colonel Durand; but perhaps not less in a desire to
make one last protest against the system of exclusion
so long practised by the Company in favour of their
covenanted civil servants, and to open up to really
public competition those imperial departments of the
Government, whose daily labours embrace the interests
of all classes of the many-coloured populations of our
Indian Empire.

The law required, however, that the reasons for select-
ing one unfitted for the post by his profession should
be reported for approval of the Government at home;
and Sir Charles Wood found himself compelled either
to disallow a principle to which he had practically
given his consent, or else indorse Lord Canning's choice.
In the consideration of this question it was but natural
he should cast his eye across the broad horizon of India's
political condition. Unexampled prosperity, the result
of but a few years' unexampled peace, had bred a wide
confidence in his decisions among the native population.
Many causes had combined to render civil administration most popular at the hands of military men. To
the martial spirit of the Punjab we had looked, and not

in vain, for efficient aid throughout our recent troubles.
To that country the name of Colonel Durand was not
only familiar, but recalled the long-cherished memory
of a great day, when the avenging tribes of Northern
India espoused with warmth the cause of our murdered
countrymen in Cabul, when, led by English officers,
they forced their way through passes hitherto regarded as
the gates of death, and received, beneath the lofty walls
of Ghuznee, a patent hostage of success in the recovery
of the Gates of Somnauth. Those far-famed gates had,
eight hundred years before, been carried off by Sultan
Mahmoud from a singularly sacred Brahmin temple
dedicated to a god in whose honour it was held that
the sea daily rose and fell in tidal homage. Their
costly weight of sandal-wood had been dragged by
victorious cannon into long exile among wild infidels,
the depth of whose religious and political fanaticism
could but be measured by their bloodthirstiness and
contempt for human life; and these gates were now
brought back in triumph, and restored, amid the accla-
mations of two hundred thousand warriors, to the bosom
of a proud nation's faith. In Lord Ellenborough's own
words, "The insult of eight hundred years had been
avenged in 1842;" and to the Punjab mind a proud
consciousness of great deeds done together was the first
feeling that the name of Colonel Durand instinctively
inspired. A second memory, with which he must ever
be associated, belongs to the history of more recent
times, when, in Central India, on the banks of the
Nerbudda, he, from a knowledge of native character
acquired among them, had leant with confidence upon

those loyal Rajpoots, among whose traditions he felt himself so much at home; for, in a word, it was Colonel Durand who, in 1857, stood to his ground, and stemmed the flood of. mutiny from bursting into Hyderabad and pouring down the Deccan.

These are some of many thoughts that must have crowded on Sir Charles Wood's mind when he turned a scrupulous attention to the claims advanced in favour of an engineer as Foreign Secretary; and to them he doubtless added his own personal remembrance of many able minutes, the characteristic penmanship of which was singularly adapted to lend the charm of easy reading to close argument

The Foreign Secretariat, however, may with some justice be regarded as the blue ribbon of Indian departmental life; and it was not without much jealousy that civilians of the Lushington and Prinsep school saw its mantle fall upon a military man.   Sir Charles Wood's Council numbered many whose advice, if followed, would not have sanctioned this emancipation; but happily the ultimate decision rested in the hands of one well used to frame and follow opinions of his own, who, from the depths of his experience, and unbiassed by the prejudices of a professional education or career, could calmly weigh each argument in turn.   Thus it was that, after some delay, the nomination of Colonel H. M. Durand was confirmed from home; and he entered on the full performance of his duties shortly after the arrival of Lord Elgin at Calcutta.

The nature of those duties has been sufficiently explained.   They embrace within their limits the whole

network of India's external policy, besides the direct
administration of one-third of our Eastern Empire.
The foreign department is indeed so large a Government machine that it has been found essential to divide
it into many branches; thus it has separate establish-
ments for its financial, military, and civil labours, each
conducted by a staff of well-trained officials, specially
acquainted with the technicalities of their respective
subjects, and presided over by such men as Messrs
Wheeler or Macleod, who, from personal experience,
combined with natural executive ability, are alone
competent to guide the wheels of these subordinate
administrations.

In the discharge of his duties Colonel Durand had the
rare good-fortune to be associated with one, young in
years, but gifted équally with power of application and
the art of making others work under him. Mr C. U.
Aitcheson was among the first of those who braved successfully the early rigours of the competition system.
Of stubborn Scotch origin, he had from boyhood set his
mind upon the East, and with a strong will had steadily
worked out his education in the teeth of many disadvantages; so that, when the doors of Haileybury were
closed for ever against the sons and nephews of influential men, and other channels were opened for the
recruitment of the Indian Civil Service, he was found
prepared to struggle for a much-contested prize with
candidates of every denomination. His early zeal had
been but whetted by a short Punjab career; and when,
to the surprise of all, and most of all himself, a Calcutta
telegram reached the distant spot where he had won

such speedy reputation, offering him the post of Foreign Under-Secretary to the Government of India, he, true to his antecedents, was found again prepared to do credit to the choice.

But to return to the three provinces to which this chapter.has been dedicated, and primarily to Oude, that crowning stroke of Lord Dalhousie's annexations —an annexation that has been so warmly canvassed for so many years, and that, while called by some an "expedient escheat," and a " *Dacoitee in excelsis*," has, on the other hand, been defended as a righteous act by calm reflective men of office of a widely different stamp from him by whom it was at last reluctantly proclaimed.

Lying on our line of northern march, Oude was inhabited by robber races who long lived by robbing one another. The rich had fed upon the poor, until finally the latter ceased to till the fields, and adopted the example set them by their betters. So long as rapine was confined within the limits of the kingdom, the East India Company only raised its voice at intervals in the general interest of humanity; but when the area of anarchy gradually extended itself, and lastly knew no bounds at all, the oft-repeated words of warning were once more spoken in the Alumbagh, and a term was fixed at whose expiry the forbearance of the British Government should end. The events that shortly after followed are well known, and have only been too often twisted into would-be inevitable results of certain policies pursued—a method of proceeding calculated to provoke distrust in native minds; where-

as, if people would cease to seek for causes and effects
so far beneath the surface, more truthful narratives
might sometimes see the light, at least where India is
concerned.

Singularly rich in all the elements of agricultural
prosperity, this country had merited a better fate than
the one its vicious rulers had entailed upon it. Its
early history had combined domestic happiness with
success in foreign war; and among the more remote
and darker pages of the past, traces are sometimes
found in Oude of a civilisation then unknown in other
parts of India. The reigns, however, of a long line of
licentious rulers had at length so degraded the condition of the people, as to render some change essential
to the continuance of their bare physical existence.
Of these rulers a graphic picture has been drawn by
Mr Kaye, in words so picturesque and forcible as to
leave no room for further comment :—

"It would take long to trace the history of the pro
gressive misrule of the Oude dominions under a suc
cession of sovereigns all of the same class—passive per-
mitters of evil rather than active perpetrators of ini-
quity—careless of, but not rejoicing in, the sufferings
of their people. The rulers of Oude, whether Wuzeers
or Kings, had not the energy to be tyrants. They
simply allowed things to take their course. Sunk in
voluptuousness and pollution, often too horribly revolting to be described, they gave themselves up to the
guidance of panders and parasites, and cared not so
long as these wretched creatures administered to their
sensual appetites. Affairs of state were pushed aside as

painful intrusions. Corruption stalked openly abroad, every one had his price; place, honour, justice—everything was to be bought; fiddlers, barbers, and mountebanks became great functionaries. There were high revels at the capital, whilst in the interior of the country every kind of enormity was being exercised to wring from the helpless people the money which supplied the indulgences of the court. Much of the land was farmed out to large contractors, who exacted every possible farthing from the cultivators, and were not seldom, upon complaint of extortion, made, unless inquiry were silenced by corruption, to disgorge into the royal treasury a portion of their gains. Murders of the most revolting type, gang robberies of the most outrageous character, were committed in open day. There were no courts of justice except at Lucknow, no police but at the capital and on the frontier. The British troops were continually called out to coerce refractory landowners, and to stimulate revenue collection at the point of the bayonet. The sovereign—Wuzeer or King—knew that they would do their duty,—knew that, under the obligations of the treaty, his authority would be supported; and so he lay secure in his zenana, and fiddled while his country was in flames."

Under such conditions of misrule as are here portrayed, any change could hardly fail to prove of benefit to the bulk of the population. The misruling class of course were doomed to suffer; and when the change, so long in vain expected from within, came finally from without by annexation, mutiny, siege,

relief, and consequent re-occupation by our armies
rapidly succeeding one another, Lord Canning's proclamation placed the British Government in a new
position as towards that country, and enabled us to
mete out life and death, rewards and confiscation, as
the ends of justice and imperial interests demanded.
Thus upon the ruins of a kingdom whose martial
ardour had· destroyed itself, by casting civil honours
into disrepute, Lord Canning laid the foundations of a
proud and peaceful province, creating from the social
chaos caused by the bloodshed of Cawnpore and Lucknow a landed aristocracy, whose Talookdaree rights
afford the surest guarantee for future loyalty.

Whether this great measure should take its place
among the world's failures or successes, and justify
the voice of general approval or the censure of Lord
Ellenborough, depended chiefly on those who were
selected to work out practically the details of a great
theoretical conception. Mr Wingfield and Mr Yule
were both well fitted to succeed in such a task. Both
belonged to the old civilian school, who, untiring at
the desk in their cutcherry, yet dearly loved the chase,
prided themselves on owning the best elephants, and
thus became identified with the pleasures as well as
the taxation of the races over which they ruled. These
were the men that Lord Canning wisely chose to heal
the open wounds of Oude.

These wounds were deep, and skill and time combined were needed for their cure; but when Lucknow
is visited to-day by one familiar with the deeds of
Major Aitken and the Baillie Guard, so great a change

is noticeable that he would find it hard to trace among the walks and shrubberies of Wingfield Gardens his recollections of the siege. The change extends more-over to every circumstance of life connected with that country. Its people are now gradually acquiring a long-forgotten industry and enterprise; while the aboli-tion of a frontier, and enhanced security for human life and property, have paved the way for English capital and immigration. The natives have shown no want of energy in aiding us in the regeneration of their distracted and exhausted land, but, headed by Maun Singh, a leading Talookdar, whose genius guided him successfully through the perilous path of mutiny, and ever earned him prominent place in the councils of the ascendant party, they have proved that Oude can still maintain her rank among the states of Hindostan, and that the mother of rebellion can be-come a loyal daughter of the Crown.

In bestowing praise on Messrs Yule and Wingfield, we must not forget to whom, second to Lord Canning, their choice was mainly due. The patronage enjoyed by Indian Viceroys is so extensive, and other claims on their attention are so numerous, that it has become the almost inevitable practice to intrust much patron-age virtually to the hands of others. The Private Secretary is usually the medium through which this power is exercised, and in this office Lord Canning had through four long years the great advantage of being served by Mr Lewin Bowring, a civil servant of Bengal who had been early grafted on the tree of Punjab administration. Upon him it was that Lord

Canning on departure bestowed the government of Mysore and Coorg; and though it might be questioned whether Mr Bowring's seniority and services alone entitled him to this preferment, his subsequent success affords the fittest justification for an appointment which many chose to read as rather savouring of nepotism.

Thus Mr Bowring entered on his duties under circumstances that could but tend to pave the way to criticism. Some there were of local reputation, who, deeming their own claims far superior to his, did not shrink from their assertion; and it was only by judicious action, and a complete reorganisation of the old Commission, that things smoothed down into the mutual confidence and goodwill so essential to the conduct of a native state, where corrupt ministers are quick to trace the signs of personal jealousy, and, by widening the breach between an officer and his subordinates, attain for themselves a practical ascendancy.

The early records of Mysore are even more obscure than average Oriental history, and no authentic chronicles have yet been discovered of an earlier date than the year 1300. But even then her reputed wealth and beauty had aroused the cupidity of the Court of Delhi, and the fourteenth century was spent in predatory invasions and eventual subjugation to the Great Mogul. From that time until the star of Hyder Ali rose in 1749, Mysore could hardly boast of much political existence. Ruled at times by greedy Viceroys from afar, at times by local princes, whose reigns were only distinguished from each other by more or less oppression and resistance, the tide of ages swept swiftly by, leaving little else than bloodshed in its wake; and then, borne on the wings of time and improved communications, came other claimants from both land and sea: the French and English arrived in ships to wage a contest with the armies of the Peishwa and Nizam, and finally to fight among themselves for the disputed prize. Meanwhile from Delhi and Lucknow came emissaries with threats and bribes and promised aid, and in the midst of the confusion Hyder Ali Khan, a Mussulman in the service of the Mysore Raja, steered a course conspicuous for its bold unscrupulous success.

Rising from the ranks to the command of his master's armies, Hyder Ali brought Mysore proper, Coorg, with the Carnatic and much within the Deccan, under subjugation. Abroad and at home he was feared with that fear most conducive to the stability of an Eastern rule. He was at the zenith of his conquests and dominion when the titular ruler of Mysore, Chumraj, died; and the events that followed cannot be better given than in the words of Colonel Wilkes:—"Hyder Ali had hitherto professed to hold Mysore in behalf of the Hindoo house, and amused his subjects, on every annual feast of the Dessara, by exhibiting the pageant seated on his ivory throne in the balcony of state, himself occupying the place of minister and commander-in-chief. This ceremonial in most countries would have excited feelings dangerous to the usurper; but the unhappy Hindoos saw their country everywhere sustaining the scourge of Mahomedan rule. The singular exception of the Mahratta State, a wide-spreading example

of a still more ruthless oppression, restrained their
natural preference for rulers of their own persuasion,
and they were soothed by the occasional condescension
which treated them and their institutions with a sem-
blance of respect.   Hyder saw and indulged the working
of these reflections, and determined to have another
pageant.   The lineal male succession was extinct, and
he ordered all the children to be collected from the
different branches of the house who, according to
ancient precedent, were entitled to furnish a successor
to the throne.   The ceremonial observed on this occasion, however childish, was in perfect accordance with
the feelings which he intended to delude, and sufficiently adapted to the superstition of the fatalist.   The hall
of audience was strewed with fruits, sweetmeats, and
flowers, playthings of various descriptions, arms, books,
male and female ornaments, bags of money, and every
varied object of puerile or manly pursuit.   The children
were introduced together, and were all invited to help
themselves to whatever they liked best.   The greater
number were quickly engaged in a scramble for fruits,
sweetmeats, and toys, but one child was attracted by a
brilliant little dagger, which he took up in his right
hand, and soon after a lime in his left. 'That is the
Raja,' exclaimed Hyder. 'His first care is military
protection—his second, to realise the produce of his
dominions; bring him hither and let me embrace him.'
The assembly was in a universal murmur of applause
the child was conducted to the Hindoo palace, and prepared for installation.   His name was also Chumraj,
and he was the father of the Raja who was placed by

the English at the head of the Hindoo house of Mysore on the subversion of the Mahomedan dynasty in 1799."

The melodramatic incident above related satisfactorily performed, the restless Hyder Ali betook himself to further conquests, and, notwithstanding some reverses, repaired by treachery, from which as a last resource he never shrank, he pursued the path of victory till death closed his unscrupulous career, in camp near Arcot, on 7th December 1782. The fact of his death was carefully concealed until the arrival of his son and practical successor, Tippoo, who was absent at the time in Malabar. To him Hyder Ali, after his reign of thirty years, bequeathed an army of a hundred thousand well-trained men, equal to the defence of an equal number of square miles, besides accumulated treasure in gold and precious stones to the value of five millions sterling. We are told that Tippoo assumed the government with extraordinary affectation of humility and grief, yet some early easy conquests did not fail to produce their ordinary effect upon a mind equally weak and malignant. His arrogance grew upon him rapidly: at length his insults to surrounding neighbours could be no longer brooked; and when he, in breach of certain treaty stipulations, invaded Travancore in 1791, a war broke out between himself upon the one side, and the East India Company, the Peishwa, and Nizam upon the other. The result of an attack from such a coalition could not remain a moment doubtful; and by the treaty of Seringapatam in 1792, Tippoo agreed to cede one half Mysore to England, to pay a large indemnity, and to give up to Lord Cornwallis his two eldest sons as host-

ages for his future good behaviour. True to his hereditary policy of display, the handing over to a conqueror of two handsome youths before the eyes of a
hundred thousand horse and foot, was an opportunity
not neglected by the crafty Tippoo. An early day was
fixed for the delivery of the princes into British hands.
They were brought on richly-caparisoned elephants to
the durbar-tent of Lord Cornwallis, and Tippoo's head
vakeel addressed the Governor-General as follows :—
"These children were this morning the sons of the
Sultan — their situation is now changed, and they
must henceforth look up to your lordship as their
father." The Governor-General made an appropriate
reply and promise of protection. This promise was
religiously fulfilled, and "the transfer of the paternal
character ceased to be an Oriental image if determined
by the test of paternal attention." A strong interest
in the captive youths was prevalent throughout the
British army and the English people generally, and
this laid no doubt the first foundation for their future
bountiful provision. They were removed to Vellore,
lodged in the fort, and allotted an abundant income.
In 1806, in the vain hope of re-establishing their
dynasty, they employed this income in corrupting the
native soldiery, who rose and massacred the European
garrison, one company strong. On the failure of this
attempt the princes were removed to Bengal, and their
residence was fixed at Russapuglah, in the suburbs of
Calcutta, where their descendants have so greatly multiplied as to render it desirable they should be en-
couraged to engage in useful pursuits and blend with

the general population; and a proposal has indeed been made by the Council of Education to establish a boarding seminary for the junior members of the Mysore family. Prince Gholam Mohammed and Prince Ferooz Shah, two of the numerous offspring of Tippoo's hostage children, recently succeeded in enlisting in their cause some members of the Indian Council; and to their plausibility and pertinacity must be ascribed the passing of the measure known as the Mysore Grant, by which a vast inheritance has been awarded to the degenerate and already wealthy children of a bold usurper.

These costly hostages for good behaviour were handed over to Lord Cornwallis in 1792. In 1798 the restless blood of Tippoo burned to wipe out the stain of his defeat by the recovery of his lost provinces. In the execution of this design he was rash enough to seek the aid of Revolutionary France, and in token of alliance to adopt the prefix citizen. Hostilities were resumed, but Tippoo was soon again defeated, himself falling by the hand of a British grenadier. His earthly remains were deposited in the mausoleum of his fathers with all the pomp with which the East knows how to honour death; and " a storm," we are told, "not an unsuitable accompaniment to the closing scene in the life of such a man, raged with extraordinary violence on the evening of the ceremony." With him ended the short-lived, barbarous, and desolating dynasty founded by Hyder Ali Khan; and Mysore with its dependencies was partitioned out between the Company, the Peishwa, and

Nizam, a certain portion being formed into a state
and conferred upon the titular Raja so long held captive by the self-named Sultan Tippoo.

In 1832 the British Government again stepped in
to quell the civil strife engendered by the utter in-
capacity for ruling of which the Raja of its choice
had afforded more than ample proof. Within a few
years of his accession, this young prince had squandered upwards of two millions sterling of accumulations, while the revenue and public debt had both
increased until all classes bordered on despair. The
country then assumed by treaty has since been held
and governed for that country's good, the Raja being
treated with great financial liberality and the political consideration to which his rank entitled him.
The executive, however, was taken from him, and
intrusted to a mixed commission of soldiers and
civilians ; and the constant intrigues of more than
twenty years to recover independence, have hitherto
been met by us with silence or refusal. Under English sway that promised land of India has attained
a measure of prosperity unrivalled in the East. Her
woody slopes of many thousand feet in altitude and
many thousand miles in area, now produce coffee
and cinchona ; and while the tiger and the leopard
of the jungles are rapidly receding before the con-
stantly-advancing strides of European planters, the
lofty plateaux have become the sites of peaceful
cities, of which the climate is described as follows :—
" At Bangalore, about three thousand feet above the
sea, the thermometer has been found not to rise above

82° in the shade, and the annual average at noon is 76°. The nights are never hot; and while the evenings and mornings are at all times cool, there is an elasticity in the air at once invigorating and delightful."

Now it happened that the Hindoo Raja of this fruitful country, when bargaining for payment of his debts and some ready money, executed a testamentary instrument in favour of the Queen of England failing lineal descendants of his own; but the childless ruler, now verging on extreme old age, has since that time so far modified his views as to request the sanction of the paramount power to an adoptive heir. The much-vexed question of adoption thus threatened to destroy the budding prosperity of Mysore; but, considering the extent to which European capital is invested there, and the daily increasing national value of the resources of the country, the Government of India, both in England and in India, steadily and very properly refused to release the Raja from his plighted word; and there is now no reasonable doubt, that whenever His Highness shall shake off this mortal coil, his territories will tranquilly become incorporated with our own.

The third great tract of Hindostan of which the government is administered by a mixed commission, is styled the Central Provinces, and comprises Nagpore proper with Jubbulpore and Saugor. It contains an area of seventy-six thousand square miles, or nearly twenty thousand more than England and Wales together. Yet of this great plateau lying be-

tween the Nerbudda and Godavery, and bounded to
the north and south by Bundelcund and the Nizam's
dominions, popular history hitherto has told us little.
In 1853 the childless Raja of Nagpore died, and the
calm historian, on perusal of the following extracts
from an official report on the character of that ruler
and the atmosphere of his court, would hardly censure
Lord Dalhousie for disallowing an adoption of questionable legality, that could only have tended to pro-
long a most pernicious state of things. Mr Mansell
writes :—

"A distaste for business and low habits seem the dis-
tinguishing features of the Raja's temperament. Any
strict attention to affairs of State paid by him has been
enforced by the remonstrance of the Resident; while his
natural inclination has again led him, when unchecked,
to absorb himself in the society of low followers, in the
sports of wrestling, kite-flying, and cards, in singing and
dancing, and in the intercourse of his dancing-girls.
A saying of his to an officer, who about a year ago was
appointed to the office of Durbar Vakeel on the removal
of the old incumbent, will not incorrectly illustrate his
character. The audience of investiture was over, and
the new Vakeel was then dismissed with these words :
'Now, go away and study the provisions of the treaty,
so as to see that they are enforced, to protect me in the
enjoyment of those pleasures of dancing and singing
that I have loved from my boyhood.'

"The addiction to the low pleasures of the harem
was always a marked characteristic of the Raja, and has
become more baneful since the habit of drinking has so

grown upon him. His time is now absorbed in the paltry conversation and the mean pursuits of the concubines, and he now with reluctance leaves the inner apartments.

"When thus the Raja has been divesting himself of much of the best part of his character, he has been acquiring habits of avarice that have led him into a systematic indifference to the claims of the administration of justice, and to the selection of merit in making official appointments. Of late years all the anxiety of the Raja and of his favourite ministers has been to feed the privy purse by an annual income of two or more lacs of rupees from nuzzurs, fines, bribes, confiscation of property of deceased estates, the composition of public defaulters, or the sale of their effects, and suchlike sources. The Raja has thus been led on by his avarice to discard all feeling, and to throw himself into the hands of the most unprincipled of his servants, who plundered the country, and put justice up to sale for profits but a slender part of which reached the Raja. He has done many cruel acts, and even carried war into the country of his feudal dependants, on the misrepresentation of those parties, gilded by the offer of a nuzzur.

"All this has aggravated the low tone of mind originally belonging to the Raja. He acts and thinks like a village chandler. Profits and pickings are to be made anyhow. The choicest amusement of the Raja is an auction sale, when some unfortunate widow is ruled not to be entitled to her husband's estate, or when some public defaulter is found to have made away with revenue collections, just equal to the sum he paid five

or six years before for his situation of revenue collector
to the Raja."

Permission to adopt having therefore been withheld
by Lord Dalhousie, the broad lands of Nagpore "lapsed"
as had done Jhansi and Satara, and became incorporated with our Eastern empire, a liberal provision being
at the same time made for the adoptive mother of the
Raja, and the other female members of the Bhonsla
family.

Though rich in minerals, and possessing all require
ments for Oriental husbandry, the inland position of
Nagpore, inaccessible by water, long told against a rapid
increase of population, and it needed both the zeal of
one whose spurs were yet to win, and the accidental
impulse which the sudden cotton famine gave to Indian
agricultural pursuits, to open up that country to imported skill and labour. In the appointment of Mr
Richard Temple the first condition was fulfilled, by the
selection of the man in India perhaps best fitted to cope
successfully with natural obstacles and native apathy.
Almost ere the ink of his commission had grown dry
and black, a powerful resemblance of the third Napoleon
might have been seen, engineering rail and cotton roads
through forests then unnamed. Like the great Lord
Peterborough in more respects than one, Mr Temple
ever far outstripped the locomotive powers of his subordinates ; and when his secretaries suspected, and indeed
half hoped, that the fair society of Kamptee still held
their slave a more than willing captive, the Commissioner was often heard of as emerging from some far-
distant swamp, with maps and long reports all ready for

the press, full of suggestions that should pave the way to contract drainage, irrigation, and an early crop of some Sea-Island staple.

The above is a faithful, though a very hurried and imperfect, sketch of Mr Richard Temple's work as Chief Commissioner of the Central Provinces;—which must not be confused by those unacquainted with the subject with so-called Central India, a country lying to the north-westward of Nagpore, ruled by native princes who enjoy a greater or a lesser share of independence and protection, and at whose courts the Government of India maintains accredited agents. The Central Provinces, being still in their political and commercial infancy, belong to the family of non-regulation states, for each of which certain laws are at present framed as suited to their individual condition. Some time hence, and probably ere long, they will have become so far assimilated to the rest of British India by the great levelling powers of steam and electricity, as to wear away the many existing constitutional irregularities, which, though they place life and property virtually at the control of the governing class, and are liable to much abuse, are practically productive of great benefit by cutting short the hydra-headed life of Eastern litigation.

A recent writer has informed us that "there is a malady common to savages in certain parts of the world termed 'earth-hunger.' It provokes an incessant craving for clay, a species of food that fails to satisfy the appetite, and impairs the powers of digestion." The East India Company suffered from this dire disorder for upwards of a century; and since it has been deemed that the excesses recorded in this chapter were those which ultimately proved fatal to its life, it is to be sincerely prayed for that the Crown, wiser than its predecessor, may, in the words of the writer above quoted, " now cease to make nobles landless," and to increase the sum of Asiatic misery.

CHAPTER VII.

THE POLITICAL DEPARTMENT.

THE broad halo of romance and genius which surrounds the Political Department, both from the nature of the service in itself and from the class of men selected to perform it, tends to make one pause in undertaking to convey some faint image of the life its servants lead. One fears lest, in the attempt to draw a fitting picture of a truly favoured class, one should yet fall infinitely short of the conception raised in readers' minds by the glowing sketches of "Our Indian Heroes," and other writings from the same authoritative pen, whose truth and power have wellnigh passed beyond the range of criticism. Yet the dreams that eager students harbour in their inmost soul of prompt distinction and personal influence brought to bear on vacillating native courts, pleasant though they be to dwell on, must not be allowed to dim the light of actual fact.

Familiarity with names like Elphinstone and Metcalfe has led men to suppose, not only that they could reap an equally rich harvest of honours and rewards, but that such fruits still hang upon the tree of Oriental life. But to very few is given the great gift of shaping the destiny of nations ; and in exact proportion as the rugged races of the East become displaced and circumscribed by the advancing nations of the West, until all mystery belonging to them is at length dispelled, must dwindle and eventually expire the opportunities that subordinates formerly enjoyed of carving out a policy of their own, and engrafting it upon the State they served. Thus the Indian Political Department, or at least the brightest and most generally accepted interpretation 'of that term, has wellnigh become a matter of past history. The deeds of Eldred Pottinger, who, fired by political fanaticism, held the wild Heratees beneath the spell of his intrepid leadership, and Central India as it was when Sir John Malcolm wrote its history for our learning, are things belonging to a period of which but little trace remains. Yet the political officer of to-day still finds upon arrival at his post work of great variety, with scope perhaps for more than even former usefulness ; and it shall be our present task to trace these labours, as they extend the line of British influence in one unbroken chain from Cabul to Calcutta.

Within the broad expanse of Hindostan two centres of our diplomatic intercourse with native states have become established, at Indore and at Mount Aboo. These we would liken unto two great planets, each describing an extended orbit round an Eastern solar system of its own, and each having in its train certain satellites dependent on its course. The first duty of the more southern of these bodies is to wait upon the courts of Holkar and of Scindia, who, from his lofty walls of Gwalior, looks down with pride, not unmingled

with contempt, upon the weaker chiefs of Central
India, though he and they alike owe one and all a
common political descent to plunder and the sword.
The second of these planets revolves around the Rajpootana States, vast tracts of territory with uncertain
boundaries that afford a constant source of bloodshed
and dispute.

These two high offices are filled by so-called Agents
to the Governor-General, accredited respectively to the
Courts of Central India and of Rajpootana. The former group includes, besides the already-mentioned
Maharajas of Gwalior and Indore, the Sekunder Begum
of Bhopal, the Nawab of Jowra, the less important
Rajas of Dewas and Dhar, together with à host of
tributary chiefs and chieftains whose extent of independence is generally best measured by the value and
geographical position of their lands. Bound by treaties,
many of the articles of which have now become inap-
plicable, the remainder being modified perhaps by subsequent agreement, the relations of the Government of
India with these states are maintained either upon an
affected footing of equality and confidence, or else on
one of open mutual distrust only tempered by expediency, according to the measure of personal influence
of the agent, or the necessities of the times.

Since Lord Lake and Sir Arthur Wellesley won the
battles of Delhi and Assaye, the Mahratta power as an
independent aggressive agency has been virtually destroyed, its martial ascendancy being crippled by very
careful stipulations as to numbers and the non-employ-
ment of adventurous Europeans in a military capacity;

yet in the van of native self-defence against annexation or an anti-caste crusade, the lance of Scindia remains still sharp enough to pierce in many places the somewhat disjointed armour of our Indian possessions.

The story of the gradual rise from vassalage to independence is one of little variation among most Eastern people. Some paternal ancestor, more or less remote, has waged successful war against his primitive allegiance, and crowned, perchance, a life of rapine by plundering the capital of some wealthy neighbour. This history repeats itself in the early annals of almost every reigning house in India; and that the Gwalior State is no marked exception to the general rule, the following quotation from a most reliable historian may be accepted as a sufficient proof: "Madhaji Scindia took full advantage of the dissensions that occurred at Poona after the death of Balajee, to usurp as far as he could the rights and lands of the head of the empire north of the Nerbudda. The detail of the progress of this system of spoliation of both friend and foe is not necessary. Suffice it to say this able chief was the principal opposer of the English in the war they carried on in favour of Ragobah. He was the nominal slave, but the rigid master, of the unfortunate Shah Alum, Emperor of Delhi; the pretended friend, but the designing rival, of the house of Holkar; the professed inferior in all matters of form, but the real superior and oppressor, of the Rajpoot princes of Central India; and the proclaimed soldier, but the actual plunderer, of the family of the Peishwa."

With these and similar historical antecedents, in

which the doctrine of indiscriminate spoliation has been too well sustained, it should not be a matter for surprise when native states adopt a code of international morality differing essentially from what European custom has prescribed; and many argue that it is the bounden duty of the paramount power to impose at least the check of good example on such predatory neighbours, rather than to perpetrate an imperfect imitation of their policy. It may be, indeed, that in the performance of this task British rule in India has achieved its destiny by preserving from the spoiler's hands the milder races of the coasts, who are far more wedded to the paths of peace than to perpetual war.

For many centuries the hill-fort that now lends a title to the Maharaja Scindia formed the curb-stone of Mahratta strength. It repulsed in 1023 the celebrated Mahmoud of Ghuznee, who, in Oriental phraseology, "finding capture hopeless, took rich presents and turned his horse's head towards the West." Between that date and 1779, when it was first garrisoned by Rao Scindia, it changed masters some ten times or more, falling in succession through treachery or stratagem into Mahomedan and Hindoo hands. These pages of its history are nowhere traceable with greater accuracy than upon its natural sandstone walls, which have retained with marked fidelity the heavy tramp of time. There the historian may read the record of the war of Tamerlane, and the geologist and antiquary may feast their eyes on basaltic columns of wondrous beauty, and colossal figures sculptured in a bold relief upon precipitous cliffs, the whole surmounted by a rampart in-

accessible, save by a flight of steps hewn from the
solid rock, of such a size that elephants may ascend
and enter through the gate called after them, of which
the approach is guarded by towers and traverse guns.
Above this rises high the citadel in heavy masses of
quaint architecture, crowned by kiosks and domes of
parti-coloured porcelain tiles, that are rendered doubly
brilliant by an Eastern sun.

Below this rock, and extending for some miles, is
Scindia's standing camp, where the present Maharaja
spends a large proportion of his royal time in military
pomp, often taking part himself in tournaments and
feats of arms. The Mahratta dress affords a marked
contrast and compares most favourably with that worn
by other Indian races. Tight-fitting in all its parts,
and nowhere superfluous in length or breadth, the limbs
being tightly laced with thongs, it displays to best
advantage the square build of Central India men, and
is equally adapted to the tedious march or to court
displays of unmatched horsemanship.

Mooktarool Moolk Umdatul Umra Alijah Maharaja Dheeraj Tyajee Rao Scindia, Sreenath Bahadoor
Munsoor Zuman, Gwalior's actual sovereign, may be
accepted as a type of the true Mahratta, and the
following picture of his Highness applies to many
thousands of his martial followers :—Slightly exceeding European middle-height, and fleshy enough to cause
anxiety to himself, but not to his medical advisers, his
square head is set upon a shapely neck resembling in
solidity some Grecian column destined to support a
mighty weight; his chest is adequately broad and

deep, and somewhat overlapped by muscular advancing shoulders; his hands and feet are rather larger than the more effeminate extremities of the races of Bengal; while his features, originally small, have, thanks to betel nut, long lost all delicacy of expression. The head, set upward, appears embarrassed by a downward cast of countenance, while the eyes, uncertain in their glance, are generally unable to regard with fixity the same object. When approached by foreigners of high rank, Scindia's haughty mien, perhaps, inspires a feeling of superiority both to himself and his attendants; yet, if contrasted with the more courteous bearing of some Eastern princes of equal rank and influence, it might be unfavourably read had we not some sterling proofs of loyal disposition to set against the prejudice of personal comparison.

In many respects his neighbour of Indore, the Maharaja Holkar, much resembles Scindia. An uncompromising pride prompts in each an assumption of ascendency, which, not recognised beyond the limits of his lands, precludes their meeting at the same Durbar. Both, as Knights of the Star of India, acknowledge "Heaven's light their guide," and both are proud of the distinction, of which each would certainly be prouder still had that honour been conferred upon himself alone and not upon his rival. Of late years, however, these two chiefs have been kept on terms, though distant, yet of useful courtesy by the tact of Major Meade, the Agent to the Governor-General, in whose presence every native learnt not only to defer to others but to respect himself, the first step needful as a prelude to reform in Eastern courts and camps. Great names have held the office Major Meade has clothed with such success, and among them Sir Robert Hamilton stands out prominently as a picture of the old political of received repute; yet the lustre of the name of Major Meade will not, we think, be dulled in the minds of Central-India men by comparison with the fame of his official predecessors.

In order to maintain any efficient political supervision over so vast and complicated a tract of country as Central India, it was not only necessary to appoint one principal officer of marked ability responsible for the conduct of affairs, but to maintain subordinate agencies in each separate state. Reasons geographical and strategical rather than diplomatic prompted the selection of Indore as the headquarters of this system; and younger men, chosen from all branches of our Anglo-Indian services, were appointed to the courts of Scindia, Bhopal, Dhar, &c., and to foster the more general and not unfrequently conflicting interests engendered by our rule in Bundelcund and Malwa. Many of these latter had assistants under them, who, in their turn, looked for high preferment; and thus was formed a school similar to that existing in the Rajpootana states, where we educate a class of men well called Politicals, who, in self-reliant energy and executive success, can boldly challenge comparison with any service in the world.

Yet the remote influence of Calcutta and Bombay, even backed by memories of more than one campaign in which the native host had been discomfited, was little likely to convince a cluster of proud chiefs, whose title-deeds were mostly acts of cession extracted from a vanquished foe, of the justice or necessity of certain measures having reference to the interests of trade and agriculture, that the Government of India deems from time to time of general expediency. To meet this difficulty, and to place within the reach of Agents to the Governor-General and their immediate subordinates the means of checking native conduct, certain names have risen into prominence borne on the wings of time's requirements. These have been intrusted with the levying of troops among the wildest clans of that wild country, who, some beneath the standard of religion required for the military service of their native states, and some from love of "Company's salt," have lent their swords to the delights of following leaders who, from their love of danger and of jungle life, appeared in every way best fitted to command such rough-and-ready men. Such was the origin of those irregular corps, whose military existence, commencing with some handfuls of ill-drilled horse, by degrees acquired consistency, until they finally became recognised as taking rank among our trustiest defenders. The Bheel Corps of Malwa and Meywar, the Bhopal Levy, and the Central India Horse, are worthy representatives of this class of troops; and Lieutenant-Colonel Daly, with Major William Gordon Cumming, have afforded fit examples of the class of man required for such irregular command. As political assistants to the Agent-Governor-General for Central India, both these officers combined high civil with military rank, and the latter's

name especially will long remain associated with the
material improvement of the once turbulent Bheels,
who under his agency have become consolidated as a
well-affected race.

Bhopal next demands attention. As Agent to the
Begum's Court the Government of India not long since
appointed Major Willoughby Osborne, an officer whose
gallantry and services had shone conspicuous throughout the earlier and more trying stages of the Sepoy
Mutiny, and won the admiration of Lord Canning,
who on more than one occasion sent a tried and trusty
surgeon many hundred miles to dress his painful
wounds. Emerging by a miracle from the Rewah
country, in which he, the only Englishman, sick and
sorely wounded, had yet retained sufficient energy to
summon the refractory Raja to what all supposed to be
a deathbed scene, and then and there dictate to the
hesitating chief a line of policy from which, to his
honour, he never later swerved, Major Osborne had
survived to reap much honour and reward. He belonged to the younger and more ardent breed of military politicals, and might, perhaps, be deemed by some
more fitted to confront a desperate situation and to
grasp some bold resolve, than to play a second part in
the administration of a well-regulated state, which,
ruled by a woman of undoubted genius and enlightened mind, affords but little scope for his exceeding zeal.

In all questions of the day her Highness of Bhopal
has evinced a shrewdness little short of second-sight
in seizing on the course which ultimately should

most conduce to the advantage of her state, not less than to her personal independence; and with such success has she listened to the promptings of an un-erring judgment, that, loving power most dearly, she wields to-day, under cover of an admirable code of laws and liberties, many culled from European sources, more arbitrary sway than any other chief in India. The part she played in 1857 has earned for her a place in history not easily effaced. She early learnt our strength, and, reckoning on it, made what to native Central India seemed at the time a desperate choice. The result has fully proved the wisdom of her policy. Since then in education, cotton roads, and the abolition of transit duties, she has set examples to her neighbours; and while adhering strictly to the many arduous observances entailed upon her by her boundless faith in her religion, she has displayed a toleration for the creeds of others that many Euro-pean powers might copy with advantage to the world at large.

Thus through fair and foul repute, the Begum of Bhopal has adhered to our alliance. Her energy of character has stood proof against advancing years, and defied the trammels which the East imposes on her sex and her religion. Not long ago, her country being blest with peace, and there appearing little scope and no necessity for her activity at home, she planned a tour that all must heartily regret was never brought to a successful issue. A long-cherished wish to visit England, and to worship at the holy shrines of the Beitullah or sacred Meccan mosque, had only grown with time, and the desire to lay before the Queen the expression of her true loyalty and gratitude for dignities conferred. The execution of this wish, more than once postponed, was planned for 1863; but though the pilgrimage so far as Mecca was happily accomplished, trifling questions as to rank and privilege, raised by Anglo-Indian heralds, were permitted to stand in the light of her approach to English royalty.

Thus are lost the opportunities, few and far between, of making England and India really known to one another. Most London seasons boast of certain Eastern visitors, the large majority of whom represent either dynasties deposed or renegades from their ancestral faith—princes and their followers who, having little left in India save the bounty of a far too generous Crown, impose their once historic names upon an ignorant and a lion-hunting public; while families still powerful, and possessing weight among the millions that surround them, are left, like the flower, to blush unseen within the limits of their mountain homes beyond the Indus. A striking picture might be drawn by one acquainted with the theme, and gifted with the power of pouring light and shade upon an artificial landscape, of two heroic women, one born to wield the sword, and one to wear the Star of India. The first was a Hindoo Ranee whose name lies wellnigh uppermost among the annals of the Indian rebellion as that of Jhansi's haughty ruler; the second a Mahomedan who, by force of her example, contributed as much to the success of our Central India columns of 1857 as did the gallantry of Sir Hugh Rose and his subordinates. But enough—the one has passed away with the scenes which she so darkly illustrated; the other happily remains to guide the judgment of her neighbours, and to reap the harvest she has so surely sown.

The above must close our present notice of Bhopal. With the exception of Scindia and Holkar, Dhar perhaps ranks next in weight among the chiefs of Central India. The importance of his state has been no doubt enhanced by the fact that the government has been of latter years conducted by a regency under the immediate supervision of the Agent-Governor-General in the person of Lieutenant Ward, an officer of promise belonging to the Bengal Staff Corps. Under his auspices, schools, both English and vernacular, have met with much encouragement, while the general condition of the inhabitants has materially improved. Yet notwithstanding these advantages, Dhar, possessing neither natural features nor marked boundaries to protect it from the encroachments of powerful and often greedy neighbours, can hardly look to any brilliant future. As a weak state of the second rank, it sees in the enjoyment of British protection its surest rock of safety and independence; and its contribution of a sum approaching to £1000 per annum towards the maintenance of the Malwa Bheel Corps may be considered perhaps not too high a price to pay for the continuance of such security. Passing now northward from the Mahratta country across an imaginary and very doubtful frontier into Rajpootana, we enter on a land deserving of much careful observation.

Boasting an area of 115,000 square miles in round numbers, the vast tracts of Rajpootana present, to the uninitiated, little cohesion or identity; yet the distinctive qualities and prejudices of the inhabitants are in marked contrast with those of the Mahrattas or Punjabees to their north and south, and as great a difference exists between these races as between the denizens of Russia and those of Italy or England. Concerning the Rajpoot people, who constitute the prevailing element of the population, very variable and indeed opposite opinions have been expressed by high reliable authorities. One thing is certain—namely, that they have known, through long ages, how to hold themselves aloof, and form a society of their own, extending about four hundred miles in each direction; that this country is bounded by the Punjab, the North-West, Central India, and Scinde; and that it contains dynasties as old, and pedigrees as long, as any other portion of the world we are acquainted with. The compiler of a book, which stands alone as 'The Sanskrit Dictionary,' teaches that "the peculiar character of the Rajpoots arises from their situation as a military class of the original Hindoo system;" thus combining military instincts with the fanaticism of religion. Again, he says, "The Rajpoots were born soldiers; each division had its hereditary leader, like clans in other countries; the rules of caste still subsisted, and tended to render more powerful the connection just described; and, as the chiefs of those clans.

stood in the same relation to the Raja as their own relations did to them, the king, nobility, and soldiery all made one body, united by the strongest feelings of kindred and military devotion;" and, in conclusion, it is stated that "they treated women with respect unusual in the East, and were guided even towards their enemies by rules of honour which it was disgraceful to violate." Yet a less pleasing picture might be drawn of the darker side of the Rajpoot character; for it was in Rajpootana that the crimes of female infanticide and suttee attained to their most hideous proportions; and some insight into the manners of these people may be gathered from M'Murdo's writings of 1818, where it is mentioned that, among the offspring of eight thousand married Rajpoots, probably not more than thirty females were alive. "To such an extent was this cruelty to daughters carried, that they were sometimes destroyed after attaining adolescence. In 1810 the Rajas of Joudpore and Jeypore became rival suitors for a princess of Oodeypore, and supported their pretensions by waging war against each other. The family of the unhappy girl at length terminated the contest by putting her to death." The above are fair specimens, taken at random, from the contrary records of this people, weighed and sifted in the balance of the well-poised mind of Colonel Tod, whose ' Annals and Antiquities of Rajast'han ' constitute the most reliable and exhaustive authority on a subject of romantic interest, containing much that the most sceptical must admit invites the fascinating analogy which Colonel Tod delights to draw between the martial followers of Odin and the not less warlike "children of the sun."

The royal family of Oodeypore, the most ancient, if not actually the most powerful, house of Rajpootana, traces its descent through the solar dynasty back to the mythological and romantic Rama, who ruled some seven centuries before the birth of Christ; and although a broad margin must of necessity be left in accepting Rajpoot legend, yet but little doubt remained upon the minds of Mill and Rennell that the reigning dynasty of Oodeypore counts upwards of two thousand years. The geographical position of Meywar, not less than its great wealth and political repute, exposed it, however, to constant inroad from without. Lying near the centre of a triangle, whose three points may be represented by the cities of Ghuznee, Delhi, and Baroda, its military strength was successively exhausted by the incursions of Sultan Mahmoud, the Mahrattas, and the Emperor Ackbar, under whom, in 1568, Chittore, the ancient capital, was given to the flames, the Rana seeking refuge in the Aravulli mountains, among the fastnesses of which he subsequently founded the city of Oodeypore, thenceforth the capital of Meywar. At a distance of some fifty miles, situated upon an isolated spur of this irregular range, and within the Sirohee Raja's territory, stands now the summer residence of the Agent to the Governor-General for Rajpootana, who, from the summit of Mount Aboo, enforces the observance of our numerous treaties, sunnuds, and engagements with the once martial races inhabiting the plains below.

In the ages, however, that witnessed the historical

transaction above related, weaker states might seek in vain protection from the oppression of the strong; and thus, for a time, unhappy Oodeypore bent her haughty neck beneath the Mogul yoke, until at length the attempt of Aurungzebe to impose a capitation-tax upon Hindoos once more fired the Meywar people, who, in the ensuing contest, overthrew the imperial hosts, and regained their cherished independence. From that time, Rajpoot history has chronicled a course of constant strife. The Mahratta States, in turn, have wasted their broad lands; and a happier condition of existence most clearly owes its origin to British agency and supervision, ever varying in efficiency, but most efficient when intrusted to the hands of one like the late Sir Henry Lawrence, who, from the depths of his knowledge and experience, was not ashamed to own, at the expiry of his first year of office, that, "as usual, he had had everything to learn. Heretofore he had had chiefly to do with one people, and that a new people; there he had twenty sovereign states, as old as the sun and moon, but with none of the freshness of either orb. His Sikh experience gave him little help, and his residence in Nipal scarcely any, in dealing with the petty intrigues of those effete Rajpoots." This was the humility required in one who entered on such varied, difficult work, and might have well been studied with advantage by more than one of his successors.

The Aravulli range, extending from the Goojeratti frontier of the Bombay Presidency to wellnigh the confines of the Punjab, in the neighbourhood of Delhi, bisects these "twenty sovereign states" into two great families lying to its east and west; the first belonging not only geographically speaking to the map of Central India, but also sharing in many of the characteristics of its people. Thus the lands of the Rajpoot princes of Tonk and Jullawar, lying to the east of this great chain, are curiously dovetailed into the surrounding states in the same manner as the Central India principalities of Dewas and Jowra—all four following apparently the example set them by Madhaji Scindia, who, in a previous century, carved out for himself an irregular kingdom by taking here and there a slice of territory as opportunity or temporary embarrassment permitted. The second group was formed in very early days by conquest by Rajpoots of the purest breed, who, previous to Mogul contamination and fear of the Mahratta issuing from their cradles of Meywar and Jeypore, crossed the chain of mountains to the west, and spread like locusts over the desert wastes between them and the burning sands of Scinde, acquiring ascendency and rule over the wild and scattered Jâts, by whom alone that country was then inhabited.

Those ancient cradles of the Rajpoot race are sufficiently curious as specimens of the extent to which superstition sometimes sinks its votaries to merit some few words. Thus Amber, the early capital of Jeypore, was formerly a city of great architectural beauty, built by Jey Singh as a lasting monument of his contributions to science in the reform of the calendar, a work intrusted to him by the Emperor Mahomed Shah of Delhi; and it has recently been thus described:—
"Imagine on the margin of a small lake in a lovely

valley, temples, houses, streets, scattered among numerous ravines furrowing the slopes of the surrounding
hills down to the very water's edge. Those streets,
intricate and gloomy by site and the shade of numerous
trees, are now uninhabited except by ghastly Hindoo
ascetics, with their hair in elf-knots, and their faces
covered with chalk, sitting naked and hideous amongst
tombs and ruined houses. On the slope of the hill
westward of the lake rises the vast and gorgeous palace
of Amber. Neither Jaquemont nor Heber ever viewed
a scene more striking, picturesque, and beautiful. Here
is the zenana crowned by four kiosks; and communicating with the palace by a succession of towers and
gateways, is a huge gloomy castle with machicollated
battlements and many loopholes; there is a small
temple where a goat is daily offered up to Kali, sub-
stituted for the human beings sacrificed each morning
during the darker and more unmitigated sway of pagan-
ism." This was the capital of a country described by
a traveller in 1835 as exhibiting "an empty treasury,
desolate palaces, stagnating commerce, a ferocious popu-
lace, and a rabble army."

The desert wastes over which the Rajpoot people
spread themselves, have now been long partitioned
among the sovereigns of Jhodpore, Jessulmere, and
Bikaneer, who dwell and have their being in walled
cities of some size but inconsiderable strength, possessed of little beauty though much interest. On
each of these the Agent to the Governor-General has
to keep a watchful eye ; and though the bulk of his
responsibility no˙ doubt clusters round the oasis of

Ajmere, which, as British territory administered by him on behalf of the North-West Provinces and surrounded on all sides by native states, affords a sanctuary for every class of Indian political offender, yet elements of disorder are not wanting in more western camps, whereto Patan and Mussulman, the soldier and the saint, alike retire, to hatch in desert solitudes schemes for our discomfiture.

With such a past as has been here described, and such a present state of things as now exists in Rajpootana, where political intrigue goes hand in hand with jealousy, creating mutual distrust, the future of the country is indissolubly bound up with the paramount sway of England in the East. To us alone experience has taught that it may look for the protection of its frontiers from trans-Indus enemies and the Mahratta; and since the British Agent-Governor-General's court has proved itself to all the surest channel for redressing wrongs inflicted by some hostile neighbours, wrongs that hitherto the sword alone could cure or mitigate, much of the necessity has passed away for the crowds of armed retainers who preyed upon the vitals of the state in times of peace, and by the mere fact of their existence made war the first and last resort, and force the only argument employed in settling disputes. Young Rajas like Ulwur and Bhurtpoor, under the guidance of a sort of tutor in things political, now attain to manhood and a sense of their responsibilities under happier influences than those by which their fathers were surrounded. Some acquaintance with the English language, and in many cases real veneration for the Agent who has nursed with care their perhaps embarrassed revenues, has prompted more than once in the minds of native rulers a desire to visit England, and become the patrons of more noble undertakings than were embraced in the ambitions of their predecessors. Yet these Rajpoot states differ as yet little in essentials from the Central India group. They are governed ill enough by some score of native Cabinets, all more or less deficient in the science of political economy. The duty of the Agent-Governor-General is much the same in both ; Scindia or Holkar are martial princes fairly comparable to Jeypore or Meywar, and Major Osborne of Bhopal found in Oodeypore a rival to his zeal in Colonel William Eden.

This chapter hitherto has been confined to pictures of two constellations of native states lying, with some trifling exceptions, north of the Nerbudda, and divided by the Aravulli range into unequal halves, inhabited by races quite distinct—entertaining for each other a fierce hatred, not unmixed with fear—who have sought in our protection a mutual defence against each other. But now, proceeding south, we shall quit the confines of these states, and, entering the Nizam's dominions, tread a soil on which diplomacy has fought many well-contested fields.

Nizam Ool Moolk, a "Regulator" of the state called after its capital Hyderabad, laid the foundation of his royal house early in the eighteenth century, in the accustomed manner, by a judicious mixture of treason and the sword. Holding under Aurungzebe high office as Viceroy of the Deccan, he deemed that a compact country counting 100,000 square miles of area might well renounce allegiance to a capital far distant; and his judgment, if not based on fealty, lacks not at least the justification of success. Thus was formed a state which at the present day stands alone in India as being still virtually sovereign; and which, though paying tribute to the British Crown in more ways than one, yet retains sufficient power to wallow in misrule to an extent challenging comparison with the darkest days of Delhi and Lucknow.

Yet when Nizam Ool Moolk, having attained a hundred years, was gathered to his fathers, the succession to this crown did not escape the fierce contests inseparable from Asiatic sovereignty; and, as usual, after many less important candidates had been disposed of, two remained—one in virtue of testamentary bequest, the second a usurper who, backed by the army, had laid violent hands upon the treasure of the state. In those days, also, France and England were contending for an Eastern empire, and it happened that each of these two candidates managed to secure the countenance of one or other party. Practical England espoused the cause that based its right on might and actual possession, while the French commander, the chivalrous Dupleix, embraced the interests of his opponent. After many complications, at length an end was put to this dispute; for the English, successful in the first instance, having withdrawn their aid by reason of dissensions among themselves, Mosuffer Jung became in fact a French proconsul. His reign was short, and then intrigue ensued, which a more lengthy narrative than this could scarce attempt to follow. For many wasting years the Deccan and Carnatic were bathed in blood; and the day of Tippoo, the son of Hyder Ali, dawned before a treaty offensive and defeusive between the Nizam, the Peishwa, and the British Government, paved the way to what was called a permanent peace.

During this fluctuating war Hyderabad attained a prominence in Indian history which she has since preserved intact; and shortly afterwards the building of a British Residency of unmatched splendour accustomed her inhabitants to red coats and negotiation. Following in the wake of these events came one Mahratta war upon the other, and the names of Rao Scindia and Lord Lake were alternately whispered in the audience-halls of the most dissolute of rulers by trembling attendants, and shouted through the streets by an infuriated mob clamouring for bread and participation in the pending struggle for ascendency. In these and similar crises it has been the duty of the British Resident to steer a course consistent with his dignity and the interests at stake, and, keeping within the Residency walls, so to conduct his correspondence and himself, as to leave the Company unfettered to act according to the ever-changing kaleidoscope of events. The names of those who led this life, and notwithstanding the difficulties of their position, backed, 'tis true, by some few Sepoys and the command of British gold, knew how to bring to a successful issue long-pending difficulties with the Nizam, whence the assigned districts, the Hyderabad contingent, and tribute paid in coin, all trace their origin—their names are known and cherished in our Anglo-Indian annals; and they in turn have been succeeded in more recent times by others, for whose memories a certain margin of respect should be reserved. These lived in happier times; their arguments could always gather eloquence by dwelling on the records of the past, they had armies at their back and still more gold at their disposal, yet it had become patent to the treasury of the Nizam that the days were different, and that this gold had already changed its master more than once. The opinion expressed in England at the outset of Secession in America, that the Union was too large, affords a not inapt illustration of the turn that native thought had taken. The Company, they argued, had grown unwieldy, and the only means at the Resident's command to dispel this fond illusion, which cost such seas of blood in 1857, was a bold front and personal ascendency: in other words, of plainer comprehension, in India as elsewhere a policy of peace at any price proved just the surest road to endless trouble and hostility. Meanwhile the times were hard and famine was abroad; and in Hyderabad this never happens without crowds surrounding the British Residency, by all alike considered as the origin of evil and the panacea for all ill. Amid these and similar scenes, weighed down by years and a deep sense of his responsibility, Colonel Davidson, the Resident at Hyderabad, died in office in 1862, and was succeeded in his duties by Mr Yule from Oude.

The antecedents of Mr George Udney Yule had

been for many years obscure. His path of duty followed in the rut of Bengal magistracy. At Bhagulpore he had devoted many years to an admixture of Shikar and scholastic life. He lived in a small house perched above the Ganges, just so high that the recurring floods of autumn and the spring passed him by unscathed, imparting to his garden-ground a rich percentage of fertility. His sister lived with him—no other human being. In animals he much delighted; and while the best - bred horses and most noted elephants grazed well cared for in his compound, his house and its contents were placed at the disposal of chosen friends belonging to the canine and the feline families. It has been said by those who knew him, that no servant's brush had ever been permitted to wipe away the cobwebs that collected in his study; yet it is on record that, while appeals from his decisions were unknown, no zemindaree difficulty within his jurisdiction was ever left unsettled. He never had arrears; and when his work was done, though not before, he rode into the jungles, and there passed his time with native friends amid the pure delights of nature until official duties recalled him to his desk. He was the Henry Lawrence of the Bengal Civil Service; and when Lord Canning appointed him to Oude as acting Chief Commissioner, a happier selection could hardly have been made. Thence he had gone to Hyderabad, appointed by Lord Elgin—an office which he, of true modesty, scrupled to accept, having, as he often said, "but a little executive experience and no political ability." More than once, indeed, at irregular intervals rumours had reached the columns of the Indian press of the mode in which the Star of India had been accepted by His Highness the Nizam. Report had said, with how much truth cannot now be clearly known, that the Nizam had with his left hand snatched the insignia of knighthood from the grasp of Colonel Davidson, and cast it unheeded on the ground beside him. At no other court in India could such a scene have been supposed and passed by without notice or refutation, yet little doubt exists that latter years have witnessed within the palace walls of Hyderabad many acts of equal if not greater insult heaped upon perhaps a too forbearing paramount power; and it is to the acute intelligence of a native Minister, the distinguished Salar Jung Bahadoor, and to the sagacity of Shums-ool-Omrah, the venerable uncle of the Nizam, that we owe alone the neutral attitude of the Deccan in 1857.

That a man of tastes so simple, and influenced so little by ambition, as Mr Yule, should shrink from entering on the conduct of a state of things so unsatisfactory to all, cannot afford much matter for surprise ; and with him the case was stronger still. At Lucknow he had become endeared to every class of the inhabitants. As years went on the Terai lost perhaps some part of its attractions; but nature, ever willing to repay with interest the debt of gratitude she owes to all that use her well, had found for him society, which changed the aspect of his life; and when the Residency of Hyderabad was offered him on public grounds, he met the call of duty upon an equal footing. One fortnight's leave he asked to pass from the condition of a bachelor into married life, and then, leaving far behind him Oude and all he loved save one, he set out for his future and far-distant home in Hyderabad.

This sketch of Mr Yule may be pardonable, perhaps, as illustrative of a class of civil servant now wellnigh extinct. The present generation may possess more learning of a classic kind; but, entering later on Indian life, they have unfortunately too often home associations that point to the accumulation of a rapid fortune and retirement, whereas in former times Hindostan became the home of the majority of its civil servants: there they lived, and there they often died—the sons succeeding to their father's office; and thus such families became identified with those they ruled, incomparably more than can now happen with the offspring of the competition system.

Quitting the Nizam's dominions and Mr Yule, we shall finally cast a hasty glance upon Nipal, as being—with the exception of Cashmere, already dwelt on in connection with the Punjab—the only native state hitherto unmentioned with which the Government of India maintains on equal terms relations of amity and commerce.

That this mountain kingdom is beneath the sway of Jung Bahadoor, is better known in England than the means whereby he reached his actual position; and these means are of a tragic character so marked, that even in an Eastern tale a simple narrative of the facts could hardly lack of interest. Jung's youth, we are told, "was devoted to gambling; and his expertness in the avocation which he chose repaired the financial

dilapidation occasioned by his wild excesses." On his
uncle becoming Prime Minister, Jung quitted the obscurity of an outpost for the capital, which he regarded
as the only field for the development of genius like his
own. There he was the subject of many remarkable
adventures, and committed sundry acts not recognised
as lawful by the moral codes of the Western world.
Among the latter may be classed "the murder of his
uncle, which he undertook and perpetrated at the instigation of the Nipalese Queen. Thereupon a new
ministry was formed, and Jung became Commander-in-
Chief. The opportunity of slaughter on a larger scale
soon awaited him; the new Premier was assassinated,
and the Queen demanded vengeance. One of the colleagues of the murdered minister was suspected of the
crime, and Jung suggested that the suspected man
should die, and the Government devolve upon the sole
survivor. But the latter, displaying hesitation, fell
pierced by a bullet from the rifle of Jung Bahadoor, his
son falling likewise in a vain attempt to save his father's
life. This was, however, but the prelude of what was
yet to follow. Fourteen hostile chiefs confronted Jung,
who levelled his rifle fourteen times in quick succession,
and at each discharge excepting one brought down his
well-selected victim. The only man who escaped his
aim was the falsely-accused assassin; but his reprieve
was short, and a few moments later he also met his
death at the point of Jung Bahadoor's sword. The
bodies of the slain were Jung's stepping-stones to
power, for before the dawn of the succeeding day he
was invested with the office of Prime Minister;" and

the historian concludes this short account of Jung's ascent to the actual sovereignty of Nipal with the trite remark that "his future reign did not prove inconsistent with its commencement."

This is the man in whose honour the London world could not do too much some few years since; on whom the Government of England of 1858 bestowed the Bath Grand Cross, a dignity till then confined to friendly sovereigns or prominent statesmen, and never once before conferred upon an Indian ruler; and it is right to state that Jung's title to this exceptional distinction has been rightly stated by Mr Montgomery Martin to consist in the fact that his Ghoorkas, "though too late for the fighting at Lucknow, were in time for the sack and the plunder;" and that when at our request they took their departure, "the whole force was a mere baggage-guard, and it was even necessary to detach a British column to escort them safely on their homeward march."

The country over which this bold usurper reigns is classed among the world's most favoured regions. Forests and deep valleys forming beds for foaming torrents, and more sluggish streams invaluable for purposes of irrigation, parcel it out in granaries and pine-clad hills. The climate is generally superb, although the frequency of fever in some of those more marshy lower Himalayan slopes known as the Terai, to which the love of sport attracts most European visitors, has gained for it a reputation far from good. Khatmandoo is its capital, and the Resident abides in a well-furnished English-looking house, surrounded by pleasant gardens, and backed by mountain-ranges rising to an altitude of eight-

and-twenty thousand feet, and stretching over two-and-twenty longitudinal degrees. The language mostly spoken is a Hindoo mountain dialect, though the aborigines, apparently of Mongol extraction, lay claim in portions still remote to a patois of their own called "Newar"—boasting, it is said, considerable richness of expression, and a literature by no means to be despised. With such a ruler and such a population, with both of whom force and selfish motives are the only available arguments, the duties of the Resident are necessarily of an elementary order, and the post is usually conferred on men qualified for so honourable a retreat by long labour and good service in the sultry plains below.

We must now conclude this sketch of the Political Department. The Guickwar of Baroda has long lost his sovereign independence; and though he wears the decoration of the Star of India, and retains the show and many of the attributes of power, his actual position is one of purest vassalage, where the Resident dictates, and is dictated to in turn by the Government of Bombay. The Poona Peishwa's fall from a dynastic seat, "founded in usurpation and terminated in treachery," made way for the establishment of the petty Raja of Sattara as representative of the founder of Mahratta rule : his line became extinct in 1848, and then his territory also "lapsed," and became incorporated with our dominions.

Following the valley of the Indus, and traversing the dark historic passes of Bolan and the Khyber, the English people have discovered that their true policy towards the Affghans is one of absolute non-intervention. At the court of the Ameer of Cabul we indeed maintain a native agent or vakeel, possessing neither responsibility nor power. He officially reports to the Foreign Secretariat at Calcutta events as they occur, and occasionally, perhaps, hands some formal compliment or protest to the Government *de facto*. Nothing he can say or do can compromise the Government of India ; and until the Queen's legation at the Court of Teheran is again taken from the London Foreign Office and handed over to the tenderer mercies of the Secretariat of State for India, it is little likely that the destiny of England will play a prominent part in Central Asian politics.

CHAPTER VIII.

THE PROVINCES BEYOND THE SEA.

UNDER this generic term we shall class those appanages of the Government of India to which access can alone be had by traversing the ocean. Although their administration is conducted through many of the departmental channels already dealt with, such as the Home and Foreign Offices in Calcutta, some being even subject to the minor Presidencies of Bombay or Madras, they may yet be treated of collectively as forming, in respect to British Hindostan, a colonial system of its own.

First among these colonies rank the Provinces of Burma, wrested from the stiff-necked court of Ava by Lord Dalhousie in 1852; and, when added to our previous possessions beyond the Brahmapootra of Tenasserim and Aracan, ceded to us at the treaty of Yandabo in 1826, these constitute a kingdom of no mean extent, now known as British Burma, and ruled by a Chief Commissioner appointed by the Governor-General. Second in size, though perhaps of first political significance, come what are termed the Straits Settlements, embracing Singapore, Malacca, Province

Wellesley, and Penang.   Next we have the interesting
groups of Andamans and Nicobars, the less valuable
Laccadives, including Minicoy, and the strongly-forti-
fied rocks of Aden and Perim, the Ceuta and Gibraltar
of the East.

The footing taken by English enterprise in Burma
dates far back among the first of our Eastern undertakings.   A country possessed of great mineral wealth
and unmatched timber, and little subject to many
noxious influences to which the European in those
latitudes too generally succumbs, naturally attracted
the attention of our earliest navigators.   In 1687
the British landed at Negrais, an island lying at
the Bassein mouth of the river Irawadi, well situated
for a commercial site, and for a space of seventy years
our relations with the local chiefs were conducted without jealousy, and confined to furthering the interests
of trade; but when the Burmese conqueror, Alompra,
overran Pegu, the East India Company awoke from
dreams of wealth alone to war and annexation.   A
rude race of "robber kings" from Aracan, called
Mughs, boasting of a "long and treacherous descent,"
shortly after came by thousands to complete the spread
of anarchy, and for many years the history of our intercourse with Ava was little but a record of extortion
on the one side and arrogance upon the other.   The
Mughs took refuge alternately with English and Burmese, laying waste the land of their respective enemies;
mutual recriminations ensued; the surrender of the
Mughs was demanded in peremptory terms, which
seldom were acceded to, and another war was the

invariable result, equally invariably terminating in some fresh addition to our territory, tending only to enhance our future difficulties. In 1852, however, India was ruled by Lord Dalhousie, who seemed to hold it for his destiny to preclude the possible recurrence of disputes like these by obtaining, either through a prompt and full submission or formal annexation, some better security for tranquillity than could be found in so-called treaties of eternal peace and amity between unequal powers. He did not, as a rule, consider in such cases the origin of the dispute of much importance; he only recognised its actual existence. He was not responsible for the doings of his predecessors; he had been sent out to " rule the Indies," and not to spend his time in a tardy investigation of our title to disputed territory or the merits of a war which had assumed the aspect of a political necessity. Thus arguing, he undertook a war against Pegu, of greater magnitude than any of our previous Burmese expeditions; and though it was one perhaps that European jurists might not have deemed quite justifiable, it was not the less successful; and after some expense of human life, and much captured prize, the conquest of Pegu was finally proclaimed in words sufficiently characteristic to merit their quotation *in extenso :—*

" The Court of Ava having refused to make amends for the injuries and insults which British subjects had suffered at the hands of its servants, the Governor-General of India in Council resolved to exact reparation by force of arms. The forts and cities upon the coast were forthwith attacked and captured; the Burmese forces have been dispersed wherever they have been met, and the province of Pegu is now in the occupation of British troops. The just and moderate demands of the Government of India have been rejected by the King; the ample opportunity that has been afforded him for repairing the injury that was done has been disregarded; and the timely submission which alone could have been effectual to prevent the dismemberment of his kingdom is still withheld. Wherefore in compensation for the past, and for better security in the future, the Governor-General in Council has resolved, and hereby proclaims, that the province of Pegu is now, and shall be henceforth, a portion of the British territories in the East. Such Burman troops as may still remain within the province shall be driven out; civil government shall immediately be established, and officers shall be appointed to administer the affairs of the several districts. The Governor-General in Council hereby calls on the inhabitants of Pegu to submit themselves to the authority, and to confide securely in the protection, of the British Government, whose power they have seen to be irresistible, and whose rule is marked by justice and beneficence. The Governor-General in Council having exacted the reparation he deems sufficient, desires no further conquest in Burma, and is willing to consent that hostilities should cease. But if the King of Ava shall fail to renew his former relations of friendship with the British Government, and if he shall recklessly seek to dispute its quiet possession of the province it has now declared to be its own, the Governor-General in Council will again put forth the power he holds, and will visit with full retribution aggressions which, if they be persisted in, must of necessity lead to the total subversion of the Burmese State, and the ruin and exile of the King and his race."

Such was the picture Lord Dalhousie drew, and perhaps unwisely, of the policy pursued by the paramount Christian power in Southern Asia, and such was the penalty he decreed to all who should presume to question the legality of a title, based confessedly upon a declaration made in Council by the Governor-General, that a fertile province had become his own by conquest. Yet a proclamation penned for Eastern hearts and minds can hardly bear the stamp of righteous dealing required by the more fastidious morality of the West; and, right or wrong, Pegu became a British province, and has since been ruled as such to its own great advantage; first by Major Phayre, as virtual Governor of Pegu alone, and later, as years passed on and brought to him increase of honours and of army rank, as Chief Commissioner for the whole of British Burma.

Colonel Phayre is one of those whose character should not be hastily slurred over with a few slender words of praise in a work that seeks especially to make apparent the high importance of a right selection of mankind for different place. Tall, thin, slightly curved, rather by much thought than by the weight of years, still light in number, his best services have been performed among that people to whose interests his whole being seems now devoted. In the expression of his countenance, at once upright and refined, those

even least versed in the science of deducing human
actions from a facial angle may read a happy combination of prudence, natural sagacity, courage of the highest
order, love of accuracy, and something like a deference
to others and slight distrust of self, which taken singly
may mean weakness, but when blended with an administrative success of twenty years can only indicate
a great superiority.

Some outline of the history of Colonel Phayre's first
years of Burmese rule may be gathered indirectly from
Colonel Henry Yule's able narrative of a special mission
to the Court of Ava in 1855. Colonel, then Captain,
Yule occupied the place of Secretary to the mission,
being given to understand that one of the chief duties
of his office would be the preparation of that narrative.
The work thus produced has since taken a high place
in descriptive literature, and has become the text-book
of all who seek for information with reference to Burmese affairs; and though the author avoids with rare
delicacy recording in too prominent a manner his own
appreciation of his chief's ability and learning, it is
evident, from the tone and language used throughout,
that the force of Major Phayre's example had sunk deep
into a mind singularly sensitive to all outward influence for good. Not less remarkable is the record of the
deep impression evidently produced upon the rulers of
those states, whether tributary to Ava or Siam, and upon Kareen chiefs, both red and white, with whom the
envoy came in contact; and taken as a whole, in its
objects, record, and results, that mission sent by Lord
Dalhousie in 1855, composed of men of modesty and

learning, perhaps at once affords the ablest vindication
of the act of 1852, and displays a kind of tacit peni-
tence for the rudeness of its mode of execution.

But Colonel Phayre's experience of the so-called
Court of Ava was not destined to be confined to the
journey undertaken in 1855; for in 1862 Lord Elgin,
wishing to establish more accessible relations with the
Burmese Government, made him the bearer of a complimentary khureta to the King. Upon this second
mission Colonel Phayre entered with undiminished
zeal; and after many weary days and nights exhausted
in delays, the flat-bottomed boats bearing him and his
attendants were seen approaching up the stream by
those who watched his advent from the towers of
Mandalay. In that city he remained some weeks in
daily intercourse with Burmese royalty and the members of the Government, and obtained from them a
curious insight into French intrigues in Burma and
Siam. These, however, partake less of a national than
a personal character; and this name of " French intrigue" in Indo-China, which rings with such familiar
sound upon the ears of Francophobists, is mainly
owing to the circumstance of many French and
Franco-Italian names being concerned in schemes for
personal aggrandisement, based upon the rendering
of some supposed service to the aggressive policy of
France on the banks of the Cambodia. As yet these
schemes have not been crowned with much success.
Some enterprising men indeed have made their way
from Ava to Saigon, crossing the Salween at spots
unknown to European geographers, and traversing Shan

states abounding in every natural product which can conduce to future wealth. These vast tracts of country, accessible alone to trade by mounting the Salween, a river known where it strikes the British territory as the Martaban, have hitherto been isolated from the ends and aims of British energy by the hostile action of the Kareen tribes, who, inhabiting dense forests, and acknowledging but little subservience to any government whatever, carry fire and sword into every camp of immigrants that ventures to intrude upon the rich and fertile tracts that they, like Lord Dalhousie, have declared their own. Not long ago an expedition headed by a learned Doctor tried to make its way from the eastern shore of the Irawadi to the Salween, passing north of the Kareen country. It was indeed successful; and there the travellers found evidence of gold and silver and of precious stones, fully explaining the source of the costly pomp in which the Burmese Court delights to clothe itself. Perhaps, also, in the exceeding riches of this country, which increase at each step taken to the east and north, some explanation may be found of the repeated migrations of the capital towards the Irawadi's source. Captain Yule wrote that "the abandonment of Amarapoora in 1822 was looked upon as an ill-omened act, and the people had a notion that the disasters of the war of 1824-1826 were connected with it. The royal residence had always previously, as least since a very remote era, been moved up the river, from Prome to Pagān, from Pagān to Panya, from Panya to Ava, from Ava to Amarapoora;" and since that book was written a further change in the same direction has been made to Mandalay. This falling back has been attributed by most writers to a resolution to retreat from the approach of Western civilisation; but whether it owes its origin to this cause or to increased knowledge of their country's wealth, and a consequent desire to keep it to themselves, may prove of interest to theorists alone—and to them we leave this fertile theme for speculation, while we pursue its practical result of paralysing the Pegu trade. The Government of India was not without the hope that Colonel Phayre might succeed in mitigating this evil by the establishment of some less exclusive passport system, and a more liberal customs' tariff than at that time prevailed; and his mission was indeed so far successful, in that extended forest rights and some responsibility for the acts of Kareen tribes were virtually conceded; but practically the wealth of Burma is not yet tapped, and that country still remains a *mare clausum* to European enterprise.

Returning from his mission, Colonel Phayre proceeded to Calcutta to render an account to his employers. That account was deemed satisfactory, and very creditable to himself; and among the rewards conferred upon him in recognition of his services, ranked by the side of a Bath Companionship the permission to retain the insignia of the Burmese Order of the Elephant, which had been sent him by the King as a special mark of favour the day he had his audience to take leave.

Descending the Irawadi to Rangoon, the traveller may select some south-bound ship, and, coasting through the Mergui Archipelago, he next sights the English flag where it floats upon the little island of Penang. Pulo

Penang, or Prince of Wales Island, was obtained by the Company some seventy years ago, on payment of a yearly tribute to the King of Queda, an independent semi-civilised ruler on the western coast of Lower Siam. In extreme fertility it makes amend for its minute proportions as a colony, and it is able to support a larger and more varied population of Malays, Chinese, Buttas, Bengalis, Europeans, Chuliahs, Siamese, and Burmese, than any spot of equal size encircled by the sea. Early in the present century a little strip of land upon the Queda coast was added to its jurisdiction, and called Province Wellesley. The arm of the Malacca Strait that separates the two is not so wide but what from time to time a tiger swims across, and in this strait a hundred ships or more may swing in calm security, protected by our guns from the pirates of Acheen, and by the ranges of the Rumbo mountains from the fierce gales wont suddenly to arise within those latitudes. Penang is a port of call for every European passenger-ship passing through the Malacca Straits, and scarcely a day goes by but some large steamer outward or homeward bound, belonging to the Peninsular and Oriental Company, or Messageries Impériales, lands its living freight to enjoy a short six hours of *terra firma*, and, if the season be auspicious, to indulge in mangesteens, the only fruit perhaps of whose merit Eastern tales do not convey an exaggerated impression. Unlike the coarse fruits of those climes—the jack, the banana, and the mango—it possesses a delicacy of taste that far exceeds the flavour of the nectarine. Its beauty of appearance is, moreover, such as to cause regret it cannot be preserved; but it is so sensitive of touch, and its clear pink and white are mingled in such pure perfection, that the softest finger wounds, and at the expiration of some hours its utility for food has ceased.

Penang is governed by an officer detached from Singapore, styled Resident Councillor, and he is aided in the administration by a legal referee, who often occupies at once the manifold vocations of counsel for defence and prosecution, of magistrate, and something like Chief-Justice. Such at least appeared to visitors the position occupied by Sir Peter Benson Maxwell, who, under the elastic title of Recorder, apparently performed a variety of duties embracing every shade of legal jurisdiction. These duties are not at all times, it is true, combined in one man's hands; but sickness or some other cause often reduces the small administration of Penang to very near a minimum, and if at intervals a case occurs which a modest man in power considers his acquaintance with the forms of justice too limited to deal with, the criminal is sent to Singapore, where the merits of the case are speedily disposed of. To this settlement of Singapore we shall now therefore turn, passing by Malacca without mention, as being very similar to Penang in many of its local characteristics, and also because, owing to its situation on the mainland, it is both less frequented and possessed of minor interest.

Singapore is a curious place, and its inhabitants have been divided by a native writer into four classes. " Malays rank first as the aborigines. These are fed upon by Europeans, who in their turn are cheated by

Chinese ; the whole three-fourths of the population being actually at the mercy of a large community of tigers, who carry off each night one human child or more, and infest the jungle ground by which the station is surrounded in such quantities as to render it unsafe to walk the streets at night." Singapore owes its importance entirely to its position. It is described as an island, but in reality it forms the extreme southern point of the continent of Asia, being separated from the mainland by what are little more than the two mouths of an unimportant river. It is the half-way house for the whole China trade, and as such its possession is a necessity for England, so long as her fleets remain the carriers of the commerce of the world. Yet it has been determined, and with wisdom, to confine its fortifications to the erection of such batteries as should prevent its falling a too easy prey to an attacking force ; and this is based upon the argument, that its possession is rather the consequence of our maritime supremacy than an abetting cause of such result.

This being the case, and applying as it does with equal force to Malacca and Penang, and the powers moreover intrusted to the government of these settlements being large enough to give scope for the exercise of administrative ability only on an unpretending scale, Colonel Orfeur Cavanagh found, on suddenly ascending to the giddy height of his Lilliputian throne, but few domestic questions of any magnitude awaiting his solution ; and it cannot afford surprise that an officer of his known activity of mind should by

preference have turned his thoughts into the more
exciting channels of his foreign policy. In this spirit
of adventure, and in search of occupation, were undertaken periodical visits to Sarawak and the haunts
of even wilder men than Raja Brooke on the rugged
coasts of Borneo. The time and labour thus withdrawn from the more immediate local interests of
Singapore were well devoted to reducing piracy in the
neighbouring seas; and in the performance of this
task he has more than once been well supported by
the strong right arm of the Christian Church, in the
person of a well-known Colonial Bishop, who, in the
exercise of his episcopacy at Labuan, oft laid aside
his cassock and exchanged the early Fathers' homilies
for the more convincing arguments of Joe Manton
or a Purdie. The works of Sir Stamford Raffles,
however, have left nothing to be desired in the description of this quarter of the globe; and having
now reached the southernmost point of our Indian
dominions, it is time to turn the traveller's head
towards home.

Before we quit the waters of Bengal one last possession calls for some slight notice. This possession
is of little value even to ourselves. Two straggling
groups of islands, separated by a channel little traversed, occupy a position which may be roughly
termed a central one as measured from Calcutta, Galle,
and Singapore. To the southern of these groups,
that bears the name of Nicobars, a melancholy interest attaches, from its having proved the grave of
many of our early navigators, who, seeking hospitality

and shelter from the burst of the monsoon, rashly landed on these coasts. Quite recently, indeed, vessels from Rangoon having disappeared under circumstances fully justifying suspicion, a search was instituted, and a history of piracy and cannibalism systematically combined was brought to light. The more northern group of islands, the Andamans, are mainly remarkable for having preserved human nature in a lower stage of civilisation than has been ever found elsewhere. They are now utilised as a convict settlement, and a small town has sprung up called Port Blair, where a Superintendent resides, who, aided by a company of Madras Sepoys, is the jailer of some hundreds of the mutineers of 1857. Attempts to civilise the aborigines have frequently been made, but still remain unattended with the least success. These savages retire by day at our approach, and hover round our settlement at night like dogs or beasts of prey. They seem too little civilised to appreciate the fact of our intrusion, and it is even a vexed question whether they possess a *bonâ fide* language of their own. They give utterance to uncouth sounds, bearing more resemblance to the cries of the brute creation than to the inflections of the human voice. They find food apparently by instinct, sleep in trees, go totally unclothed, know the rude use of a club as against the beasts by whom they are surrounded, though scarcely against their fellow-men, and are equally incapable of organisation among themselves, and of individual resistance to white enemies. Yet missionaries have not been wanting to approach these islanders, and well-meaning members of the Society for the Diffusion of Christian Knowledge have sown their coasts with Bibles, whose use the finders could certainly but ill conjecture.

The office of Superintendent at Port Blair is one not widely sought for. Hitherto it has been almost always held by military men. Colonel Houghton, now known to fame from his suppression of the Jyntiah Cossiah Rebellion, once occupied this place, receiving twelve hundred Company's rupees per month in exchange for utter banishment. On his departure there ensued a kind of interregnum, during which the convicts had time to get accustomed to lax discipline; and then there suddenly appeared among them a Colonel of the late Company's army, called Robert Christopher Tytler, who had won for himself a certain reputation in some obscure transactions in 1857. Colonel Tytler's merits were better known, and certainly had been better appreciated, at the London India Office than in the Military Department at Calcutta. Some merits he no doubt possessed; but he was not the man to inspire a feeling of security amongst an isolated few. Neither did it appear, when he became the head of such an isolated few, that he had it in his power to feel much confidence in himself. The Anglo-Indian officer of many years' experience in comfortable stations of burra khanas and of iced champàgne was ill at ease among a people who fed on roots and wore no clothes. Port Blair offers but few resources for a devotee to social life. The settlement is composed of a few mean bungalows scattered under cocoas on a sandy shore. On one side stretch the lines of some Madrassee Sepoys; while on the opposite are seen a tiny cast-iron

church, but recently imported, and the white man's
graveyard, well tenanted for so limited a community.
The convict settlement occupies a central place, raked
by the imaginary fire of an hospital ship, two store vessels, and some few coasting craft, peaceably at anchor in
the horse-shoe bay. Certain people have it not in them
to endure an existence to which they deem themselves
superior; and it is to be supposed that Colonel Tytler
belonged to this large category. However this may be,
he first applied for leave, and almost ere his application
was received his health broke down, and he left the
Andamans after a reign of short duration and of few
results.

Corresponding to these groups of Andamans and
Nicobars, and occupying, with reference to the coast
of Malabar, something of the same position they hold in
respect to that of Coromandel, we find the Laccadives
and Maldives, separated from each other, like their
prototypes, by a channel of about a hundred miles,
whose value for purposes of navigation is lessened by
the existence in its centre of a coral formation, to which
the name of Minicoy has been given. This island is
uninhabited, save by native fishermen, who visit it
from time to time, and form a floating population,
which hitherto has shown but little tendency to expand.
Minicoy, like all mid-channel islands, is not without
its fair average of shipwreck tales, though happily
the half-savage mariners frequenting it have shown a
marked humanity to all whom accident has cast upon
their coasts.

The Laccadives, until lately, formed a portion of the

inheritance pertaining to the Chief of Cannamore, subject to the payment of an annual tribute of a thousand
pounds to the British Government.   With the growth,
however, of our dominion in the East, the power of
native princes to enforce their rights at the hands of
distant vassals has very much decreased; and hence it
followed that not long since, the tribute having fallen
into many years' arrears, the Government of India
absolved the reigning Beebee from all responsibility of
its collection past and future, assuming the administration of the islands.   With them, as with the Maldives,
fish is the sole produce.   They are not reported as possessed of mineral or vegetable wealth.   Gold-dust is not
found upon their surf-bound shores; neither do costly
spice trees cast a perfumed shade upon their sun-burnt
soil.   Their wealth consists of palms and cocoas, and
the inhabitants obtain imported clothes and articles of
luxury, in quantities limited by their inaccessibility, in
exchange for the shells called cowries, that are used as
money for small payments throughout the length and
breadth of Hindostan.   It has been stated, on the
authority of a careful investigator, that the inhabitants
of the Maldives are Mahomedans, probably of Arabic
descent; that they live under a Sultan paying tribute
-to Ceylon, who, according to Hamilton, resides in Malē,
an island about three miles in circuit, fortified by walls
and batteries mounting upwards of a hundred pieces
of artillery.   But this account must be received with
caution, as ill according with the piscatorial simplicity
and indigence that form the leading characteristics of
their brethren of the Laccadives.

Aden and Perim are now all that remain unnoticed of what we have termed the Indian provinces beyond the sea; for the rich island of Ceylon forms an isolated colony, having no dependence on Calcutta. It is ruled by a Governor appointed by the Queen, upon the advice and responsibility of the Secretary of State charged with the Colonial Department, and corresponds with India on equal terms on matters of a mutual interest. Often it has been suggested that Ceylon physically belongs to continental India, and forms as much an integral part of the Presidency of Madras as the isle of Anglesey does of Wales. Indeed more so, the latter being now at length connected only by a triumph of engineering skill, the former by a succession of broken rocks or islands worn away through long ages by the break of the monsoon, known to geography as Adam's Bridge, and uniting the island to the main shore with the exception of a pass one hundred and fifty yards in width, dignified on charts by the appellation Paumben Channel, where at low tide, thanks to an expenditure of fifty thousand pounds, we have now succeeded in obtaining a depth of water of about thirteen feet. Other breaks and irregularities exist, it is true, in Adam's Bridge, but over many of them a boy could leap with ease; and geology has surmised that the interruptions in this natural causeway were originally the result of some slight terrestrial convulsion early in the fifteenth century.

The fact of the island of Ceylon being constituted independent of the Government of India, was no doubt mainly owing to the circumstances connected with its

acquisition. The Portuguese established themselves
there early in the sixteenth century, and were succeeded in the seventeenth by the Dutch, from whom
the island was wrested by the British in the course of
the wars resulting from the great French Revolution.
Yet the conquered portions were confined to fortified
points along the coast, and the King of Candy until
quite recently ruled in the mountains of Muralia.   In
former times Ceylon was mainly prized as a convenient
point to touch for wood, water, and provisions; it
boasted more than one good harbour, and was inhabited
by a peace-seeking people who knew few wants.   Its
interests were Imperial, being bound up with those, not
only of East India, but of China and the whole extensive Australasian group; and it was argued, that if
made subordinate to the Governor-General, these interests might be farmed for local ends which might
not so well reconcile with general requirement.   Lord
Wellesley early saw the shortsightedness of such a
view, and used his influence, though in vain, to counteract the claims to this pet island which the Colonial
Office was advancing on the strength of its colonial
antecedents.   But at that period our Indian possessions had by no means formed themselves into the
ring-fenced estate they now resemble.   The process of
consolidation had not indeed commenced, and conquest
was still the order of the day.   The Cingalese themselves, no doubt, have benefited by the course pursued.
They have escaped all share in the vicissitudes of war,
pestilence, and famine which waged beyond that narrow
belt of sea.   Neither have they been compelled to con-

tribute towards the maintenance of Indian finance a quota corresponding to their wealth. As an independent colony their taxation has been light and easy to be borne; and though the progress they have made in arts and agriculture has been small compared with that of Madras or British Burma, it has proved sufficient to satisfy the humble cravings of an unambitious race. A market for their pearls is all that they require, that a family may buy some five-and-twenty cocoas, and build beneath their shade a rude abode composed of sticks and matting—the trees themselves supplying all their wants; one tree, perchance, is hollowed out to form a rough canoe, by aid of which still more pearls and fish may be obtained; and with such treasures, and an iron pot or two, they contentedly eke out the burthen of their existence. Still Ceylon is not without drawbacks, mainly incidental to its independence. It has a civil service of its own, an ecclesiastical establishment both overgrown and overfed, and a mint, accompanied by all the ramifications of a fiscal system on a scale commensurate with the necessities of Imperial shipping interests, but far exceeding those of the inhabitants themselves. One argument used in former days against the incorporation of Ceylon with British India was, that such a step would immediately be followed by granting to Trincomalee the patronage bestowed on Point de Galle: the latter undoubtedly the worst haven into which the shipping of the East habitually puts, and only maintained as lying handy at the extreme south of the island, so as to save each China and Australian ship some half day's coal; the former styled by Nelson "the finest harbour in the world"—a reputation endorsed in the following words by one of the ablest navigators of our day :—"Almost entirely landlocked, the water is so deep that it is practicable to step from the shore on board the largest vessels moored alongside.   During the north-east monsoon, when all ships on the Coromandel coast and in the Bengal Bay are compelled to put to sea, Trincomalee is their main place of refuge.   The town," it is added, "well fortified by the Portuguese, may be considered as the military capital of Ceylon."   Galle, on the other hand, is assailable both by land and sea, and annually submits to the appreciation of mankind a list of accidents and loss of life so long that nothing but the influence of Peninsular and Oriental Company directors and of the agents for Australian mails, combined with the ignorance of the general public and of the holders of East India stock,—nothing less than such a powerful combination of ignorance and wealth could have preserved, beyond the middle of the nineteenth century, Galle harbour from its inevitable doom of utter and complete abandonment, and kept closed to trade for upwards of a hundred years "the finest haven in the world."

It so happens that public opinion in England concerning India is mostly formed by men whose paths have lain in Bombay or Bengal; for not only numerically speaking do they form a stronger phalanx than those who toil within the precincts of Madras, but the commercial and military ascendency of the two northern Presidencies has tended to absorb the interest expressed in England in what relates to British India. Of these two Presidencies the servants of Bengal alone set eyes upon Ceylon, where they spend in transit some few hours, just sufficient to enable the more energetic to visit the so-called Cinnamon Gardens, and Wockwallee, in the immediate vicinity of Galle, being thus alone enabled to form an opinion worthy of the name, as based on personal observation. This opinion is palmed off upon their brethren of Bombay, by whom it is adopted, partly from deference to the superior wisdom of Bengal, partly from the fear of being bracketed perhaps with the benighted denizens of Fort St George, and most of all, no doubt, from the innate love, common to peoples as to individuals, of dissenting from the preconceived opinions of their nearest neighbour, when circumstances enable them to do so without incurring responsibility. To men thus fresh from Calcutta or from Europe, Ceylon's palm-clad coast affords a marked contrast to the Hoogly's muddy shores or Aden's scorching cinders, and they endorse in daily conversation the belief existent, that the island of Ceylon is distinct from continental India in language, manners, and religion ; whilst the Anglican of Madras, who occupies, both from his minority and the accident of geographical position, the place of smallest interest and influence at home,—he alone can trace a similarity between the Cingalese and the southern races who occupy the lands beyond the Cauvery, from Tanjore to Cochin.

The fact is, Hindostan must be regarded as a continent, of which Ceylon forms but one component part.

The mountain races to the north are rude-spoken and rough-mannered; as you travel south, they soften at once in character, language, and appearance. They are less martial, less fanatical, and more effeminate. The patois of the Hills gives place to the full-mouthed Punjabee languages, which ₐre superseded in their turn by the more cultivated Mahratta and Hindee; and finally all give way to the softer sounds of Canarese and Tamil. These dialects again, as the coast is gradually approached, merge, through stages not always very clearly traceable, into Cingalese, which, when spoken in its purity, is peculiar to the island whence it takes its name, but when written and termed Pali is in general use in Burmese literature, and has much analogy with Malay and Siamese. Further, we are told that throughout Ceylon and Travancore, "gatherers of fruit," "drawers of toddy," or fermented sap from the palm, and low-caste fishermen called "Moognas," form a large proportion of the population; and again we have on high authority "that the Malabars of Ceylon and the Cingalese of Malabar are so closely allied in manners and religion, and both resemble in such degree their congeners of Southern India, as to form one people, evidently descended from the posterity of Hashem, who was expelled by Mahomet from Arabia; and though Candy, from its isolated and inaccessible position at the summit of the Kadaganava Pass, still remains a stronghold of the Buddhist faith, yet little physiological importance should be attributed to a circumstance so local in its operation and accidental in its origin"— owing, as the priests themselves allow, to a very flying visit once paid that mountain by the divine Buddha, who condescended, we are told, to purchase the eternal sanctity of so beautiful an island, hitherto inhabited by demons, at the costly price of a holy tooth.

Thus race, language, manners, and religion seem to culminate in the most southern portion of the peninsula of Hindostan. There, within the space of two square degrees, are found living side by side, in friendly intercourse and commercial prosperity, representatives of every creed from Ghuznee to Juggernaut; and England, far from seeking to sink the nationality of Ceylon, and class her by the side of secondary insular possessions, ought on the contrary to cast her weight into the scales of British India, with whose destinies she must ever be inseparably associated. Their products are the same; and unfortunately there is but little difference in their climate. The same Eastern sun shines on both, and, recent experience has taught, with almost equal detriment to European life. The last two rulers of Ceylon have been brought to early graves by reason of the noxious influences there imbibed. Sir Henry Ward, it is true, succumbed to cholera a few days after his arrival in Madras. And that Presidency unjustly has his blood upon her hands; for no less surely did his labours at Colombo predispose him to the grasp of the disease than was the case with his successor, Sir Charles Macarthy, who after lingering long, apparently unwilling to leave his work ere its completion, was finally compelled to ship himself for England, which he never lived to reach.

But interest in Ceylon has made us stray from the

path prescribed, and Aden, with Perim, have claims on our attention that brook no further of delay. The acquisition of the former dates from 1849, when Captain Haines was authorised by the Government of India to demand redress for some indignities suffered by Mahomedans, under the protection of Bombay, bound upon a pilgrimage to Mecca. The local Sultan was accordingly addressed, and his reply was of so insolent a nature as to provoke hostilities, which terminated in our acquisition of a town and seaport of Arabia Felix in the province of Yemen. "The geological formation of Aden is of pure igneous origin, the whole peninsula being little more than a huge mass of volcanic rock. Aden has been styled the eye of Yemen; it is certainly the key to the Red Sea from the south, its harbour being the finest in Arabia." Since the possession by Great Britain of this exhausted crater, vast sums have been lavished in the erection of fortifications, which render it no doubt impregnable, if not to any attack that might be made from the sea or the mainland, at least to any force the Arabs could collect. Indeed it has been said by competent authorities, that what Aden has most to fear in the event of war, is that its lofty walls might be brought down by the concussion caused by the discharge of its own artillery. Such as it is, however, Aden is governed by a military Resident appointed from Bombay. The wonders of the tanks, by means of which the rain that falls once in three years or so is carefully preserved for the use of the inhabitants, are too well known to need description here. They have been supposed to be of Roman origin, and their excavation is mainly due to the energy displayed by Captain Playfair, now Her Majesty's Consul at Zanzibar, who, being left long in charge, spared nothing, and money least of all, in the successful execution of this work.

The island of Perim is dependent upon the peninsula of Aden, being situated in the centre of the Strait of Bab-el-Mandeb. It is small, flat, arid, and worthless; and the meagre company, detached from the garrison of Aden for its defence, would be of less value to serve the guns commanding the narrow entrance to the Red Sea, than they actually are as a security for the burning of the light watched for with anxiety by every pilot as he nears that channel. The blustering menace expressed by France at the date of our attachment of the island of Perim was so much capital expended on an unremu nerative object. It has since become palpable to all that for offensive purposes Perim is powerless; while its defence could not be maintained in so isolated a position without a force vastly superior to its strategic value. Perim is not a fortress, but a light-station; and the eloquence of France and the threats of her colonels have failed to construe the encouragement of commerce into an act of political aggression.

CHAPTER IX.

THE MILITARY DEPARTMENT.

IN previous chapters some space has necessarily been devoted to military deeds and men, but without encroaching on the place reserved for notice of the profession whose history they adorn; for in the East a soldier's duties cannot be kept within the limits of camp life, and the force of his example extends far beyond the small circumference whence his watch-fires may be seen. Half a century ago the duties of an Indian soldier to the English Crown embraced even wider fields of action than is the case to-day. Less liable to barren criticism, a broader scope was left for the unembarrassed exercise of character and genius; and while it was impossible for a commander to shield himself from the responsibility attaching to his office by endless reference to headquarters, no general could be blind to the fact that the prestige of the blood shed by Clive and Warren Hastings might easily be sacrificed in one campaign. Thus place and power then really went together, and each conveyed some sense of its responsibility to him who held it, by force of actual fact, and not by reason of the fear of having tardy tactics watched with ill-disguised impatience, and military distances measured upon the Horse Guards' maps by the light of letters from a correspondent of the 'Times.'

A combination of the difficulties of both these positions may be said, however, to have been embraced in Lord Clyde's Indian career. He, perhaps more than any of his predecessors, might feel that one day's insuccess, or even doubtful gain, would more than neutralise the prolonged victory of a century; and he moreover entered on his duties at a moment when national anxiety for India in England had reached its highest pitch, and when each British tax-payer considered that his status as a free-born Briton, not less than parental fondness for a younger son who had perchance embraced an Eastern life, entitled him to know the programme of reconquest. Sense of responsibility is of two kinds—legitimate, for the ultimate result of the interests at stake; and illegitimate, for fear of the discredit entailed by failure. Both of these Lord Clyde might well experience. He had been essentially the soldier of good fortune, who, raised to high command by past successes dearly won at the hands of worthy enemies, might not unnaturally be supposed to shrink from the possibility of dulling in some Indian fight the lustre of a long life's achievements. Besides, though suffering less than many from a morbid consciousness of the magnitude of the game he played, he yet possessed a full and healthy knowledge of the heavy liability incurred by one who led the vengeful hosts which England had sent out to buy back with still more blood a land already reddened by the sword. To this just appreciation of his own position, Lord Clyde's good fortune further added the not inconsiderable advantage of having to narrate his doings in the East the pen of Dr Russell, who, from long familiarity with both the pains and pleasures of campaigning, knew how to keep the British public satisfied with accurate details, without assuming, as he might, the easier part of censor and reformer. Finally, the condition of events was such as to leave Lord Clyde more untrammelled than any General in the field since the era of the first Napoleon. The Indian telegraph by sea was not then laid, while that by land was everywhere destroyed or in the enemy's hands; he had at his beck and call men devoted to himself by past association, and in Sir William Mansfield he, first alone, but later joined by all the military world, recognised the ablest soldier of our time.

But it is not our intention to emulate the zeal of octogenarian heroes, who never tire of fighting well-fought battles yet once more. Too many books have helped to cast an insufficient light upon the acts in which their authors played at best a poor third part; and we must rest content with the attempt to trace some faint outline of the relative positions occupied by soldier and civilian—showing how each now wears the other's mask, how the civilian of an earlier day, having the command of soldiery, was martial to excess, while now, that the rupees he monthly earns are owing to success in arms alone, but little love is lost between the services.

This mutual jealousy has constantly afforded cause

for scandal, and not unfrequently produced results most baneful to the public interests. Formerly, in times of great excitement, or when some long-pending measure required immediate carrying-out, the difficulty was often met by joining in one man's hands the reins of military and civil rule. The biography of Lord Cornwallis affords more than one example of such a combination, necessary at the time, but invariably dissolved when the necessity had passed away. But when two men of equal ambition and genius for usurping every field of action meet on the theatre of Indian life, difficulty invariably ensues. The last instance of such difficulty, growing from a mere personal feeling of dislike, or what Sir Cresswell Cresswell might have termed "incompatibility of temper," into a public animosity, such as to make it impossible for civil and military authorities to work in double harness, occurred in Lord Dalhousie's time, when Sir Charles Napier, rendered the weaker vessel by the glowing administrative successes of the Governor-General, was shattered in the contest and recalled.

A much-abetting cause of these dissensions doubtless may be found in the constitution of what are termed the "Civil Regiments." These consist of corps enrolled rather for political reasons than as arms of Imperial warfare or defence, and as such they are subject to the sole control of the Governor-General, to the exclusion of the authority of the Commander-in-Chief. Queen's officers are appointed to them as vacancies occur; and these appointments being highly paid, and affording special opportunities for distinction, are much coveted, and constitute a valuable branch of patronage. The "Punjab Irregular Force," raised in 1849, ranks first among these troops for efficiency and importance, being composed of horse and foot and guns; and since 1857 it has earned for itself an honourable place in the military history of India, beneath the iron hand and silken glove of Brigadier-General Neville Chamberlain, an officer whose daring and ambition found an ample field in the belt of country known as the Derajat, that separates the river Indus from the frontiers of Cabul. Many other corps belong to the list of "Civil Regiments;" the duty of some of them lies in obedience to the commands of the Resident at Hyderabad, and some receive their orders through the Agents to the Governor-General at Indore or Mount Aboo. Some are still more local in their character, like the Mhairwarrah battalion; and the special service of others, like the Viceroy's body-guard, and that of the Resident at Nipal, consists in the performance of perpetual escort-duty. There is, however, no necessity to name or number these personal and local military bodies. They all differ in externals; some are clothed in scarlet and gold, with jack-boots and plumed head-gear; others wear the dust-coloured khakee uniform and turban peculiar to the native infantry, and prefer to remove their European ammunition-boots before proceeding on a march; yet, though distinct in outward show, they have the fact in common that all of them wear swords, which one and all know full well when and for whom to draw. Though the anomaly of this system is no doubt very great, it has hitherto been found practically to work well, and has proved itself of almost priceless value in these days when so much of the real power of a Governor-General has been laid low—first by the creation of powerful subordinate administrations, and secondly by the system of increased subservience to home, even in matters of minute detail, such as the granting of a paltry annual pension;—thus rendering it doubly necessary that the office of Viceroy should be clothed with martial attributes, and all the outward pomp and circumstance of an Eastern Court.

With men of the stamp of the Governor-General who annexed the Punjab, and of the Commander-in-Chief who conquered Scinde, it was not unnatural that difficulty should have arisen; but Lord Canning at the outset of the Indian Mutiny had for Chief Commander a man of the heroic caste, who, had he lived, might by the force of his prompt action have crushed in its first infancy the wide-spreading conflagration. But the sudden illness of a few days closed the life of General Anson, and he died in Northern India on the very day our countrymen exchanged the line of their intrenchments at Cawnpore for the river-boats so treacherously provided for them by the Nana of infamous repute. Thus Lord Canning lost the services of one above jealousy like himself, and for a time was left alone to battle with events.

Then it was that Sir Colin Campbell, the first and last Lord Clyde, appeared upon the scene, bringing with him in his train a host of junior commanders whose personal confidence he had acquired in what Mr Kinglake calls Crim Tartary. Yet a little, and Fort St

George sent a representative in the person of Colonel Neill, while Sir James Outram, having put a hurried termination to the Persian war, hastened up from Bombay Presidency. Troops now poured in from every side, and every nerve was strung in expectation. The brigade of the "Shannon," and the other troops diverted from the second Chinese war, played their part right nobly in the struggle. Lord Clyde, however, from the first set his hard face rigidly against advance, reserving his whole forces for defensive operations, until the white troops at his command should number seventy thousand souls. Many have since questioned the wisdom and necessity of such a resolution, and, *ex-post-facto* arguments being of special ease in application, it has not proved difficult to spread a crude belief that Lord Clyde might have done his work with less; and that even had he failed, though England might have lost some prestige in the East, she would at least have been relieved from the necessity of sending half her army to a distant sepulchre. Yet these criticisms are of little value, either for purposes of history or to enable one to form an approximate appreciation of Lord Clyde as a soldier. He came rapidly from England, and formed a just decision from the first. From this decision he never swerved by the width of a camel's hair. He was obstinate, he had his own way, fought his battles on spots selected by himself, and brought us through a doubtful crisis in our destiny without a moment's hesitation and with success impossible to controvert.

The rebellion thus subdued, Lord Canning could

afford to cast an anxious eye around, and see how much was gone, and what remained of former institutions. The first grand conclusion at which he speedily arrived, and which when taught by him soon found a general acceptance, was, that India, though reconquered by the sword, should now be ruled alone by legislation. Yet many a brigadier who holds command at some up-country station still clings with moribund tenacity to the style quoted in 'Cawnpore,' by Mr George Trevelyan—a style remarkable for inhumanity, and boasting little force but that derived from bare alliteration " Peafowl, partridges, and pandies, rose together—the latter," it is added, " affording the best sport." It is to be regretted that the class of thought to which such writing owes its origin still boasts of numerous advocates in our Anglo-Indian army ; yet thrice happy is it that the practice of the human race divine to trim its sails by the prevailing breeze, whichever way it blows, is strong enough to modify the mischief ; and hence, so long as wise discretion is displayed in the selection of officers for high command, for staff employ and civil situations, no general impression adverse to our interests can be produced upon the masses of Indian population by the unchristian language of the few.

When Lord Clyde left India, a short military reign devolved upon Sir Patrick Grant, the then senior General commanding ; and he was soon succeeded by a name wellnigh synonymous with success. The career of Lieutenant-General Sir Hugh Rose has been too lately laid before the public in a fascinating form by Major Mallison to call for any biographical detail. But queries, perhaps, it may not be deemed presumptuous to put, in order that the picture of this great man may form a pleasing object for the eye to dwell on, as perfeet both in light and shade. If we would, therefore, criticise Sir Hugh's career, we might be tempted to dwell less leniently upon the amiable defects in which his character abounds—defects glossed over even by a hypercritical Review as casting the tenor of his life within a mould better fitting the past century than the present day. Again, some say that personal friendship may be carried to excess ; and the enemies of Sir Hugh delight in pointing at many of his omissions and commissions as the results of causes certainly not professioual. But these are personal questions, and of little import when compared with the administrative reforms which mark this period ; for it is denied by none that throughout four years of peace Sir Hugh devoted his considerable genius, and an activity that knows no bounds, mainly to improving the condition of our Indian army, by each and every device that could occur to an ever-thoughtful brain. Prominent among these ranks the grand experiment of regimental workshops, where the private soldier may spend profitably some hours each day, otherwise probably devoted to pernicious sleep, or to still more baneful idleness when awake, in the construction of small articles either for his personal use or for sale in the bazaars, thereby enhancing the modest revenue from which the better class contrives to set aside a fund against some rainy day.

The sanitary condition of British troops in India has,

however, received of late a liberal measure of attention from the English public. The statistics furnished by Mr Strachey and Sir Sydney Cotton, contrasted with reports supplied by various departmental heads, have now afforded upwards of one year's study to those who can devote some time and consideration to the task of criticising and comparing compound sums like these, containing elements that assume a widely different aspect, when seen from one or other point of view.

The fact is, white life in India has become so costly of importation and of maintenance, that the ablest minds have racked their ingenuity in endeavours to lay down conditions for its preservation at once humane and economical. Thus various dogmas have been promulgated, asserting that a length of service varying from five to ten years might be looked for from each white soldier transplanted to Calcutta at a cost of £90 ; and when Lord Clyde reached India the financial question had attained its zenith. A country then in debt, had to be recovered by expending money raised with difficulty at six per cent. Some there were who ventured to predict that, even if recovered, India would henceforth have lost its fascination as a mercantile investment ; and Threadneedle Street eyed with doubt and hesitation the opening of loans, although secured by Government, for sums which far surpassed what they supposed the value of the stake. The funds were ultimately raised however, and fifty thousand men were sent to India in six months. Though India was thus saved to us, she had to bear the debt incurred ; and little wonder if Lord Clyde's successor, as Sir Hugh

Rose may almost be called, felt his first care in time of peace to be the preservation of white life.

The tables framed by various statisticians have so differed as to complicate the question of mortality and sickness in India, as compared with corresponding entries laid before the House of Commons from other portions of Great Britain and her colonies; and the result has been, first to mislead those who sought with difficulty for truth, and secondly to discourage all who might have wished to understand what climate can effect when brought to bear on military immigration. As has been said, Sir Sydney Cotton, Mr Strachey, and others possessed of equal claims to our attention, have presented to the thinking world reports so differing as to preclude a true comparison on which to base a radical improvement. In the face of all these complications, Sir Hugh Rose adopted, when in India, the only course consistent with his own experience; and sought by zeal, and what approached to omnipresence, to counteract the harm of theories opposed or practical neglect. Often at Murree or Nynee-tal he might be heard of as arriving; yet ere the small and mixed community had decided on the mode of his reception, it would suddenly be known that he had reached Delhi or Mean Meer, where cholera had appeared. Few could overtake or even trace him on these rapid marches. Correspondents of the press were almost invariably at fault. His Excellency might be reported on his road to seek a moment's respite from the toils of office at Simla or Mount Aboo; but only Colonel Haythorne and his satellites of the Adjutant or Quartermaster General's

Department might know that, with a chosen Staff, he at that moment was riding hard towards the valley of the Indus or the Ganges, where his troops were sickening in inaction, and needed the reviving presence of their Chief Commander.

Those whose knowledge of Sir Hugh has been confined to passing visits paid to Barnescourt or Mahasoo, where he was wont to spend some shady weeks each year, stolen from the arduous cares of Indian office, and who but saw him reclining on a mossy bank ten thousand feet above the level of the sea, beneath the shade of cedars trained by the artistic hands of Mr Courtenay and Lord William Hay, could ill suppose that so refined, almost effeminate, an exterior contained a mind remarkable for ardent enterprise and great strategic combinations. The easy flowing life and many pleasures of an Indian sanitarium were but bright oases in the daily drudgery he for years performed at cost of health and strength; and the real light in which Sir Hugh appeared the most at home, was amid the gleam of hostile hosts, or the darker shades of tented hospitals. Essentially a soldier, the country now possesses the combined advantage of his vigour in a field where much lies in active military prevention, and of knowing that in peaceful India his successor, not one whit less the soldier, brings ripe statesmanship and a still rarer knowledge of finance to the solution of those mixed equations where the letter x is still affixed to men and money, as unknown quantities yet to be adjusted.

The changes lately made in the Indian military world have been so numerous and important as to con-

O

stitute the dawn of a new era in its history. Not only have different and opposite systems of administration succeeded one another with a rapidity rarely seen before upon so large a scale; not only has advance in science introduced organic changes subversive of almost every preconceived opinion, and pregnant with unnumbered theories in the arts of war; not only has the march of education, which in its infancy has proved that with natives as ourselves a little knowledge is a dangerous thing, steadily progressed, until its ripening buds burst forth and bore the fruits of confidence restored; but the individual agents of all these transformations have, from one cause or other, disappeared from those scenes wherein they played so prominent a part. Lord Clyde, Sir James Outram, Neill, Havelock, Nicholson, Sir Henry Lawrence, and too many more, have been gathered to their fathers. Sir Patrick Grant, Sir Sydney Cotton, and some others, have retired to well-earned rest at home; while Sir Hugh Rose, Sir Hope Grant, and a chosen few, now occupy some of the highest military offices within the British Isles. On the other hand, Sir William Mansfield has not disappointed the high hopes formed of him when chief of Lord Clyde's Staff, but has succeeded in his turn to the sword and mantle of his former master; while Sir Robert Napier, the Bayard of the Punjab, has found, first as military member of the Viceroy's Council, and later as Chief Commander in Bombay, ample scope for the exercise of his great ability and zeal. Thus in a brief survey of the characters brought into historical prominence by the events of 1857, Sir William

Mansfield, Sir Robert Napier, and one other name, stand forth almost alone as still fighting India's battles with accustomed obstinacy and success. The third name is that of Colonel Norman, who understands better perhaps than any one the intricate mazes of amalgamation. Upon his shoulders has devolved the adjusting of incomprehensible accounts, and claims opposed. His brain alone seemed large enough to contain without confusion the cadres of upwards of a hundred corps, with military furlough regulations and retirements old and new, the whole surmounted and embarrassed by that royal warrant, dated January 16, 1861, to which England owes the somewhat rash formation of its hybrid staff corps.

But let us leave the heads of action, and dwell a moment on the comparatively subordinate officers who were mainly instrumental in carrying out the countless changes they, each day more and more bewildered, read of in army general orders. A divisional command in India is singularly well calculated to embarrass one who, without experience of local facts, should undertake its charge. Yet reference to recent Indian army lists will show that the combined agency of the Horse Guards and the India Office has had for one of its results to place some names upon the roll of Generals of Division in satisfaction of claims not merely local. From this roll two major-generals have elected to follow the fortunes of Sir Hugh Rose to England and across St George's Channel: their names are Lord George Paget and Major-General Thurlow Cunyghame. For the appointment which has devolved upon the former, a fitter man could not have been selected ; and it is no disparagement to add that, as Inspector-General of Cavalry, he has passed into a more congenial field of work, and one for which his genius better recommends him than it did for the Sirhind command of troops, with whose drill and language he could boast of little previous acquaintance. His stay in India was short, however, and but a passing though unpleasant dream to Indian soldiers who had borne the heat and burden of the day ; and he has now been permitted to exchange a sphere of almost forced inaction for a post of high responsibility that he is admirably qualified to fill. The latter's term of Indian service was marked by none of the characteristics above mentioned. General Cunyghame fought his way to high preferment in fields beyond the Sutlej, and was long officially connected with one of England's military Governor-Generals of India. Upon him reposed successively the divisional commands of Mooltan and Lahore ; and we only see in his transfer to Dublin a much-envied post conferred upon a much-deserving officer. Of others who have rendered good service throughout a long career we may here briefly mention Sir John Garvock and the late Major-General Showers, both of whom owed ultimate promotion to the Presidency and Peshawur commands more to years than patronage or the performance of great military miracles.

Yet as the earth's crust hardens by the unseen effect of time, so gradually pass away the opportunities and necessity for feats of arms. Few military incidents of modern days, if we except the defence of Kars and the deeds of Hodson's horse, are of such a character as to stamp their actors' names on the records of our history; and, practically, the utmost that authorities can be required to do is, to select such persons for the performance of a certain class of duties as may reasonably be supposed competent to discharge them by force of professional experience. Yet we find that when some cause removes an officer from command, the choice of his successor is made in different ways by different men. A timid general often seeks to shield his personal responsibility by a blind endorsement of the praise awarded by his predecessor, the importance of which praise is, however, much diminished by the fact that too many writers of military despatches deem it incumbent on them in all cases to record appreciation of several members of their general staff, and half the number of field-officers engaged, recommending a very large proportion for promotion or the Bath, and not unfrequently concluding with the used-up phrase, that where all are so deserving it is invidious to make distinctions. It is this method of despatch-writing which proves in modern days the greatest bar to the discernment of true merit; and very much is to be said in favour of the system of filling up a vacancy from personal knowledge of the officer himself, thus assuming all responsibility, and risking the aspersions of a greedy and place-hunting multitude. Lord Clyde's Indian appointments were generally made in accordance with the principle laid down in time of need by all the greatest captains of the world. Sir Hugh Rose, succeeding to a time of peace, pursued a different course, and, in the absence of heroic exploits, often framed the roll of his promotions upon past records, easy in their application to those whom he himself preferred. Yet when all is told, Indian military patronage is so hedged in by reference to home, and the necessity of concurrence with the Governor-General in Council, as not only almost to exclude the possibility of pushing favouritism to a serious fault, but rather to confine a Chief Commander's choice within limits too restricted for the reward of genius or the true requirements of each case.

Explanatory of this assertion, which may at first appear easy of disproval, an instance may be cited that, but for sake of argument, might well perhaps have passed unnoticed. Sir Hugh Rose had selected a young subaltern to conduct the office of his military secretary—a place in which it obviously is of the first importance that a General on active service should possess the man who suits him personally best in the discharge of confidential business. His choice had fallen on Captain, then Lieutenant, Burne, whose ability and tact alike it was impossible to impugn. Yet the Horse Guards held the post was one demanding a field-officer, who, while drawing higher pay and military allowances, is also entitled by his rank to partial aid in the maintenance of a stud at Government expense —advantages that are denied to subalterns not unfrequently superior in years and understanding, and that, taken by themselves, are certainly no crucial test of merit. The exception, however, that the Horse Guards took to the proposed appointment, though it ousted and retarded for a while a most deserving officer, was in this instance but a source of personal hardship to

Lieutenant Burne; for the field-officer replacing him was Lieutenant-Colonel Sarel, whose attainments as a linguist, a soldier, and a man of business, would have rendered him an acquisition to the staff of any army in the world.

But to discuss at any length the individual merits of recent nominations falls not within our province. Such a task would be at once too comprehensive and invidious for a civilian to undertake; yet a host of names must rise instinctively to the lips of any one acquainted even partially with our Anglo-Indian armies, and some of them must find utterance every now and then in illustration of views expressed. Some there are whose services are too prominent to be passed over in sheer silence; and there are those whose services, though not less brilliant in themselves, call for observation as having heretofore been less prominently recorded. On one point, moreover, a civilian may perhaps be left unshackled by the wholesome knowledge of his technical ignorance of military discipline, and express appreciation of a now restricted class of officers of whom but little is generally known. As a type of these heroes whose fame has been obscured without being dulled by the passing clouds of mutiny, and who, from the circumstances of their position, were then so surrounded by temptation that it is indeed a miracle, considering the prejudices then existing both on their sides and our own, that any of their number proved faithful to the Queen, it behoves us here to mention, in terms of high respect and admiration, the name of Ressaldar Sirdar Bahadoor Mahomed Buksh Khan. The services of this officer date from the Affghan war; and both in the earning and the wearing of the Ghuznee medal, and the clasps for Moodki, Aliwal, Sobraon, and Ferozeshah, he has ever shone conspicuous for courage and fidelity. As native Aide-de-Camp he has now served upon the Staff of several successive Governors-General of India; and Colonels Blane or Bowie, and all who served with him, will willingly bear evidence to the value of his precept and example. Our Indian armies, as at present constituted, afford but few openings to native officers of advancement to anything approaching high military distinction; and it should be the aim of every man in India, with patronage at his disposal, to seek out and discover those of this numerous band whose obscurity, if such it can be called, is essentially the result of their misfortunes, and endeavour to apply the remedy of fitting place to improve their hard position.

The day must come when some yet hidden cause will operate in the reduction of our British force in India. It cannot be supposed that England will for ever be content to stop in silence the gaps which each year makes in the more than seventy European regiments there maintained. Neither can it be supposed that, when the memory of recent struggles shall have grown remote, or been succeeded by events nearer to our homes, that the House of Commons will willingly expend so large a portion of the Indian revenues on measures of precaution; while it may be questioned whether even Dr Cumming would venture to predict so speedy an approach of everlasting peace throughout the continents now most advanced in civilisation and the arts of war, as to warrant the conclusion that a large proportion of our Anglo-Indian forces may not some day be sorely needed in another quarter of the globe. With the prospect of such an inevitable future, though how far distant none can tell, it surely would be little less than folly on the part of those in power to blind themselves to such eventualities; and, on the contrary, it should be their aim to use these years of peace and calm security in gathering a chosen nucleus of well-proportioned native weapons of defence. The elements of danger have been discovered, and may henceforth be avoided with some degree of certainty. The completion of our railroad system will render thirty thousand English troops in India sufficiently omnipresent for all practical purposes of aid where aid may be required; and although we may forget as victors the events of 1857, the recollection of the bloody lesson then learnt, by ill-starred Hindoos and Mahomedans alike, will not so soon be lost to native hearts and minds.

With the existing conditions of to-day, the English troops that were in India in 1857 before the mutiny broke forth would not only have been sufficient to guarantee the life and property then sacrificed, but even might have proved unnecessarily numerous. Strategic points, magazines, and arsenals, in European hands, added to the lever of native legislation and our increased commercial interests in common, afford together an array of power surpassing our requirements, and ill comparable with the facts that led to the rebellion. The truth of this assertion is happily so patent as to render argument superfluous; and in concluding this disjointed picture of the fabric of our military ascendency in India, we may without presumption express blind confidence in the stability of our rule from the Himalayas to the sea, so long as the balance of power established by the long-suffering treaties of 1815 remains unchanged in Europe. From natives we have naught to fear; with them we maintain a debtor and a creditor account, and to them our paramount duty is honestly to pay the interest long since fallen into foul arrears, and due on borrowed land. The last sun of our sword-rule has set on Hindostan; her fruitful plains no longer lie at the tender mercies of hungry martial younger sons; her woods are cleared, and jungles drained, and have become vast fields for raising crops of indigo and cotton, farmed, 'tis true, by dint of English energy, but on fair payment of a rent, which, while it leaves a large and profitable margin to the tenant, is high enough to guarantee undisturbed possession, so long as all conditions of our permanent lease are punctually fulfilled.

CHAPTER X.

FINANCE AND PUBLIC WORKS.

THE word Finance must here be read as having mainly reference to Revenue, "Expenditure" being represented by "Public Works," a department that of itself admits of a division into at least two distinct classifications— those works which are remunerative, and those which are the contrary. These may be regarded as natural foes, each ever opening its greedy mouth to swallow up the lion's share of our cash balances ; and one of the most delicate tasks devolving on an Indian Chancellor of the Exchequer, is the steerage of his financial bark between this Scylla and Charybdis in such a manner that the public should not give tongue and follow with a hue-and-cry each sum allotted to the one or other, nor raise its angry voice against imagined misappropriation.

It is not, however, at all times a very easy matter to discover to which class a given work may appertain. It frequently changes character more than once in course of progress ; and an undertaking designed for raising revenue may actually prove an encumbrance to the State, while some system of highways, originally commenced for the sole purpose of opening up remoter provinces, and bringing them beneath the eye and hand of the ruling power, may prove upon completion a source of prosperity and gain, not entering into the barren calculations of the projector. Within the last ten years we have had in India two grand specimens of these classes. The military works rendered necessary by rebellion are directly unremunerative in their character; while the railway system that has followed our reconquest of the country, though constructed at a vast expense, must ultimately prove reproductive in the truest sense.

In the division of available funds between the antagonistic claimants, it is more than probable that an unfair proportion has been dealt out to those most unremunerative in their character: for barracks, arsenals, and purely military roads have until quite lately been deemed to constitute our strongest hold upon the country, and hence entitled to the first consideration; while each outlay of a lakh on one of these not only brings in no return, but entails the future payment of an annual sum for bare repairs and preservation. Again, it is not unreasonable to suppose that the military genius which long guided the councils of the Company made the most of military necessities, and the constant practice of appointing to the chief control of public works in India some military man may well have tended in the same direction.

But let us turn from generalities to facts. The Ganges Canal is undoubtedly the grandest isolated reproductive work in India. At Hurdwar the sacred

river breaks from its mountain source, discharging, it
is estimated, when at the lowest ebb, seven thousand
cubic feet of water every second; thence its course
points near due south to Delhi, nature having apparently ordained that the tract of country known as
The Doab should reap but little benefit from its fertil
ising power : but art willed otherwise. A plan of
irrigation was originated, first by Lord William Ben
tinck, but little practical result then followed.   Lord
Auckland next renewed inquiries as to its feasibility,
the subject having been painfully pressed upon the
notice of the Government by the occurrence of repeated
famines; and at length the persevering genius of Sir
Proby Cautley elaborated a splendid scheme, combining
irrigation with a navigable canal.   One of the most
serious hindrances to its execution existed in the low
level of the land across which the water from the
Ganges must in the first instance be carried by artifice
towards the districts most in want.   Moreover, this low
land was seamed by three broad watercourses, dry in
the thirsty season, but rapid angry rivers when swollen
by the rains, and so differing in level that each had
to be traversed in a peculiar manner,—the canal had to
be borne across the first, through the volume of the
second, and literally beneath the bed of the third.

Some notion of the costliness of these several undertakings may be formed from the following brief account
of one among their number:—The Solani river has
been bridged by an aqueduct of stone, affording transit
to the canal.   It rests on fifteen arches, each spanning
fifty feet, leaving a clear waterway of seven hundred and

fifty feet. The strength of the work is enormous, and its duration appears destined to be coexistent with that of the rocks on which it rests. It is supported by blocks of masonry sunk twenty feet below the river-bed, and measuring twenty feet in length and breadth. Huge piles protect each part from injury by the current; and a full description of all the contrivances, multiform and ingenious beyond conception, by which it has been sought to secure the fabric from every accident imagination could anticipate, would fill a moderate volume. This aqueduct alone has cost not less than thirty lakhs.

In its still unfinished state one cannot arrive at an accurate estimate of the total cost of the canal, but the best authorities consider it can hardly fall short of two millions sterling. It is, moreover, worthy of remark that competent persons to whom the question has been submitted coincide in the belief that the fact of tapping the Ganges at Hurdwar, and the consequent abstraction of some 75 per cent of its sacred volume, will not materially enhance the difficulty of navigating the inferior Ganges—the fact being, that the outpour at Hurdwar is small compared with the surface-drainage of the plains, and that this last is materially increased by the division of the original source. Thus, notwithstanding the gigantic difficulties nature strewed in the path of this great enterprise, and the yet more imminent dangers of administrative jealousy and studied opposition, energetic science, combined with British capital and credit, have carried it to near upon completion; and the fertilising element is already conveyed in countless branches, dykes, and channels, to almost every village throughout a tract of country upwards of eight hundred miles in length, and is supplied to every tiller of the soil on payment of a trifling tax, quite out of all proportion with the benefit diffused.

This work alone might well suffice to stamp on us the character of Indian benefactors; and though it is but one of many undertakings of a similar nature, projected for the interest of the country, it yet may, from its proportions and the ability displayed in its construction, be not inaptly termed the father of remunerative public works in India. Its remunerative character is of the truest kind, as steadily augmenting by the lapse of time; its cost has been prodigious, and the revenues derived from it can hardly yet afford a full set-off against the money sunk: but in years to come, the constantly increasing density of population and value of the soil must ultimately adjust the balance, and leave it equally entitled to our admiration, whether as regarded from a mercantile or philanthropic point of view.

The school founded by Sir Proby Cautley has been well maintained by his successors in influencing the Indian Government in favour of non-military public works. Cawnpore was the point fixed for the canal to rejoin the sacred stream, and below this the ingenuity of man has been directed rather to repelling than attracting the waters of the Ganges. At Benares, after the river has received the waters of its tributaries, the Kallee-Nuddee, the Goomtee, and others, the average discharge, each second through the year, has

been estimated at two hundred and fifty thousand
cubic liquid feet; and by the latter end of July all
the lower parts of Bengal contiguous to its banks
are overflowed, forming inundations of a hundred
miles in width, where little appears above the surface
of the flood save isolated villages and trees. Embar-
kations of every kind then traverse the inland sea,
those bound northwards availing themselves of a
direct course, with comparatively still water, at a
season when every stream has become a foaming torrent. Husbandry and grazing are alike suspended,
and the peasant sculls his boat across the fields that
he, in other months, was wont to plough, happy if
here and there an elevated slope still yields him scanty
herbage, for otherwise his flocks and herds must die.
Where nature has afforded some slight assistance, large
tracts are guarded jealously from inundation by means
of costly and elaborate dams; and here again abundant
proof is given of the benefit of Western rule, and above
all of the habits introduced by us of organising labour
for a public object, in the performance of a task from
which all private enterprise must necessarily shrink
in prudence or despair.

Passing from the Ganges to the valley of its sister
stream, we find the white man's ingenuity again at
war with nature. A thousand miles above the sea
there stands the ancient town of Attock, whose name,
signifying "obstacle," is said to have been given it
under the presumption that no scrupulous Hindoo
would venture farther to the westward. Here the
Indus runs between banks so high that the enormous

increase of its waters during rains and meltings of the snow affects its depth alone. The rocky banks are formed of blackish slate, polished by the stream until they shine like marble, and between them one clear blue stream shoots past, with great rapidity, and an average depth of fifty feet throughout the year. Its speed is fatal to all ferry-transit, while its breadth and inaccessibility preclude as yet the possibility of bridge - construction. The river - bed is formed of boulders, washed from the feet of the Hindoo Koosh, and ever travelling south by the action of a powerful under-current. Nature, with her usual profusion, has thrown these many difficulties in the path of an easy access to the central table-lands of Asia. We, in our turn, have sought to overcome them by evasion rather than by conquest, and, led by the fertile mind of Colonel Robertson, have bent our efforts to carve out a subterranean passage. This tunnel has not yet attained completion. Simultaneously commenced from both sides, some years witnessed satisfactory progress, and even wild Sittanas and Beloochees, whose instincts were opposed to such attempts at circumventing nature, looked forward to a speedy termination. Finance alone willed otherwise. The work was costly ; partially, perhaps, to disprove a native prophecy it had been undertaken, and who knows but what partially in obedience to such prophecy it has been now neglected ? The pumps have ceased their work, and water has obtained possession of the caverns excavated for purposes of communication. It may thus afford no inapt example of that class of undertakings which

P

change character more than once in course of execution : left in its condition of to-day, it only represents
so much capital expended idly and without return ;
and yet it is probable that further appropriation for
its prosecution might have the result of verifying
the sanguine expectations of its original designers,
who fondly dreamt of a grand highway for Indo-
Persian commerce, combining a political object with
the raising of imperial revenue.

Among recent occupants of the post of Secretary of
Works in India, the names of Colonels Yule and
Strachey will long remain associated with the spending
of the largest sums disbursed within the memory of
man on any single undertaking ; and the outbreak of
the mutiny and its suppression proved the more immediate source of this expenditure. It was generally
felt that our future hold upon the country was much
dependent on more rapid means of internal communication than Dâk Gharries or the Government bullock-
train afforded, and the rendering accessible of certain
districts either for the sake of health or the eradication
of any local disaffection. The spending of the money
thus determined on, was, after some discussion, placed
under the control of the Government of India in the
old established office of its Public Works. This was
preferred for certain reasons to the organisation of a
separate Railway Department, conducting operations
on an independent footing under the authority of the
Governor-General, as part and parcel of the great
machine of Government itself. The construction of
these railways was regarded as a national object, de-

manding national aid, it might be even sacrifices; and
Lord Stanley and his colleagues of that day boldly
grappled with the stern necessity, and set their shoulders
to the wheel to raise by loans and bonds and guaran-
tees, and every kind of credit and debenture, capital
commensurate with the immensity of the task.   But
although the working of the machinery required for
the design and execution of a strategic system of rail-
communication between Madras, Bombay, Calcutta,
and Mooltan, was intrusted to the Public Works
Department, yet within that office, already overgrown and overworked, it was necessary to constitute
an *imperium in imperio*, charged alone with railway
business; and the House of Commons coincided with
the Secretary of State for India in the advisability of
appointing one possessed of technical qualifications
Government Director of Indian Railway Companies.
This office, requiring deep acquaintance with almost
every branch of human industry, was well conferred upon
Mr Juland Danvers, who for some years past has spent
his time according to requirement in personal inspections
throughout the length and breadth of British India,
and in rendering accounts, accompanied by *viva voce*
explanations, to the powers supreme in Westminster.

One of the most interesting results the public
derives from the punctual performance of the duties
intrusted to Mr Juland Danvers, is the annual pre-
scntation to both Houses of Parliament of a report,
addressed by him to the Secretary of State for India in
Council, on Indian railway progress during the previous
year.   From a perusal of these reports it appears that

up to 1850 the coin spent on rail-construction in Her
Majesty's Indian dominions was within two hundred
thousand pounds; and the amount of miles opened
within the year referred to, 1850, was simply *nil;*
whereas in both 1861 and 1862 upwards of seven
hundred miles of rail were opened to the public, at a
cost averaging in each case six millions sterling. Further, it is shown that the capital that has already been
expended on Indian railways falls little short of sixty
millions sterling, whereof a third at least has accrued
directly to the benefit of England through exportation of
machinery and rails. For an expenditure of capital so
ample we have, however, a fair share of labour done to
show; for the natural difficulties overcome by Indian
rail-contractors rank second to none within the range
of engineering skill. The works which bear the iron
horse across the Thull and Bhore Ghâts are perhaps
unparalleled in boldness of design and happy execution; while the Sone viaduct, and the hundreds of miles
of brick embankment through the Bengal flats, are
probably unsurpassed in durative power and cost of
workmanship.

The sections here referred to are but links of inter-
communication between Calcutta and Bombay; and to
form any adequate idea of the work performed by railway kings in India, of the numerical strength of the
imported artisans therein employed, and of the firm
hold upon the country and its inhabitants thereby
acquired, it would be necessary to dive deeper into the
recesses of Parliamentary blue-books than is consistent
with our immediate purpose. Still it is impossible to

consider with attention the remarkable figures above roughly quoted without arriving at some slight conception of the sudden impetus the introduction of the railway system must have given, in the substitution of a mutual commercial interest for one-sided military dominion.

It is, moreover, fortunate that the introduction of this system should have taken place within the sequent reigns of Lord Stanley and Sir Charles Wood—both statesmen of a practical type, superior to mere party strife, and who, following in the same broad track of progress, unbiassed by the narrow chains too often cast by a life's experience of power or opposition, have viewed with calm discussion the rival claims of many a vexed item of expenditure, as placeable to capital or revenue account, or as to whether this branch-line or that should be admitted to the receipt of certain subsidies, by driving a far-fetched quibble in a coach-and-six through some obscurely-worded Act of Parliament. Happily indeed for the great interests involved, Lord Stanley and Sir Charles Wood have been permitted to direct the march of Indian railway enterprise very much according to their own convictions, and have, of their wisdom, drawn a medium line between the oft-opposed requirements of strategy and commerce.

Having reached this point, which tends to prove that, in the distribution of the sums at their disposal, neither remunerative nor unremunerative, martial nor pacific enterprises have seriously suffered at the hands of recent Indian administrators, it may not be amiss to

pause a while from more immediate considerations, and
enter on a brief comparison of the mode pursued by
ancient despots in expending revenue and contracting
debt with that which has distinguished Anglo-Indian
rule.   It is, we think, in the broad field of finance that
India reaps the greatest benefit at our hands. Taxation,
if higher in densely populated or singularly fertile
districts than it was in former days, when these same
districts were less thickly peopled and their wealth had
not attained maturity, is now at least more equally distributed, and presses with greater ease on all.   On the
other hand, history bears record of the lavish sums that
Ackbar squandered on the construction of vast palaces,
destined to become nurseries of vice for the many
thousands who could claim consanguinity by reason
of polygamy or adoption, and who, ever multiplying
and extending their fell influence farther and still farther from the palace gates, ultimately converted busy
cities, like Delhi and Lucknow, into sinks of infamy
and disorder.

Such were the objects to which, in those days, the
taxation of a State was too often primarily directed.
Some there were indeed, like Shahjehan, who exalted
its use in the construction of buildings dedicated to
their titular deities, or priceless mausoleums, like the
Taj Mehal, rearing its proud head through three succeeding decades, and swallowing up more wealth than
could have been raked together, at that early date, even
by oppression, for any other than a religious object.
Yet both palatial and ecclesiastical structures, though
essentially unremunerative in their character, may at the

time have rendered service by the employment of hordes
of labourers and the consequent spread of skilled workmanship; but their termination was invariably followed
by the results necessarily attendant on a heavier taxation,
both in men and money, than the circumstances of the
land permitted. Masses of men had been brought together
to complete with all speed some shrine to an emperor's
patron saint, in order that the old man's ashes might
be laid upon the altar of his own creative fancy; but
almost ere the ringing of the hammers was hushed in
its completion the country fell a prey to famine and the
sword. Agriculture had been neglected, and the hands
that should have tilled the fields had been employed in
carving stone; while peace, perchance, had held so long
dominion in the minds of men as to breed reactionary
desire for war. Then came the winter of that country's
discontent. The marble screens afforded no protection
from the pangs of hunger or the spread of dire disease.
In the nation's eye they remained, for a time at least,
objects of deep veneration or contempt, according to the
appreciation of the sovereign by whom they had been
reared and the fickle sentiments of an ever-changing
multitude. However this may be, the accumulated experience of past ages shows that ancient public works
in India, eloquent as they are as ever-living monuments
of bygone dynasties and thrones, as surely paved the
way to broadcast misery and want as our remunerative undertakings of to-day prove themselves unerring
heralds of enhanced prosperity.

A solitary example may suffice to illustrate this.
On a spur of the Aravulli range, already noticed in a

former chapter, there stands an ancient celebrated place of pilgrimage, which, according to the high authority of Colonel Tod, ranks beyond controversy among the most superb of Indian temples. It was, we are told, erected on the site of other shrines, dedicated in far gone days to Siva and to Vishnu; and tradition records how the original founder obtained the site from the Sirowee Raja, by covering with silver coin as much ground as was required. In the centre of a court, that forms an outskirt of the main edifice, is a pagoda containing a colossal statue of the deified Coryphæus of the Jains, composed of an alloy of several rich metals; and before the temple is an equestrian statue of its founder, Bimul Sah. It is estimated that this temple occupied a period of fourteen years in building, at a cost of eighteen crores of Company's rupees, besides some sixty lakhs spent in levelling the site itself. In close proximity there stands a second and more modern temple, dedicated to Nemminath, which those learned in inscriptions assert was built in 1236; and this is in its turn supported by two others, of still less antiquity and price, all, however, showing nearly equal symptoms of decay. The total cost of these buildings, into which must have entered largely the transport of the marble whereof they are constructed, must have exceeded twenty millions sterling, or one-third of our actual expenditure in Indian railway enterprise; and it should not be overlooked, that in the distant ages when these mines of wealth were worked to such pernicious use, the country could have offered no comparison with its smiling aspect of to-day; while its people, ignoring the advantage of a foreign commerce, could but compare unfavourably with wealthy Indian planters of the nineteenth century. Lastly, it must be remembered that but one instance has been quoted of a long array of ruinous works; and it would be an easy matter to establish that the comparatively unimportant sums we have raised and spent in India for India's own advantage, are, to use an Eastern phrase, but as the ear of corn to a barley loaf, when weighed against the bound less expenditure of an unproductive past.

Ere we quit the subject of recent Indian rail-con struction, space must be found to record the triumph of a principle which occurred during Lord Elgin's term of holding the viceroyalty. At first sight it forms but a trifling link in the great chain of rail-communication between Calcutta and Mooltan, but in reality it is susceptible of extended interpretation, if taken as an individual fact whereby to read the spirit of the times we live in; for in it the march of progress may be traced, bringing remote military considerations into due subordination to the immediate needs of commerce by the conversion of a massive bastion into a city railway station. The last siege of Delhi was sufficiently protracted to inspire respect in England for the lines of her defences; and the Cashmere Gate, with other spots, will probably remain familiar to many generations, from their having been the salient points of our successes. Yet there are other works less generally known, because of their strategic strength and consequent avoidance by our engineers. Foremost amongst these ranked the ancient Patan fort of Selimgurh, on the eastern bank of the Jumna, and communicating with the royal palace by a narrow bridge of stone. On this side Delhi was impregnable, at least to any means at our disposal in 1857, and the military world was loath to cast away this advantage, questionable as it was in a fort which had so frequently changed hands. The money, therefore, granted to restore the battered works was concentrated on other weaker parts, and Selimgurh was guarded with all jealousy from base contamination by the arts of peace, until at last the waves of railway enterprise broke with fury uncontrollable against her storm-proof walls. Much discussion then ensued. Those there were who, loving Delhi dearly, loved their military prejudices more; the formation of the ground, however, was such as to leave the railway engineers a choice of evils admitting of but little compromise. If Delhi was to reap the full advantage of a railway, Selimgurh must sacrifice her hostile character; and, after some years of doubt and indecision, the question was finally set at rest on personal inspection by Lord Elgin, who knew how to weigh improbable eventualities in the scales of practical requirement.

The conversion above referred to could not be effected without considerable expenditure; and the expectation of saving some few lakhs was not without its influence on those who estimate works of public utility by the rate of interest to be obtained on capital invested. The English House of Commons often thinks, that when it has accorded sanction to an outlay of some millions on Works or Education, it has done a liberal thing—pluming itself upon expending larger sums on foreign than domestic soil; and country members often measure plans and undertakings by the standard of the local interests with which they are themselves associated—for, after all, opinions must be formed more in accordance with one's own experience than on the pleading of an interested counsel. Thus, while great safety lies undoubtedly in the necessity of home sanction, if only from its impedimentary action, at times a heavier drag may be thereby applied to the national wheels than is counterbalanced by the benefit derived from what is often really over-caution and a false economy. The main remedy lies, of course, in local legislation; and it is our firm belief that in this respect a wider scope of power should be left to the supreme and presidency councils in determining on the conduct of local enterprises than has been previously the practice—subject of necessity, however, to ultimate control by the prescribing of an imperial margin beyond which neither debt nor guarantee might be incurred.

The system now in force is the cause of constant trouble and delay in the passage of a scheme, in all its stages of design and execution, through the widely ramifying weary channels of local, supreme, and parliamentary legislation, and the prodigious difficulties growing out of a closer knowledge of this subject have hitherto been powerful enough to impede a simplifying process. Mutiny and debt, and the great names of Wilson, Laing, Trevelyan, have succeeded one another with such rapidity in the last few years, as to leave, one would imagine, little time for passing more than measures of paramount importance; and the only cause for wonder is, that so much has been effected. We cannot tell whether history will pronounce the credit of the manifold results obtained due to one man or to many; but until the wisdom of the future shall have passed its sentence on events still recent, we may be permitted to retain a firm belief that, after making ample discount for some errors, the untiring zeal displayed in the administration of India by the Maharaja Wood of Westminster affords, perhaps, the readiest key to the solution of this problem.

Abandoning this train of thought, we shall now proceed to a short examination of India's financial status of to-day. Her annual accounts are presented to the House of Commons in two parts—the one comprising finance transactions within the limits of continental India; the other, styled the home accounts, consisting mainly of interest on debts incurred and credits held or due in England. Part I. is far the most comprehensive, and its first care is laudably directed to presenting to the world a complete tabular statement of the gross and net revenue for the year, the charges of collection, and other payments for which those revenues are responsible —the whole for more general comprehension being converted into sterling money, at the rate of two shillings the rupee.

The total income varies with the circumstances of each year, but probably may, for some time hence, be roughly stated as bordering on five-and-forty million pounds. A glance at this account shows at once the large proportion of revenue derived from land, amounting, as it does, to 45 per cent upon the total income.

The remaining 55 per cent of gross receipts is subdivided under headings similar to those which enter into every European budget.   Assessed taxes, customs, interest on capital accounts, and mixed incomings from remunerative Departments, such as the Post Office or Telegraph, each has its assigned place in this tabular statement. The two great Government monopolies of salt and opium represent over five and eight millions sterling respectively, and these, together with the large proportion derived from land, form the special characteristics of our Indian budgets.   From this hasty survey it may be gathered with what anxiety Indian finance regarded Lord Canning's latest measures for the sale of waste lands, and the ultimate redemption of the land-tax. The carrying out of these measures, and their practical adjustment to the necessities of the State, was left as a legacy to his successor, who was moreover pledged to the removal of the uneasy burden of the income-tax from native shoulders at the earliest moment compatible with financial pressure, and, if not sooner, certainly at the expiry of the five years for which it had been imposed.   A cry had, moreover, gone abroad against the continuance of Government monopolies as a source of revenue ; and unless the hand of the Governor-General should stem the revolutionary tide then bearing down upon our treasuries, it would be left to the devices of Mr Laing's successors to meet an annual expenditure approaching five-and-forty millions, from practically little else than the resources of their own unaided brains. But things were not permitted to arrive at such a pass. The action of the Government was stayed in Waste

Lands Sales, and practical restrictions were so imposed as to impede the future legislation by which alone these measures could too hastily be carried out.

Revenue has here been dealt with at greater length than is necessary for an account of Treasury outgoings, and this for two reasons : first, because expenditure has already had its say, and must now be left to plead its own great cause; and, secondly, because it is marked by none of those protective peculiarities incidental to our Indian incomings.

Part II., or home accounts, may briefly be disposed of. They include the payment of about two millions interest guaranteed to railway companies. Further, a charge of £120,000 per annum for the establishment of the Secretary of State for India in Council, numbering near four hundred souls; and prominent on the list of expenditure we find a long array of charitable allowances to widows, orphans, invalids, who by their number prove that India is a costly appanage to England, at least in human life.

Thus India under the Crown is something more than a mere commercial enterprise, and her agency is now directed to something higher than that at which the Company aimed. The ambition of the Crown concerning India is not so much that her stocks should be quoted so superior to par as to enable bond-holders to realise colossal fortunes, as that the destiny of a hundred and forty millions of her subjects should be worked out in accordance with the usages prescribed by the combined civilisation of the East and West; and therefore it is that the total of the revenue affords fair index

to the actual expenditure. The days of old are counted
out, when galleons laden to the water's edge with treasure were regarded as the natural products of colonial
possessions. India no longer forms an orchard of
pagoda trees for England's younger sons to shake : her
value to us is that of an almost boundless field for the
investment of energy and capital ; and hence the bal-
ance-sheet at the termination of each financial year
shows a long array of figures, wellnigh matched in
every proportion—the revenue but slightly in excess of
all legitimate requirements, whatever small excess there
is being carried to the credit of ensuing years in the
substantial shape of hard rupees.

Surely these things are worthy of being written.
The outside world has not yet fully realised the high
importance of the transfer from the Company to the
Crown. It is argued that events repeat themselves,
and that even as the Company to-day has been compelled by accidental pressure to give way, and ultimately retire from action, so later commercial interests
must reassume pre-eminence, driving political philan-
thropists from the scene of India's future. But be
this as it may, let each theory be heard in turn, if
only to its own detriment. We have it on right
good authority that "all this world's a stage," wherein
we all are players, having entrances and exits in accordance with set rules which we happily for us ignore ;
and the day must come at length when dreams of
perfect trust, between what mischief-mongers love to
call the subject races and ourselves, shall attain real-
isation in mutual bearance and forbearance, based

on confidence in a common future and the wealth of past experience.

In conclusion, we permit a native statesman of great experience and ability in dealing with finance, to speak for his country and himself on the question of the *modus operandi* for raising annually what moneys are required under the present *regime* to keep our Government of India alive. The memorandum wherein he has expressed his views was prepared while the oppressive weight of the income-tax still remained upon the shoulders of the Indian people. In the removal of this unpopular source of revenue, which Mr Wilson first imposed for a limited period only as a war tax, or we might almost say a retribution on the Indian people for the calamities of 1857, the Government of India has but kept its pledged troth; and it must be very many years before our Indian accounts display such a surplus, after providing for the extinction of debt incurred, as to justify those by whom public burdens are imposed in reducing a taxation which the country becomes each year more able to sustain, and of which each year a larger share falls, directly or indirectly, on European immigrants, who derive from the stability of our rule equal if not greater benefits than the native subjects of the land.

Under these circumstances, the removal of the hated income-tax but opens the approach to other means of raising money; and so long as more than half of what we want comes straight from the pocket of the native into our own, in the shape of land-tax and the Government monopolies of salt and opium, so

long shall we maintain that the native has a right
to make his feelings known, even outside the walls
of those mixed Council Chambers established for the
purpose.

A few words here on the subject of this land-tax
may not be out of place before proceeding to the
consideration of the memorandum with which this
chapter closes. The fact is that the Land Revenue
System, on which so many lances have been broken
by anxious students of Anglo-Indian Injustice, is one
that recommends itself to the native mind by imme-
morial practice, based on the doctrine that the original
proprietory right to the soil is vested in the Government *de facto*. Owing, however, to the prodigality
of long lines of dynasties, by whom, in token of approval or reward, lands free of revenue had constantly
been granted, it happened that great tracts became
exempt from their due share of taxation, causing either
considerable loss of revenue to Government, or enhanced burdens on unexempted lands. This trouble
grew with the extension of our rule, and at length
Commissioners were appointed to examine all titles
to exemption. The sphere of their action, limited
at first to provinces on attachment, was gradually
extended to those long subject to our dominion; but
the principle involved was so familiar to the native
mind, that though it might cause private vexation
to landowners whose documentary or other evidence
had disappeared with lapse of time, it was insufficient
to produce a general irritation. Without, however,
entering into the propriety and policy of a measure

that natives at least can understand, and far prefer to many of our more elaborate fiscal systems, we would only plead that the fact of its existence, causing as it does half our Anglo - Indian revenue to accrue directly from the soil, entitles the children of that soil to a voice in all decisions of a nature to affect their welfare.

"The experience," one author tells us, "which enables a man to write on the subject of Eastern government tends to blunt his sympathies, and in some degree to injure his moral sense." "Torture and lawlessness" were so familiar to this writer, as to render him "conscious of not feeling as he ought when wrong is done to individuals and nations." This truly is a sad picture of a human mind after a very few years in India; but were the condition of moral obliquity described confined to the producers or consumers of such highly-flavoured literary food, it might not be necessary to undeceive a sensation-loving public. When, however, the disorder affects the minds of men in office like Mr Seton Karr, late Secretary to the Government of Bengal, making him write of certain land-revenue-raising machinery, " that each day produced its list of victims, and the good fortune of those who escaped but added to the pangs of the crowd who came forth from the shearing-house shorn to the skin, unable to work, ashamed to beg, condemned to penury ; " and when we are further told by the graphic Mr Kaye that " of 3500 estates, great and small, three-fifths were confiscated," in the course of but one local land-tenure inquiry,—we must confess that the truth-seeking world is under great obligation to the calm judicial pen of Sir Charles Jackson, for demonstrating in a recent work that the title here set aside was not the title to land, but the title to hold it free from the payment of land-tax ; that there was no ousting from possession in these cases—a resumption of the right to the land-tax only, and not a resumption of the land itself.

From this digression we shall now return to the salt monopoly, to which, second only to the income-tax, the writer of the following memorandum draws attention. In the days we live in, this is perhaps the greatest abuse of power extant in any civilised portion of the globe. Along certain frontiers of the North-West Provinces and Rajpootana, a boundary-line is drawn, cutting off the sparsely populated producing districts from the neighbouring lands, densely peopled by consumers, the nature of whose food demands a liberal use of salt in its preparation, not only to render it wholesome, but palatable to the taste. This line has been drawn upon arbitrary principles that render the most elementary conditions of existence dissimilar in adjoining village hamlets. Along it a hedge of thorn, strictly emblematical of the duty it performs, has been planted, winding for many hundred miles across an open country, sometimes fertile, sometimes barren, heedless of mountains, streams, and all those marks by which the hand of nature traces lines for the division of mankind. This hedge is kept intact by a large and costly staff of customs' officers, and represents, in its eternal presence to the view, a cordon more intolerable to the freedom of native thought and action than any Continental octroi, passport, or other fiscal system, since the abolition of the gabelle or the hated corvée. The people of those districts live, as it were, in permanent quarantine; smuggling is of course extensively practised, and each day gaps are found to need repair along this rude financial hedge, or men and women are detected in the act, and made to pay a penalty, certainly not likely to spread a general belief among the poorer classes of the benefit our sway confers. The monotony of the hedge is only broken at intervals by gates, where roads are crossed, and here and there by stations of police. The whole system is known as that of salt chokees; and considering the inconvenience and injustice, and the heavy charges for collecting the revenue accruing from it, we must confess, and not without regret, that the writer of the memorandum now before us has treated the abuse with an exceeding moderation, that might, who knows, perhaps not unjustly be attributed to his ignorance of our desire to govern righteously, or else to familiarity with other modes of raising revenue equally questionable in morality and political economy.

In this memorandum it will be also seen that the native mind conceives that indirect taxation lies easier on the shoulders of the Indian people than any kind of direct taxation, in the equitable collection of which domestic sanctity must be invaded, and "minute inquiries" are rendered necessary. Still natives must remember that our administration of India is a costly one, that security for life and property is a plant requiring in Asia much artificial training and support, and that we also are labourers worthy of our hire. A large voice as to the least objectionable mode of raising this hire we willingly accord the native; but if he selects, on mature reflection and by gradual legislation, the system of accumulated indirect taxation, he must be prepared for a period when the condition of India will resemble that of England, where, in the words of Sydney Smith, "Taxes were piled on taxes until they reached every article which enters into the mouth, or covers the back, or is placed under foot; taxes upon everything which it is pleasant to see, hear, feel, smell, or taste; taxes upon warmth, light, and locomotion; taxes on everything on earth, and in the waters under the earth —on everything that comes from abroad, or is grown at home; taxes on the source which pampers man's appetite, and the drug which restores him to health; on the ermine which decorates the judge, and the rope which hangs the criminal; on the poor man's salt and the rich man's spice; on the brass nails of the coffin and the ribbons of the bride. The schoolboy whips his taxed top; the beardless youth manages his taxed horse, with a taxed bridle, on a taxed road; and the dying Englishman, pouring his medicine which has paid seven per cent into a spoon that has paid fifteen per cent, flings himself back upon the chintz bed which has paid twenty-two per cent, makes his will on an eight-pound stamp, and expires in the arms of an apothecary who has paid a licence of a hundred pounds for the privilege of putting him to death. His whole property is then immediately taxed from two to ten per cent. Besides the probate, large fees are demanded for burying him in the chancel; his virtues are handed down to posterity on taxed marble, and he is then gathered to his fathers to be taxed no more."

Finally, it must be remembered that Persian is the language in which the writer of the memorandum has been accustomed to prepare state-papers, and that division by ten is the simplest method of calculating rupees in pounds sterling.

*

MEMORANDUM BY THE HONOURABLE RAJA DINKUR RAO.

ON THE FINANCE OF THE GOVERNMENT.

From the Budget it will be seen that when the population of British India, which is about 140,000,000, is compared with the income, which is 420,000,000 rupees, the average will be about 3 rupees per head. When this average is compared with that of the native states, the population of which is about 48,400,000, and the income 130,000,000 rupees, it is equal to it, if not greater. But from the estimate of the receipts and expenditure of the year 1856 it is seen that the total income was about 300,000,000 rupees. It must be considered that during this short time the income is much increased. It is clear that this increase is not merely from the land revenue, but from the taxes and duties also. Now, judging from this, it does not appear proper to increase this amount beyond what may be added from the improvement in the land revenue. It is necessary for the Government to give attention, as much as practicable, to decreasing the taxes and duties.

It will be deemed right to give attention in certain cases to decrease the expenditure. The amount thus saved will be usefully applied to continue to some officers proper amount of pay suitable to their stations, and to maintain chowkees on roads and in cities, towns, &c., which are at present reduced. It is also necessary that some balance should remain in the hands of the Government for the use of the State and to pay the interest and some amount of the debt. But from this Budget so much appears impossible. Such being the case, it is obvious, from the remission of the license-tax, how much the comfort of the people is at the heart of the Government. The subjects should understand from this that, when an opportunity will present itself, the Government will no doubt lessen, as much as possible, their burden of taxes and duties. From the present Budget it is seen that, although the Government has reduced so much its expenditure, still the expenditure amounts to the same sum of income, which is 420,000,000 rupees. From this the reflecting persons will think that the Government necessarily requires this amount of income, and they must therefore pay it. It is also just for the subjects to pay the Government for being protected. Though this is the case, still the Government must pay attention to relieve the subjects from the pressure of several kinds of regulations on taxes and duties, considering that the people of Hindostan do not like them. By this means the people will be left free to perform their occupations with ease. The Government, therefore, instead of increasing that pressure, should decrease it as much as practicable, in such a way that it should not incur loss to itself, and the people should be satisfied.

In receiving money from the people it is difficult to please all entirely. There is no transaction which shall not be open to some kinds of objection. But it is proper for the Government to take money from the people and also to look at their convenience.

Though I am not acquainted with the Government financial system, yet what I think better to be done is as follows :—

Some of the following items that will appear proper may be made a source of income in lieu of those that should be abolished. This system will be, to some extent, in accordance to the native custom. Though, owing to their being long abolished by the Government, these duties will be less liked at first, still, owing to their being of the nature of an indirect tax, they will be liked by the people when all other imposts that are hereafter mentioned are totally abolished.

My opinion also is that indirect taxes should be taken, because, though an indirect tax affects all, yet it is taken from a few persons. But the process of realising these duties should be easy. The Government should pay attention only to make up the amount of its income, and not to the extending its interference and making minute inquiries, which prevent the people from following their occupations. There is no need to describe this here in detail.

Tobacco.—Supposing that a person requires about ten seers of tobacco annually, so, at the highest rate of five seers per rupee, he spends about two rupees every year. Were he obliged to buy at the rate of four seers, he would not find it very inconvenient. From this, in proportion to the population, exempting thóse that are not to be taken into consideration, an estimate can be formed of the income that can be realised. Though the people will feel a little inconvenience from this duty, because tobacco is used by many, still this article is not so useful as the salt in his nourishment. The use of this article is generally a matter of habit. But when the income-tax, the duty on salt, and all other direct taxes and duties, are abolished, this indirect tax, without being more inconvenient to the people, will, I think, be conducive to their comfort.

Betal Leaves.—The same is the case with betal leaves. Estimating that each man consumes about two leaves every day, or 750 per year, their value to the highest rate will be about 12 annas.

Stamp Papers.—If it be deemed impossible to abolish all the stamps and fees, the following only should be kept and all others abolished:—

1. A fee at the rate of half an anna per rupee should be taken from the decree-holder after he has obtained money in satisfaction of his decree.

2. A bond of sale or mortgage of immovable property.

3. A warrant of pleaders.

If it will be said that, owing to there being no stamps to mark papers, opportunity will be given to commit forgeries, there is already a law to punish such offences; or, if it be deemed proper, a paper having a Govern ment seal affixed to it should be sold for such purposes at the price of other common papers.

Cloth.—A fee on stamping new cloth should be taken. Each man requires on an average two rupees for his cloth annually. From this an estimate can be made that at the rate of ½ anna per rupee on common cloth, and one anna on silken and embroidered cloth, ¾ of an anna at an average rate will be levied from each person. But the cloth that comes from England should be exempted, because customs duty is already taken on it; but in order to have a mark on it, it should be stamped.

The same system of stamping should be observed with regard to weights and measures.

From all this it appears that the deficit in the Government income, which will occur from abolishing other taxes and duties, will be made up from these imposts. If something should be wanting to make good the income, a small fee should be imposed on weighing all articles. This system is prevalent in India from the earliest days. The British Government has abolished it. It will not be difficult to bring this system into operation, for it is now a practice that those who weigh things receive something from those in whose behalf they weigh. The same persons will receive the contracts for the tax and pay to the Government the amount. This will be less inconvenient to the people than other imposts, and it is also according to their customs.

ITEMS THAT SHOULD BE ABOLISHED.

Income-Tax.—Though it is necessary for the Government to take income-tax from the people, yet it is evident how much all classes of people complain against it, and it is clear that they are obliged, besides paying the tax, to suffer much inconvenience from the regulations connected with it. It is therefore necessary to abolish it at once. There is no doubt that the income which is realised from this impost can be made up from some of those items that are above mentioned.

Salt.—It is necessary to decrease the duty on salt, for salt is the principal thing in the nourishment of all classes of people, and, owing to its being dear, the poor are exposed to much inconvenience. For instance, each man consumes about 9 seers of salt annually. At Agra the rate of salt is about 6 seers per rupee, so that each man requires $1\frac{1}{2}$ rupee per annum for his salt; while at Bhurtpore, Kurrowlee, &c., it can be obtained at about 18 seers per rupee, that is, each man expends $\frac{1}{2}$ rupee per annum; so that the people are obliged to buy salt so dear within such a short distance of where it is cheap. In such places the duty must be so much reduced that the salt may be obtainable at not less than 12 seers per rupee.

Opium.—The increased duty on opium will not, I think, stand at the present rate; for this article is generally consumed by the Chinese, who, perceiving the high rate of Indian opium, will commence to produce it in their own country to supply their wants—consequently the demand for the Indian opium will be less, and production stopped. This case, therefore, ought to be taken into consideration, and the duty to be reduced to the former rates. By this reduction the future deficit in the Government income and loss to the people

will be saved, and an obligation will be conferred upon
those cultivators who pay lakhs of rupees of land-
revenue, and indeed on many labouring classes of
India.

On Stamp.—The stamp-duty is considered by some
only an easy source of realising the Government income; but it is obvious from the stamp regulation that
the former stamps, together with those that are recently
introduced, do not leave the people to perform their ocen-
pations freely. They are required to buy stamps in every
transaction of life, and at every step of every proceeding. Besides this they have also to bear other losses
on account of stamps. It is not proper for the Government to take any duty, or wish to have money for
giving justice, but it is right to keep the way of justice
open as much as possible. For these reasons this
impost must be reduced as much as practicable.

Municipal Taxes and Chowkeedaree.—The municipal taxes and chowkeedaree should also be, if possible,
abolished. If it be impossible, the Government should
reckon the chowkeedaree tax, which is established for
protecting the people in its income from other sources.
And, if the municipal system is to be continued, there
should not be several sorts of taxes and duties imposed
on the people for this purpose, except that which shall
be approved by the inhabitants of the locality. The
Government should also become a sharer in the work.
The authority on the spot should act as one of the
municipal body.

These and all other taxes and duties which may prevent people from following their occupations freely

should be abolished. As the Government income can be made up from the taxes and duties on the items above mentioned, there is no objection to abolish all other imposts. What I mean is this, that there should be no other tax or duty except those that are described as the sources of income. I hope that by this means there shall be left little cause for the people to be discontented, because they will be saved from the oppression and left to perform their occupations unmolested. This system is in accordance to their custom, and will not, I think, be much different from the policy of the Government.

CHAPTER XI.

FOREIGN SETTLEMENTS IN HINDOSTAN.

THE dreams of the chivalrous Dupleix were not destined to fulfilment, and French intrigues in the Carnatic and Mahratta States were ultimately buried in the graves of Bourquien and of Lally. All that now remains to mark the past designs of France are some few specks on the horizon of our Indian possessions, the names of which are seldom quoted in the marts of policy or commerce.

Of these Pondicherry claims pre-eminence to-day as still boasting of some slight mercantile importance, the more political settlement of Chandernagore having long since fallen into insignificance and decay, by reason of its close proximity to Fort William. Yet beyond this statement of the *de facto* prominence of Pondicherry as the commercial and political mainspring of French possessions in East India, naught remains to tell of interest to the general reader. Her exact position, population, and pretensions are items that concern herself alone, and as such need no comment at our hands.

Seventeen miles above Calcutta, and further removed from the insalubrious mouth of the Hoogly, the traveller catches sight, on turning a long reach, of what appears a large well-built emporium of trade. Chandernagore, with its ruined quays and past remains of greatness, contrasts strangely with many of our modest Indian coast-stations, and the system of commercial makeshifts frequently resorted to by the practical merchants of Great Britain.   Still this is not surprising, for the endeavours of France to plant her foot in India were prompted by national pride and jealousy of the rapidly increasing colonial importance of other nations in the seventeenth century; while in our case a company of merchants sued for and obtained a quasi recognition from the English Crown, with leave to establish factories within certain geographical restrictions, and enjoy specified monopolies, imperilling their own lives and capital at their own sole risk.

Herein lies the radical difference between English and French colonial enterprise.   Both started from the principle that the rights of the infidel inhabitants of foreign climes were subordinate to those acquired by Christian discovery and conquest; but whereas England contented herself with giving tardy encouragement and a scant support to her successful adventurers, not heeding those who failed, France ever took upon herself to organise each struggling settlement in distant and uncongenial climes upon a Governmental basis, and deemed it incumbent on her to sustain her sovereign rights, and the honour of her flag, wherever it had once been rashly planted.

The most successful of French colonies originated in the days of Huguenot contention, when some patriotic leaders of the persecuted party conceived the idea of a refuge beyond the sea, where they could still work in peace for the glory of the mother country; and the Government, surrounded by embarrassment, was not sorry to accept an outlet for disaffected elements. With repeated change at home, however, came changes in the character and composition of the joint-stock companies then trading to the West. But though Jesuit influence eventually supplanted Calvinistic, Canada still grew and flourished. The unerring genius of Colbert rendered him a stanch supporter of maritime and commercial enterprise; and it was not till the war of 1756 that Canada, after a gallant struggle, accrued to the British Crown. Yet the memory of France did not altogether die with Montcalm on the heights of Abraham; for now, after a century of our dominion, blue-books are printed by Her Majesty's command at Montreal, Quebec, and Ottawa, counting money in pounds sterling, but written in a foreign tongue, which has outlived a change of masters.

From this somewhat irrelevant digression on the failure of France in the West to reap the fruits of colonisation and foreign industry, we may turn in a fitting frame of mind to the study of her doings in the East, where she had to grapple with still greater difficulties, and failed yet more conspicuously.

The two positions are indeed somewhat opposed. In the West, France found far-spreading sparsely-peopled plains thirsting for the colonising element. She, flattered by the returns which the virgin soil yielded to the emigrant's first touch, bestowed much gratitude upon this country, and ultimately struck so firm a hold as to leave the impress of her nationality on large masses of the population. In the East a very different combination of conditions awaited the arrival of her explorers. There old-established faiths and empires vied with one another for mastery in the hearts and minds of forty separate peoples. Moreover, of all European nations, France was the last to take the field in India. Her first efforts to establish herself there were repulsed at Surat by the united action of the Dutch and English, and a subsequent attempt to seize on Trincomalee was likewise unsuccessful. Later she maintained herself at Mailapur, "the City of Peacocks," near Madras, for a period of two years ; but it was not until 1672 that she made good her title to consideration as an Indian landholder by the purchase from the Bejapoor Raja of the town of Pondicherry and ninety-two adjacent villages, tolerably well watered by the little river Gingy.

Having, however, once acquired a footing, the French backed more directly by their Government than we, had larger means at their command ; and French gold, working in a political sense, for a time outbade individual Anglo-Saxon enterprise. It must remain a doubtful problem whether, had not European wars, tapping the sources of her wealth, ended in constant maritime defeat, France might not have played the Eastern *rôle* which happy accident appears to have reserved for us. All we know is, that so surely as war broke out in Europe between France and England, those small isolated spots in India where the Bourbon flag or tricolor waved changed hands ; and

history records that Pondicherry and the other settlements were captured by the British on the outbreak
of hostilities in 1761, 1778, 1793, and 1803. They
were finally restored to France at the general pacifi-
cation of 1815 ; but since that date their rights and
boundaries have been confined within certain narrow
limits and restrictions.   Dupleix's capital of Chandernagore, for instance, has been deprived of the sanctity
of asylum, and only permitted to maintain a specified
number of municipal police—the French flag being
hoisted without the right of military enlistment within
the territory it covers.   Ruined buildings, grassy
quays, a swollen river, ill-kept within its rotting
banks by mouldering sea-walls ; a commandant with
nothing to command, an administrator with little to
administer ; such are the leading features of one and
every French settlement in India to-day.   In Mahé,
Carical, and specially Yanaon on the Orissa coast,
these characteristics are enlivened by ecclesiastical adventure, these places being professedly rather stations
for influencing native minds through missionary channels, than outlets for the pent-up commerce of a continent sighing for relief and foreign wares.   Yet if
France now bases her colonial dominion on the suffrage
of religion, she builds her house on sand : for having
herself passed through the ordeal of unbelief, she has
lost much of the strength of personal conviction ;
while should she on the contrary seek to flatter the
religious prejudices of others, she would find that
natives have become too much accustomed to religious renegades to attach a vast importance to the arts

of those, like Kleber and Desaix, who hastily embrace the forms of worship that prevail at any Eastern shrine.

The position of Yanaon is equally curious and instructive, regarded from a social, political, or ecclesiastical point of view. The tortuous Frank appears to have sought a spot, equally well suited for the propagation of commerce or the Roman Catholic faith; and in this vain pursuit has failed in the attainment of either end in view. The eldest son of the Church, ever attempting to distil influence from the headquarters of some foreign creed, was little likely to overlook entirely the sacred Delta of the Mahanuddi, the cradle of Hindooism. Hence missionary fathers turned to the discovery of some inlet on that rugged superstitious coast whence they might sally forth to fulfil their destiny. Combining Juggernant with trade, and hoping to conciliate both God and man, they hit upon Yanaon, situate at the bifurcation of the Godavery and Coringa, in a low-lying land seamed by sluggish streams and reeking with ague and pestilential fever.

At the convenient and safe distance of little more than two degrees northward along the coast, and equally accessible by land or water, stand the far-famed Poorie temples, dedicated to Krishna, Balorama, and Kali. These, with their co-deities, including the monkey god Huniman, exemplify the realistic tendencies of Hindoo mythology, if we may credit the following record of their appetites as officially published in the 'Transactions of the Asiatic Society' :—"The provisions furnished daily for the idols consist of 220 seers of rice,

97 seers of kallai, 24 of mung, 188 of clarified buffa loes' butter, 90 of molasses, 35 of vegetables, 100 of milk, 13 of spices, 20 of salt, and 22 of lamp-oil. So insatiable are the appetites of the idols that they eat fifty-two times a-day, and give occupation to nearly four hundred cooks; the gates are cautiously shut during the presentation of food, and none but a few personal servants of the idols are allowed to be present. While the meal lasts the hundred and twenty dancing-girls attached to the temple dance and sing in the room of many pillars." We are further told that a grand festival which these gods annually hold occurs in the month of March, when the moon is of a certain age after the sun has entered Aries. On these occasions many thousand men, women, and children harness themselves to the sacred cars, and Brahmins stationed on the platform sing and repeat fanatical stories, accompanied by appropriate gestures, which are hailed by the multitude with sounds and movements of applause. It was on these annual excursions that, according to our old belief, a large proportion of the votaries of the cause and glory of Poorie were wont to immolate themselves; but a careful writer has stated his opinion, that "this excess of fanaticism which prompted pilgrims to court death by casting themselves in crowds beneath the wheels of Juggernaut, either never existed or else has long ceased to actuate the worshippers of the idol;" and he attributes the fact of the roadsides being for many miles white with human bones to the general practice among Hindoos of dragging their failing bodies at the approach of death to this sacred

neighbourhood, so that they may end their days within sight of the holy edifice, and purchase everlasting bliss at a price within the reach of the poorest in the land.

The gods that are the object of this popular veneration are grim enough in shape and colouring, and lay no claim to wealth or beauty. They are of wood, painted white, black, and yellow respectively, and are publicly exposed twice a-year, when " Juggernaut and his brother, after undergoing certain ablutions, assume the form of Ganesa, the elephant-headed god, by means of masks, and are placed on the terrace overlooking the temple, surrounded by crowds of priests who fan them to drive away the flies, while the surging multitudes below gaze in silent awe and admiration."

This was the society which France ambitioned in acquiring a *pied à terre* in the vicinity of Poorie; yet even here, where nature wears morally and physically an unusually sombre garb, she has not departed from that law of compensation which renders her so fond a mistress. The dark alluvial soil rewards the husbandman with heavy crops of fruit and grain, the turbid streams teem with excellent fish, and every fowl of the air and beast of the field good for man as food appears with laudable punctuality at its appointed season. Notwithstanding, however, that all material wants are thus bountifully supplied, it can afford little cause for wonder that, in a climate so singularly prejudicial to white life, the French community should have remained stationary within the narrow limits of eight thousand acres, counting seven thousand souls. But these may hug with satisfaction the fond reflection that, though they live and have their being in a land of foreign misbelief, they remain subject to the parti-coloured flag which history will hand down to future ages as the incarnation of ideal government.

Between the lands occupied by the tolerant yet proselytising Frank, and the more worshipful Hindoo, there lie the broad estates of Vizianagram, whose young Maharaja, thus brought up in contact with exaggerated forms of Eastern and of Western life, has marked out for himself a path of happy compromise. Dearly wedded to European tastes, this native noble has recently been raised by the fiat of Sir John Lawrence to a seat in his Council for legislative purposes, for which, though somewhat young perhaps in years and consequent maturity of thought, his character, educational attainments, and great wealth fully fitted him. Seen the other day in the Town Hall of Calcutta, his not very swarthy countenance set, as it were, in a turban of elaborate simplicity, the admirable proportions of his figure displayed by the becoming folds of Oriental drapery, his outward man contrasted most favourably with the servile imitation of European dress that marks the fallen dynasties of Mysore and Oude. To these advantages he added knowledge of the English tongue, in which he had a well-turned phrase for all; and, from association in the habits of our daily life, he had acquired the knack of social intercourse with aliens in creed and colour, without derogating from the dignity of his high descent.

Clad in these amiable and manly attributes, we must now leave the Vizianagram chief to take his part in the legislation of his country; and, pursuing the thread of colonial experience, we shall next turn to the fortunes of those ambitious burghers of the Netherlands, who at one time monopolised the carrying trade of the East.

What little of romance remains associated with the doings of the Dutch in India is connected with the exploits of one Hantman, under whose command a small squadron of four Dutch-built craft approached the Coromandel coast in 1594. In those days the weapons in the hands of Eastern people were not a match for the arms and armour of adventurous Europeans, and the slight resistance at first opposed to Dutch aggression was exactly of the kind best suited to stimulate their passion for mercantile dominion. Hautman and his followers moreover strove to impart that confidence by which alone the trade they sought could be obtained; and the peace-loving people of the coast were far more inclined to accept his conciliatory measures with gratitude, than to descry enemies in the hardy whites sent them by the winds and waves, from whence they could not tell. But though the lukewarm opposition of the native race of itself proved no insurmountable obstacle to the prosperity of the new-comers, it happened that a southern European people had preceded that Dutch captain by a hundred years or more, and now regarded with a jealous eye the advent of a rival, of a hated faith, in those Eastern Indies, which she deemed her own by every title human and divine. Hence ensued a tedious cruel war between the Portuguese and Dutch, wherein the latter ultimately triumphed, though at a heavy cost. While this struggle for ascendency was pending, the natives had insensibly become embroiled in our dissensions ; for not unnaturally seeing a source of gain in the mutual extermination of the intruders, and in their resort to mercenaries, they proved apt scholars in the art of selling their sword-arms to those who bade the highest price, and often by playing a double game became involved in indiscriminate slaughter by both factions.

Thus, by a happy mixture of audacity and skill, the Dutch obtained the mastery over Portugal in India, established factories at Negapatam, Sadras, Pulicat, and Bimlipatam upon the Madras coast, and thenceforth saw in British energy the only serious obstacle to their attaining the monopoly they sought. For several decades matters took their course of intermittent peace and war ; the genius of the Dutch, however, seemed to point more to maritime adventure than territorial extension, and, so far, the real interests of England and Holland clashed less than their pretensions. To this cause may probably be traced the long forbearance of the British people with the arrogance which characterised Dutch dealings at this period ; and it was not till the nation's ire was fully kindled by the massacre of inoffensive unprotected English on the island of Amboyna in the Banda Sea, that serious collision proved fatal to Netherland dominion in East India.

Negapatam was taken by the English in 1781, and thus descended from the rank she occupied as capital of Dutch Hindostan to the condition of a ruined town, mentioned in Gazetteers as " situate within the district of Tanjore, Presidency of Madras, of rare resort except to ships in want of water"—which, however, we are told "is both plentiful and excellent." The decadence of Pulicat and Bimlipatam, though less prominent, has not been less complete; the former now "lies within the jurisdiction of the British magistrate at Chingleput" —a spot, we infer, of more importance; while little information is accessible with reference to the latter, save and except the fact that its geographical position may be laid down on any chart with tolerable accuracy, since its latitude and longitude are known, and stated at 17° 52′ and 83° 30′ respectively. Sadras alone remains to be described in its actual state; and here we have the benefit of a more detailed account by an excellent authority: for, according to Heber, "it is a large but poor-looking town, once a Dutch settlement, and still containing many families of decayed burghers, the melancholy relics of a ruined factory, some of whom are in receipt of little pensions charitably awarded to them by the British Government."

Only one more northern power has set her seal on Indian soil; and though, by the agency of time, the seal itself has been removed, its impress still remains for good, and merits some remark. This power is Denmark; and we would refer those who ask what part the Danes have played in India, to the early history of type-printing as applied to Eastern languages. It was at Serampore, an ancient Danish settlement on the Hoogly, opposite to Barrackpore, that William Carey first set up his missionary press, whence issued translations of the Scriptures in forty different Indian tongues,

bringing the Bible within the range of three hundred
million additional human beings. For this civilising
service we are indebted to the good offices of the then
Danish governor, who promptly placed the small resources of his administration at the disposal of so general a benefactor. The good influence thence diffused
flourished and bore fruit throughout our empire in
the East, paving the way to many of our subsequent
achievements in the interest of peace and education;
and it behoves us, in here endeavouring to trace the
march of causes and effects in British India, honestly to
acknowledge the advantage we derive from the example
of a literary and scientific neighbour in an era of bloodshed and dismemberment.

The end of Serampore as Danish property was honourable to herself and all concerned. . She did not fall
a prey to the grasping policy of a powerful neighbour,
by conquest or surrender; she did not primarily pass
through the gradual stages of decay, which have sapped
the broad foundations of the French and Dutch in
India; neither did she tenaciously adhere, like the
colonies of Portugal, to a state of things long since
become a burthen to the mother country. She was
vigorous even to the end; and so distinguished for the
excellence of her manufactured fabrics, that we English
of Calcutta still print our better publications, and the
Government Gazette, upon the paper she continues to
produce. Yet she had the good sense to know that
the benefit of her industry was reaped by us, and that
constant correspondence on extradition questions was
embarrassing to the cause both of justice and morality.

In other words, Serampore had become troublesome to the jurisdiction of the East India Company as being the. Alsatia of Calcutta, where schemers, insolvent debtors, and reckless spirits of all kinds, sought refuge, when circumstances rendered it expedient for them to disappear from the metropolis.   It was, in consequence, we are told, a bustling, lively, gay, and dissipated place enough.   This condition of affairs at last became so onerous to both parties, and so subversive of good government, as to lead to negotiations, which, undertaken in mutual good faith, ended in 1845 in the cession by the Danes of Serampore to England, for a pecuniary equivalent calculated at five-and-twenty years' net revenue.

Tranquebar, another Danish settlement, distinguished for its neat cleanliness and picturesque appearance from the sea, whence the white walls of the Dansborg Fort still gladden the eyes of every mariner who hugs the Coromandel coast, likewise passed by purchase into British hands about this time—thus severing another link which bound northern men together in a southern clime.

Yet however much, from sentimental reasons, we may be loath to part with these isolated foreign stations in East India, completing, as they do, the picture of a little world perfect in all its parts, with revenues internal and external, foreign governments and native states, a colonial system and a penal settlement of its own, there can be no question but that the gradual extinction of their independence by purchase is sound policy, and would tend more to consolidate our hold on India than might be at first imagined from the mere acquisition of an additional 1254 square miles of territory, with a population of 517,000 souls.

Of these figures France claims 188 square miles, with 204,000 subjects only; and these her possessions, from their isolated and scattered character, are so inconvenient to the many practical details of our administration as to render it most desirable that the earliest moment should be seized to purchase their fee-simple. The remaining area and population included in the statistics above quoted represent an element more difficult to deal with; for the Portuguese settlements are both more compact and more identified with the surrounding native races, besides which they rank first in priority of intercourse with Hindostan, and second only to ourselves in influence on her history.

A study of the *rôle* of Portugal in India takes the student back to those discoveries which closed the middle ages. The improvements made in navigation, to which it was primarily indebted, received their first impetus from Henry, son of John, the first King of Portugal of that name. Under his auspices several fleets were fitted out for the purpose of exploring the African coast and the adjacent seas. The first discovery was not important, but was yet sufficient to afford encouragement and stimulate perseverance. It consisted of the little island of Puerto Santo, so named from the fact of its having been discovered on the Feast of All-Saints A.D. 1418. Shortly after, the adventurers were rewarded by the discovery of Madeira; but for more than half a century the voyages of the Portuguese were continued in the same direction without more important results than occasional additions to the small stock of geographical knowledge then existing. Little progress seems to have been made towards the attainment of their grand object—the discovery of a new route to India—until the latter end of the fifteenth century, when Bartholomew Diaz eclipsed the fame of all pre ceding navigators by his success in reaching the southernmost point of Africa, and doubling the famous pro montory called by him the Cape of Storms, but more happily and permanently designated by his sovereign the Cabo de Bona Esperanza. Emanuel, the successor of John I., inherited the maritime ambition of his predecessor. An expedition was fitted out and intrusted to the care of Vasco de Gama. It sailed from Lisbon in 1497, doubled the Cape in safety, and finally reached Calicut, thus achieving the triumph so long and anxiously sought. Landing under cover of his guns, and in full view of a large and waving crowd, the Admiral was forthwith introduced to a native prince of Hindoo faith, whom Portuguese historians denominate Zamorin, but who among ourselves is more generally known as Samari. After a short stay, marked by rapid alternations of friendship and hostility, Vasco de Gama returned to Portugal, where he was received with well-earned honours. Some Portuguese, however, had remained behind, with permission more or less specific to engage in commerce. Disputes arose ere long, and acts of violence were committed on both sides; yet the power and influence of the Portuguese continued to increase, and the assistance afforded by them to the

neighbouring King of Cochin, in his quarrel with Zamorin or Samari, was rewarded by permission to erect
a fort for their protection within the territory of the
former ruler.

Thus was laid the corner-stone of a Portuguese
colonial empire, which, with the sanction of a Papal
bull, extended itself not only in India, but in China,
Japan, and the uncounted islands of the Pacific.   Following in this track of domination, the little town of
Goa fell into the hands of Albuquerque in 1510, was
strongly fortified by him, and became ere long the
capital of Portuguese Hindostan, the centre of commercial intercourse, and the residence of an archbishop,
the acknowledged Primate of all India.   Throughout
the first three-fourths of the sixteenth century Goa
grew and flourished, gradually assuming the character
she still retains, of a city of churches, in whose construction the wealth of provinces seems to have been
expended, and which surpass in grandeur and in taste
all previous and subsequent architectural efforts of
Europeans in the East.   The chapel of the Viceroy's
palace was built after the modest pattern of St Peter's
at Rome; the church of St Dominic is adorned with
paintings by the most esteemed Italian artists of the
time; the Jesuit church contains the costly tomb of the
sainted Francis Xavier; and the cathedral is only to be
classed with that of Antwerp for richness of decoration
combined with purity of design.

The temporary annexation of Portugal to the crown
of Spain in 1580 gave a fatal and a lasting blow to her
colonial supremacy, for the Dutch were not loath to

take advantage of the occasion thus afforded of mon-
opolising Eastern trade; and Goa, with her sister
colonies, gradually fell from their high estate into
wretchedness and degradation.

Goa lies, as all the geographical world is well aware,
upon the coast of Malabar, midway between Baroda and
Cape Comorin. In the course of centuries she has
assumed a character peculiar to herself; for the Portuguese have mingled more extensively with the native
population than any other Western people, and have
succeeded, by means of proselytism, in teaching their
Eastern subjects a regard for Western intercourse,
which through two centuries both French and English
have failed equally to instil. They have besides enforced a moral code that holds its own with some success
amidst the ancient faiths around, and practically cries
shame upon our own past efforts. Indeed it would
appear alone attributable to extraneous causes that
Goa has at length, through no fault either of her own
or her administrators, but by the sheer accident of her
position, sunk to a level of comparison with Pondicherry
or Yanaon.

On the western coast of India, between latitudes corresponding to those by which Orissa is embraced, lies a
tract of rugged country, formerly included in the territories of the so-called puppet Raja of Sattara. This
country, known as the Concan, was little prized previous
to the sixteenth century. It was bordered then, as it is
now, by the Portuguese possessions of Goa and Damaun;
and, considering its fertility and happy site between the
Western Ghauts and the Arabian Sea, it need not excite

surprise that a nation so ambitious of colonial possessions, and grasping in its policy, as Portugal in the
middle ages, should have availed itself of the absence
of other foreign powers and of native combinations to
fertilise this field for enterprise, and thus cement its
northern and its southern settlements by a strong commercial link. This would be only the more natural
when we remember the proselytising character of Portuguese emigration ; for the pious Johns by whom it was
conducted no doubt dreamed of grand results to Christianity from contact with the Poona Peishwa. In the
execution of this project many difficulties had to be
surmounted, but one and all eventually gave way to
Portuguese energy and daring : the contact with the
Peishwa was attained, and a fort was built upon the
little island of Bombay, a central and convenient point
of occupation. But ere the full advantage of the situation could be reaped, Portugal herself had lost her independence ; and when in 1540 she at length shook off
the hated yoke of Spain, her first object naturally was
to regain her former European status, and to fortify
herself therein by treaty and alliance. So it was that
when Catherine of Braganza became the bride of Charles
II. the island of Bombay was fixed on for her dowry.
The marriage took place in 1661 ; and though the
Portuguese inhabitants of Bombay held out from recollections of a former pride, and long refused to recognise
the transfer and to cede possession, the English East
India Company eventually secured by force the trading
privileges of the island, and executed them under letters
patent from the English Crown.

Thus was inserted the thin end of ‘the wedge of foreign dominion, severing Goa from Damaun. The city of Damaun lies at the mouth of a river bearing the same name. It is the frontier town of the Concan to the north, and an insignificant spot enough. It contains nine Christian churches, and the Castle of St Hieronymus, surrounded by a ruined rampart with ten bastions and two gates. The surrounding country owns the peculiarities common to coast districts, being subject to prevailing breezes from the sea, and not unfrequent inundations.

On the other side of the Cambay Gulf, at the southernmost point of Kattywar, directly opposite Damaun, and at a distance of a trifle more than a hundred miles, stands the ancient fort of Diu. This is but another ruined emblem of the past ambition of Portugal in the East, an ambition that has crumbled into dry religious dust, and ended in a very limited missionary influence, and the carrying on of a small coast commerce. Portugal has, however, reaped the richest fruits from the introduction of Christianity in India ; and it is worthy of remark that, while in Calcutta or Madras the term of "native Christian" does not entitle those who claim it to consideration as specially intelligent or credible as witnesses, throughout the length and breadth of the Bombay Presidency it affords a sort of passport to its bearer, as possessed of some rudimentary acquaintance with the meaning of the words honesty and labour. The half-caste Portuguese of Goa make excellent domestic servants, and, when treated with humanity, become easily attached to good, and too often to bad masters.

Of all classes whence the Anglo-Indian has to pick his menials, there is certainly none which, taken altogether, ranks so high. Hindoo castes form a barrier to the performance by their holders of much of a servant's work. The Mahomedan religion, less absolute in its requirements, and perhaps a shade more tolerant of others, is still apt to be associated with fanatical habits, which render it a disturbing element in the white man's house. No nation has intermarried to such extent with natives as the Portuguese, and borne such ample increase as to constitute a race apart or national family. The English have indeed intermarried and borne children, but, not possessed of sufficient numbers to form a distinct class, they are, as a race, lost sight of, and exist now only as isolated human beings. To such an extent is this the case, that throughout the length and breadth of British India but one child has been found of later years the colour of whose hair and eyes was so dubious as to justify a doubt on the part of the district Assistant-Superintendent of Police, by whom she was unearthed in Central India, as to whether she could boast of white or black extraction.

The history of this little child is generally supposed to be associated with the darker side of our common national history, when flight by night, aided by the faithful services of a native nurse, was the last escape for the hated child of the Feringhee. This child, possessed of national characteristics peculiar to the Anglo-Saxon race, was suddenly discovered, hid in the bosom of a mountain Indian home. For some months she was discussed by Anglo-Indian newspapers as a curiosity of nature. Her dark brown skin, it was argued, contrasted strangely with the light blue windows of her soul, while her golden locks seemed out of place on the head of a little maiden whose only tongue was a Hill Mahratta dialect. She was ultimately taken from her *quasi* parents, and passed through more than one Commissioner's hands into the maternal care of the Bombay Government. Yet her history, here lost sight of, tends to prove, that throughout a population of a hundred and eighty millions, embracing every shade of colour, a child of questionable English origin is next thing to unknown ; while it did not enter into the brains either of the Assistant District Superintendent of Police, or any of the Commissioners through whose hands she passed, to argue that the circumstance of her peculiarity could be accounted for by mixed blood. This fact, taken by the side of a Goanese hamlet, where some hundred little urchins lie baking in the sun, with skin and eyes and hair of varied tints, unquestioned and uncared for, seems to afford strong evidence in favour of the aptitude of southern blood to stock a still more southern soil.

The subject of the aptitude of certain races to domineer, assimilate themselves, or become subordinate to each other, is however one, the treatment of which may be left to natural historians and scientific writers, as quite beyond the limits of a practical view of human happiness, tested by the sum of annas and rupees at which the taxation of a country is assessed. We shall now, therefore, take leave of Foreign Settlements, and in the following and last chapter our efforts shall be bent to prove that, seen from a point of view where mere fancy themes do not encroach upon the space reserved for solid interests, India, as ruled to-day by an Anglo-Indian Administration, enjoys far greater material advantages, national identity, and political weight, than the positive facts of her existence could admit of under any other form of government than our own.

CHAPTER XII.

NATIVE INSTITUTIONS.

OF all the institutions by which national character is moulded, religion probably exercises the deepest influence upon mankind. Now it happens, that so far back as history can be traced in India, faiths opposed have constantly waged war for paramount dominion. Some six centuries before the birth of Christ, the Buddhist worship raised its head, some say in Cooch Behar, displacing the uncouth religion of the Jains, whose origin is obscure. The slow and complicated growth of Hindooism takes the inquiring theologian back to times of which the history is recorded in fabulous narratives of most questionable veracity; and the sudden introduction of Mahomedanism alone stands out as a landmark by itself, in striking contrast to the gradual development of other Indian creeds. Following in the train of bloody conquest, it could not be withstood; and it had taken a considerable hold upon the minds of Hindos tanees by the commencement of the eleventh century.

These may be termed the three parent faiths of India, and from them at different periods a variety of schismatic churches have branched forth, such as the Seik heresy first preached by Nanak, at an age contemporary with our own domestic Reformation. Mahomedanism, once powerful and compact, lost in the lapse of ages much of its ancient strength, by reason of its own dissensions; and the temple of the Prophet became divided against itself by Shiah and Sunni sects, who occupy positions of mutual antagonism. Some idea of the confusion now prevailing may be gathered from the fact, that the Hindoo Pantheon has grown and multiplied, until to-day it counts within its walls upwards of three hundred and thirty-three million deities, worshipped according to capricious custom in different modes, by some hundred and forty-four castes of human beings, pursuing different trades, not permitted to intermarry, and quite incapable of social or political combination.

A population so rent by different beliefs, the votaries of each bred to the use of arms and habituated to the thought of propagating their own particular ritual at the point of the sword, their only lesson of toleration being derived from the unchristian conduct of Christian creeds towards one another, offered an arena for invasion too tempting to be withstood by the lax morality of trans-Indus tribes when led by men like Sultan Mahmoud of Ghuznee, or Nadir Shah. The country thus peopled, and thus invaded, was further parcelled out among a host of rulers, often chosen by the accident of adoption; and in the absence of natural boundaries, at times a jungle, and at times a forest, did duty as a frontier, proving a refuge for the criminal and destitute alike, and breeding abundant evil in the land.

Yet one more condition remains to be recorded to complete the chaotic character of the picture now before us. This is the additional fact, that the forty distinct races inhabiting Hindostan worshipped their almost countless gods in fifty-eight distinct living languages, of which some twenty-eight possessed a literature and historical traditions of their own. Race, language, and religion thus combined to disintegrate the East Indian people, and pave the way to their acceptance of a foreign yoke. The infliction of this yoke, with its conditions and results, has been well epitomised by the late Mr J. R. M'Culloch, whose words upon the subject are so characteristically broad and sound as to merit their quotation at some length :—

" The great body of the Indian people had, for six centuries before the commencement of our government, been under the dominion of foreigners more energetic than themselves, and a good deal more civilised. Upon a fair retrospect of what they have lost and gained by the Mahomedan dominion, they must upon the whole be considered as having been considerable gainers ; the conquerors being Asiatics, and approaching to themselves in manners, language, and complexion, became to some extent assimilated to the subject races ; while even in matters of religion, where the difference was widest, a considerable share of toleration was established, and Hindoo converts to Mahomedanism became in time admissible to the highest offices of State. This condition of things was superseded by the British rule. The British Government, as established in India, may be considered an enlightened despotism, a good deal controlled by the public opinion of Englishmen on the spot, and to a less extent by Parliament at home, and possessed of some advantages, but also many disadvantages, when compared with the Mahomedan Government by it superseded."

Mr M'Culloch next proceeds to divide our reign in India into three periods : the first terminated by Pitt's India Bill, by which the Board of Control was established, in 1784 ; the second from that date until the practical reorganisation of our Indian institutions in 1814 ; the third extending to the present day, or at least the time at which he wrote.

The first, we are told, was a period of pretty general anarchy ; the government was carried on upon the Mahomedan system, the taxes were levied with more than Mahomedan rapacity, and the Mahomedan law was administered with less than Mahomedan intelligence. Everything depended at that time on the moral and intellectual character of a few functionaries, while the industry of the country was subject to a commercial monopoly, exercised by the government itself, for the sole purpose of obtaining possession of the produce of the country at less than the original cost price, in order to re-sell it for more than it was really worth ; and Mr M'Culloch rightly judges that this period could hardly have been productive of beneficial results to the native inhabitants so ruled.

The second period was marked by the establishment, throughout the greater part of Indian territory, of the land-tax, the basis of our revenues, and the heaviest burden ever borne by the Indian people. On the other hand, regular courts of justice were instituted, and the Mahomedan system was so far modified that judicial and fiscal administration became distinct, after the fashion of European nations. The commercial monopoly continued, but was exercised with less extortion. During this period, Parliament did not interfere in the affairs of India, where everything was presumed to be going on prosperously. Meantime, if wars doubled the extent of our territory, they also more than doubled the amount of our territorial debt; and so far from reaping any direct advantage from its new acquisitions, Parliament was compelled to exonerate the East India Company from a long arrear of tribute which it was wholly unable to discharge. The advantages conferred upon the people of India during the period now mentioned, may be resolved into some ameliorations in the administration of justice, and freedom from all foreign aggression save our own, minus the additional burthen of the oppressive land-tax. England for herself derived no advantage whatever. Her commerce remained stationary, and was of trifling value; we paid a monopoly price for every Indian commodity we consumed, and were ultimately compelled to forego the tribute money we had bargained for in exchange.

The third period has, however, been one of vast improvement. The influx of Europeans into India at the close of the Napoleonic wars, was accompanied and followed by a still greater influx of British capital. A public opinion next sprang up at the principal seats of commerce, not quite inadequate to cope with the despotism of a practically absolute government. This public opinion found expression in a press formerly subject to a rigorous censorship. Native education assumed a practical shape; and those who had previously considered all education to be comprised in the study of Persian or of Sanskrit, now betook themselves with ardour to the study of our language and its literature.

It must not be forgotten that the preceding paragraphs are little more than extracts from opinions, formed and written some years before the Company was succeeded by the Crown; and a writer of to-day might prefer that the history of the intercourse of England with East India should, at some future day, be written down in two broad columns side by side, the line of division being very clearly traced by the terms of that Royal Proclamation whereby the Queen assumed the government for better purposes than those for which the country had been farmed by a sordid board of East India directors.

The remark above quoted with reference to the measure of intelligence displayed in the administration of Mahomedan law, by Mahomedan and Christian conquerors, tending as it does to the disparagement of British rule, should not be permitted to go before the world without a practical set-off favourable to our own repute; and happily one is ready to our hand, sufficiently conclusive to dispel the cloudy views of those who yield the preference to the Persian yoke. With all the merits, real and supposed, that, according to M'Culloch, tended to render the rule of Nadir Shah acceptable to the native population, it bore too much resemblance to traditions of the scourges inflicted by the heavy hands of Tamerlane and Genghis Khan, to pass muster as a pattern of good government. It is recorded that so late as 1738, upwards of a hundred and fifty thousand persons perished by the orders of Nadir in a general massacre at Delhi; subsequent to which little episode in the life of an Eastern king, he carried off gold and precious stones to the value, it is computed, of a hundred and twenty-five millions sterling. The greater part of this enormous sum was actually deported from the country; and, so far as India is concerned, the reign of Nadir Shah, far from raising the tone and temper of the people, decimated the native population, and reduced the country to a condition of bankruptcy and bondage, whence it is but just beginning to emerge.

Under the Company a widely different state of things prevailed. For a century its servants reaped rich harvest from the ruins of a crumbling Empire. During this period many families and individuals acquired considerable wealth, salaries and retirements being calculated on a singularly lavish scale. Yet these were personal abuses, and not national connivance in the plunder of a people. Indian gold often found its way to England in the pockets of her adventurous sons, at times no doubt through channels not strictly constitutional; but these sums, though sufficient to sap the broad foundations of the revenues of the Company, and reduce it, as we have seen, to inability to pay a paltry annual tribute to the mother country of half a million sterling, were small compared with the extortionate

rulings of the past.   During this period, and under this
system of personal accumulation as opposed to imperial
plunder, India acquired, thanks to the infusion of our
trading energy, improved communications, additional
security for life and property, and a greater measure of
national consistency than she had known before.   The
not very unnatural consequence was a passing thirst for
independence.   This was much enhanced by vague religious terrors, and the spectacle was for the first time
seen in India of the country rising almost like one man.
Those who rose, however, had exaggerated their resist-
ing power, and relied too much upon their recently
cemented bonds of national cohesion.   The fruit of this
erroneous calculation was the Sepoy War, which ultimately brought about the existing happy state of
things, and landed us, with peace and plenty, in a
period distinguished by a feature new in Indian history—that of gold returning to the hands of native
populations, in the shape of a hundred million English
sovereigns, spent on works of general utility, and the
opening up to native industry of roads to wealth and
power, in the production of the raw staples so essential
to our national existence.

Thus it would almost appear that India has at length
attained the turning-point and crisis of her destiny.
For the first time in her annals, the importance of what
is known as Sovereign Independence has dwindled into
small dimensions by the side of the material benefits
accruing from our rule.   The golden tide has turned,
and now rolls back towards the East in search of profitable investments on good security ; and so long as such

are found for British bullion, the native mind will not easily revert to fevered dreams of restoring the dominion of the Great Mogul.

If, however, the greater influences on mankind in India have only acted negatively in our favour, in that political, social, and religious discord, paving the way to the Persian conquest, brought about the deliverance of Hindostan from a foreign yoke by incorporation with our dominions, at any rate the lesser influences by which a people is developed have been more positive in their operation on our behalf. Among these rank the national conditions of prosperity that are included in the growth of education, art, science, literature, and police both moral and municipal. Now, in each of these branches of Anglo-Indian civilisation a very nearly equal part is played by natives and ourselves. The observing traveller in India may learn, for instance, on inquiry, that the unfinished building with a broad verandah and capacious halls, on which the masons are actively engaged that it may be tenantable by the ensuing rains, was designed for this or that scholastic purpose by the munificent Rampore Nawab or Puttealla Raja. At the seat of Government itself the same movement is discernible. The Calcutta Madrissa, under the active supervision of Captain Nassau Lees, has turned out latterly each year a good percentage of well-trained Anglo-Persian scholars, most of whom embrace the service of the Crown or the profession of the law. Art and science we find fully represented, in the definition, by Sir William Jones, of the bounds set to the investigations of the Asiatic Society of Bengal, said by him to be "the geographical limits of Asia Magna," and within these limits, we are told by him, that its inquiries are extended to whatever is performed by man or produced by nature. The council and committees of this society are composed of Europeans and natives of both prevailing creeds, according to the specialty of the subject under treatment; and among the Hindoo gentlemen who have actively participated in furthering its interests and utility, the name of Rajendralal Mittra should not be omitted.

The formation of societies of men for purposes of deliberation and self-government is a habit that has taken deep root in the Bengali mind. Several such societies exist in the township of Calcutta; but two among their number are of a character so marked, and have been productive of such good results, as to merit the careful study of all who desire to make themselves acquainted with the working of the native brain. The first to which reference is here made is the Bethune Society, established in 1857, in order to promote among the educated natives of Bengal a taste for literary and scientific pursuits, and to encourage a freer intellectual intercourse than can be accomplished by other means in the existing state of native society. The second, to which we would direct the most attention, bears the name of the "British Indian Association." The object it keeps steadily in view is the improvement and efficiency of the British Indian Government, which it seeks to further by memorialising the Imperial Parliament and the local powers for the removal of existing, or prevention of proposed, injurious measures, and for the introduction of such measures as may tend to promote the interests of all. This society has had for many years the great advantage of possessing the counsels and support of the Rajas Radhakanth Deb and Kalikrishna, both recognised leaders of the orthodox Hindoos of Bengal Proper. This position is hereditary to them ; and that Hindoo blood and breeding have for very many generations lent a willing hand to cast fitting representatives of their faith and its nobility, no one can doubt who has conversed with these patterns of austere simplicity. Robed in spotless drapery of white, they take their place at the Governor-General's Durbars amidst respectful silence. Devoid of all external ornament, save perhaps some solitary ancestral stone of purest radiance, their druidical appearance contrasts most strangely with that of the jewelled chiefs by whom they are surrounded.

Before taking leave of these associations, it behoves us to record two European names that will long be held in reverence by all classes of the mixed community of Calcutta. The first of these, in rank ecclesiastical, is the venerable Archdeacon Pratt, whose depth of learning in every branch of science and theology is equally appreciated by those who follow in the footsteps of the late Bishop Wilson, and those who make the differential calculus their study. The application of his reasoning powers to the solution of material problems outside the limits of his own cathedral church inspired his Aryan brethren with feelings of respect, and often led them to seek the benefit of his opinion on the issues of their daily lives. It is not, indeed, too much to say,

that in the religious conciliation of antagonistic principles he, as Archdeacon of Calcutta, has rendered as
good clerical service by abstaining from accepting too
prominent a place in propaganda as any member of
the Anglo-Indian Church has done by an ascetic faith;
which, after all, in outward show is as naught compared
with the austerities of fanatical Fakirs in Oude and
Rajpootana.

The second ecclesiastic to whom we here refer is
Dr Alexander Duff, a Scotchman of the best Scotch
type, in whom missionary zeal was only curbed and
held within the bounds of wise restraint by the working of an iron will. The good that he has done in
India cannot be overestimated. He did not shun his
countrymen and bury his wan cheeks in the remotest
corners of the earth in search of martyrdom and
visionary results—the conduct of his life in India was
far different. By active participation in native cares
within the foul Mahratta ditch, he gathered round him
in the course of years crowds of stanch believers. He
wisely chose for the field of his operations that part of
India where European contact was most familiar to the
minds of men, and where many of the deepest prejudices of the Eastern heart had been erased by the
gentle action of natural causes on five succeeding
generations. On such ground he might not unreasonably hope that his energy would create large and
wealthy institutions, based on the sound proselytising
principles of diffusing comfort to the poor and needy,
providing hospital accommodation for the afflicted, and
offering the rudiments of education to one and all

without distinction. This plan of action Dr Duff preferred to despising the advantages of his position and working in the dark, where the light of his own intelligence would be obscured by the surrounding ignorance, and where, though by sheer personal ascendency he might turn some few souls from the worship of carved images, there could be little doubt but that the results obtained would gradually expire upon his own removal from the theatre of life. At any rate the course pursued by Dr Duff has been crowned by the most entire success. He lived and laboured long enough in India to found a Christian congregation worthy of the name, as well as many philanthropic institutions on self-supporting bases of a gradual development, likely to retain their influence for good so long as the native population in Calcutta shall stand in need of corporal or spiritual aid.

Of what we have ventured upon terming the lesser influences on mankind, we shall only touch upon one more—Police. This brings us to the threshold of a question of great import, at a time when the wheel of public thought once more revolves upon the axis of military reduction, both in men and money. It has recently been argued with much vigour, that the European force in India should decrease, in just proportion with the increase of improved media of communication; that climatic influences are so various, and locomotion is now so easy, that one-third the actual number of white regiments might practically combine hill stations with the necessity for omnipresence. The only argument alleged *per contra* is the large proportion of natives

still in arms for purposes of municipal police and the
maintenance of village law. These, to the number of
three hundred thousand, still carry weapons of no mean
defence, are daily drilled, and, being officered by
Europeans, resemble to no small degree the Sepoy of
our recollection. Yet some items in their actual condition have been overlooked, whereby their power for
harm is restricted within the narrowest limits compatible with efficiency against . Pindaree robbers or the
more organised Dacoits of the plains.

First, the Indian police, large as it is numerically,
is three-fourths composed of men whose loyalty was
proved in 1857 ; and of their officers about the same
proportion were witnesses of the events for which that
year is memorable, and are thus no novices to the pre-
monitory symptoms of extended disaffection.

Secondly, the police force is more local in its character, and has less of class or caste cohesion, than
characterised the Sepoy hosts. Its employment is not
directly connected with political affairs, such as the
chastisement of some refractory Raja, or the occupation
of a territory recently annexed, but is almost invariably
confined to measures for protecting life and property,
in which the natives, as the basis of the population,
themselves have most at stake.

Thirdly, with very few exceptions, these police are
quite domestic in their habits, are bound together by
no common tie except the prospect of promotion, and,
instead of herding in bodies of ten or twenty regiments,
reduced by the influence of inaction to seek excitement
in sedition, they are distributed in companies and

patrols throughout the length and breadth of India, and very generally ignore their own numerical importance.

When this force was constituted on what may be termed the local basis, with a view to the absorption of many loyal native corps, after the reduction of the Sepoy army, Lord Canning planned the nomination of a superior officer to be called Inspector - General of Police in India. To this appointment Sir Charles Wood demurred, partially on constitutional grounds, and partially as tending unwisely to centralise the infant system; and thus it happened that an officer was lost to this department to whose directing skill its growth and most of the results obtained were mainly due. This officer was Lieutenant - Colonel Bruce, whose singular good fortune it was to be appreciated by three successive Governor-Generals of India. One of Colonel Bruce's greatest merits was his willingness at all times to cope with the most opposed and difficult of situations. It was indifferent to him whether the service of the Queen required that he should be attached to the intelligence department of a flying column about to penetrate into the obscurity of Central India, or that he should be selected to report on some abstruse financial or commercial problem. He was so constituted by nature that his powers seemed always best adapted for whatever labour was committed to him. Subsequent to the Indian mutiny the doctrine of ruling India by a military police had found favour and encouragement, almost irrespective of the cost to be incurred. Those who then advised Lord Canning turned over in their minds the pages of their past experience in men, and finally recommended Colonel Bruce as perhaps the readiest officer at their command. At first his duty was confined to the collection of materials for the building of this structure, and later, these receiving high approval, he was ordered to elaborate the rudiments of a service by itself, that should combine the force of military law with civil obligations. The arm of power thus sketched out for holding India bore upon the face of its previsions much promise of success, and the experience of some years has proved that the expectations of its authors were not unreasonably sanguine. Colonel Bruce, however, had to meet and overcome much local jealousy. Up to that time police had existed in a form subordinate to Lieutenant-Governors and Chief Commissioners; now it was to be an imperial force, at the immediate control of the Government of India. The programme therefore drawn up by Colonel Bruce made enemies of almost every subordinate administration. Military privileges were to be enjoyed, without rendering those who profited by them subject to divisional or brigade command; and while in Bengal and the North-West two members of the Civil Service, Mr C. F. Carnac and Mr Court, were appointed to the office of Inspectors-General of Police, and thus relieved from all subordination to their seniors the Lieutenant-Governors, in Oude and the Punjab two military officers, Captain Aitken and Major Hutchinson, escaped, through their selection for the performance of similar functions, from the control of the Commander-in-Chief.

At the crisis when these impartial schemes of Colonel Bruce were given to the world, and angry men of all classes and opinions were clamouring for his removal, the call for general economy had succeeded to the passing cry for national defence. In a letter therefore from the Government of India, Colonel Bruce was summarily told that his efforts should in future be directed to the reduction of previously approved-of estimates. To this thankless task of pulling down the work of his own creation, and pruning the branches of the tree that he himself had planted, he proceeded with his usual successful zeal; the budgets for police again assumed proportions within the possibility of payment, and Colonel Bruce was told in laudatory phrases that his work was done. He reverted then to other things, and his name appears for the last time in the history of India, as occupying the post of political officer appointed to accompany to Bhotan the army destined to erase the stain ·on our escutcheon caused by the fiasco of Mr Ashley Eden. To this service he devoted the remains of a frame and constitution once remarkable for vigour, and there he contracted the Terai fever, under which he sank on his homeward journey, undertaken in the hope to recruit his health beneath the shady oaks and cloudy skies of England, which none but those who have felt the burthen of an Indian sun can value at their own high price.

Another indication of the spirit of the times and their requirements may be gathered from the gradual decay of a department, the duties of which once embraced the supervision of every village inn and mountain-path from Poona to Lucknow. The class of crime for the suppression of which this department was intended is known as Thuggee; and Dacoitee, or highway robbery, was shortly after added to it. According to the legend, Thuggee had its origin as follows :—" Kali encountered a monstrous giant, every drop of whose blood as it fell became a destructive demon. The blood of each demon thus produced possessed the same property, and an enormous brood was generated, threatening the world with destruction. The evil would have been without remedy—for the more they were slain the more they multiplied—had not Kali fallen upon the notable device of creating two men, and giving them hand-kerchiefs or waistbands with which they were able to strangle the demons. As by this process not a drop of blood was shed, the race of demons, which could only be propagated by blood, was extinguished. The instruments of strangulation became the property of the men who had used them so successfully; and to make this gift of value, the goddess authorised them and their descendants to make strangulation their trade." In accordance with this strange legend, " the Thugs became hereditary murderers, and spread throughout Central India and into part of the Deccan. Though formed into fraternities by initiatory rites, and able to recognise each other by the use of particular signs, they lived as the ordinary inhabitants of the country, following the peaceful occupations of agriculture or trade." The reports of the officers charged with the prosecution of a crusade against this crime, that rendered travel in time of peace and plenty a matter of even greater risk

than when war was raging, and trade and merchandise
moved from place to place under martial escort and
protection, long teemed with interest to the general
reader in search of entertainment or instruction; and
the insight they afforded into native character, proved
hardly of less value than the actual services they
recorded. Foremost among the most interesting and
valuable of these reports rank those of Colonel Slee-
man, under whose administration some of the earliest
and busiest years of this department were passed.
Throughout the native states of Central India, and
specially in the Nizam's dominions, this crime was most
at home; and though it is one of rare commission now,
yet in many parts of India remote from the intercourse
of white men, travellers are still wary of accepting prof-
fered fellowship on a journey, much preferring the fear
of solitary hunger, thirst, the wild beast at night, and
maybe open pillage, to the dread of being decoyed and
strangled by a fancied boon-companion. Of late years
Colonel Hervey has filled the office of General Superintendent of Thuggee and Dacoitee; and even if it be true
that he inherited a moribund machine whose special
labours, it might be thought, had been sufficiently performed to admit of their being handed over to the various local services and administrations, yet it is but
naked justice to a never-tiring public servant to record,
that it was under his directions that a final blow was
dealt at the hereditary existence of a sect of professioual men, by whom the fact of taking life without
the shed of blood was deemed a cardinal tenet of
religion.

Thus, under the conditions of which the barren outlines only have been roughly sketched within the pre-
vions chapters, Anglo-Indian administration certainly
possesses in itself numerous elements essential to the
life of what are sometimes termed " permanent institutions." The powers that be, however, should not too
far indulge themselves in this gratifying reflection ; for
it is not the less true, that many little surface clouds
still interpose between the native races and their own
contentment. One prominent cause of dissatisfaction
exists perchance in the greater taste and aptitude for
splitting hairs that past prestige, and the fact of framing their own laws and penal code, have generated
among covenanted civilians, as compared with the
handy, free-and-easy justice dealt out by military or
native agents engaged in the conduct of affairs. Probably it is to this fact that the preference exhibited by
natives for non-regulation government may in some
degree be traced ; for though this invention of Lord
Dalhousie places at the control of one individual a
wider field, both for good government and for abuse,
than could exist under the more tortuous formalities
and conditions of divided responsibility maintained in
the system of Bengal and the North-West Provinces,
yet, not unlike ourselves, natives often prefer a speedy
and practically irrevocable decision at the hands of a
local judge, to the prospective satisfaction to be derived
from the tardy revision of a sentence by remote machinery with whose working they are but imperfectly
acquainted. In the support of these assertions some
extracts from the correspondence of native ex-legisla-

tive members of both prevailing creeds, and of councils both local and supreme, may not be here considered out of place ; and these, if analysed, will appear to lead to the conclusion that our native legislators do not think so highly as we do ourselves, of the progress we have made in conciliating the Eastern races confided to our rule and governance.

One of these legislators writes from India under date of December 21, 1865, in a tone in which it is not difficult to trace a vein of bitter disappointment. "The present general condition of affairs," he writes, "combined with my thirty years' exertions, induce me to prefer devotion-to the Almighty in seclusion to anything else. Still it affords me pleasure to give now this general abstract of my own opinion about the administration of India. The affection of the subject, and attention to the prejudices of the people, regarding which the Queen of England spoke in her gracious Proclamation, the preservation of custom, appointment of selected and experienced officers, fixed laws and regulations, are essential to the wellbeing of a people. It must also be borne in mind that the system of constantly imposing or abolishing different taxes, in order to maintain receipts and disbursements within a condition of equilibrium, is not generally acceptable in India. It is a custom in almost all our native governments to leave sufficient balance from the income of one year to supply any probable excess of expenditure in the next; and some such scheme is necessary to insure the happiness of the Eastern subjects of the English Crown. These unhappy subjects are at a long distance from the throne, and are of a different disposition, possess different prejudices, different habits and customs, and live within the influence of a different climate. The true principle of all good government consists in the affection of the subject and the preservation of good faith. Since the mutiny of 1857 many appear to think that it is difficult to gain the affection of the subject; but I do not agree with them, because the subject here is poorer than anywhere else. Their poorness and affection is self-evident from the fact that so vast a continent as India has come so speedily and easily beneath the rule of the British Government. You say that the attention of the great statesmen in England is directed towards the real improvement of India; but you should bear in mind that it is but little use to repair the upper storey of a building the foundation of which has been damaged. After the mutiny, when I and my friends suffered many difficulties which will never be forgotten, Lord Canning had the opportunity to bring the whole of British India under non-regulation system, and thereupon depend the fortunes of the subject."

The foregoing expressions were penned by one whose character for extreme loyalty towards the English Crown ranks second to none in India. There seems no reason for withholding from the public that the man referred to is Raja Dinkur Rao of Gwalior; and since the services which circumstances have enabled him to render have been so continuous and conspicuous that modesty in glossing over his deserts would be misplaced, we venture to transcribe the following from the pen of

Major Meade, Agent Governor-General for Central India, dated Indore Presidency, April, 1865 :—

. . . . "I can have no hesitation in stating that I fully concur in, and can endorse every word of, the late Sir Richmond Shakespeare's memorandum, and that it is simply impossible, in my opinion, to do adequate justice to Raja Dinkur Rao's services and admirable character in such documents.

"His administrative ability and thorough knowledge of the people generally of the Gwalior State (including his own class, which filled most of the offices of the Government, and the various tribes and clans making up the two millions odd subject to the rule of Maharaja Scindia), and of the measures and policy which were best suited to their requirements, and the real interests of the State and his chief, aided by his singular acquaintance with, and appreciation of, the merits and defects of the system of British administration, enabled him, from the date of his assumption of the Dewanship, to introduce improvements, order, and organisation in every branch and department of the State, and in a wonderfully brief time, under the circumstances, to establish a Government such as had never before existed in the territories of his master, and which gave promise, if maintained in the spirit and on the principles in which it was conceived, to make Gwalior the first of native kingdoms.

"In all this the Honourable Raja had much to contend with : for his measures were necessarily opposed to the traditional policy of the governing classes of the country, and to the interests of the many influential

persons who had fattened on the abuses they were
specially intended to abolish; but his tact, calm temper,
and good judgment, aided by the example of unimpeach-
able integrity he set to all around him, enabled him to
effect what to those acquainted with the circumstances
of the State might well have appeared hopeless.

"The people of the country were relieved from the
system of oppression and misrule which had made
some.districts, as Tourghar, a prey to the most lawless
disorder, in which the Durbar possessed no real authority but such as was exercised under the guns of a large
military force, and the revenue was periodically collected at the point of the bayonet; and had made others,
as Esaghur, which had formerly been prosperous and
flourishing, in many parts a desert, and abandoned by
its impoverished and ruined inhabitants; and a general
feeling of contentment and satisfaction, and of love
and respect for the Minister who had so changed their
condition, prevailed among all classes.

"To this policy the safety of Maharaja Scindia and
his Government during the troubles of 1857 may
assuredly be fairly and justly ascribed: the people
generally, instead of taking advantage of the disrup-
tion of authority consequent on the mutiny and
rebellion of the British native troops (including the
local contingents), on whose presence the peace of the
territories of Central India had previously principally
depended, and who were openly sympathised with by
all, and actively aided by many of the troops and
armed police of the native states, remained obedient to
the local officials; and the presence at the capital of a

large number of them, hastily collected and summoned by the Minister for the purpose, enabled Maharaja Scindia to overawe his own disaffected troops and to withstand the otherwise overpowering force of the Gwalior contingent, which, confident of the full support of the Gwalior army and of the many influential people in the Luskier and about the chief, for upwards of three eventful months endeavoured to cajole or compel his Highness to comply with their objects and demands.

" The triumphant manner in which Scindia emerged from these difficulties was, viewed by the light of former times, the best proof of the wisdom of the measures of administration previously adopted by the Minister. Throughout the trying events of 1857-58 Raja Dinkur Rao's devotion and services to his master were beyond all praise. He was in truth an impersonation in his own territory of loyalty to his chief, and of order amidst the wild anarchy then raging, and which threatened to sweep away all before it ; and his attachment for, and friendly good feeling towards, the British Government and its officers when the power of that Government was for a time at its lowest point of depression, can never be forgotten by those who experienced or benefited thereby, or were acquainted therewith.

" With the complete suppression of the mutiny, and amidst the changes in the administration of the Gwalior State which followed, the position of the Minister unavoidably became greatly altered.

" The Maharaja desired to direct the Government

himself, and to retain the business of administration wholly in his own hands; and after a time Raja Dinkur Rao withdrew, not without grief and disappointment, from the laborious post he had filled for eight years with unmeasurable benefit to his chief and the State, and with lasting credit and honour to himself.

"In truth his work for the time was done, and it was but fitting that he should take some repose from the wearing fatigues of the business' and struggles incidental to the high position he had held for so long a period.

"He was not, however, suffered to remain unnoticed; for on the establishment of the Governor-General's Legislative Council in 1861, he was among the first members selected to sit therein as representatives of the native community of the Empire.

"His services and usefulness in the lofty and novel sphere to which he was thus transferred were such as might have been expected from his previous career and character, and are well known to have been much appreciated by the Viceroy of India.

"At the date at which I am writing, the Honourable Raja's term of service in Council having expired, he is unemployed and living in retirement, and there appears to be at present no prospect of his return to the business of public life in a fitting position.

"It is a subject of the deepest regret to me that the services of one so experienced and gifted, by far and in every respect the ablest native administrator I have ever met, should be thus lost to the public; but there seems to be no help therefor at present.

"Whatever the future may have in this respect in

store for the Honourable Raja Dinkur Rao—and that the time will sooner or later come when, if spared, he will reoccupy a public post suited to his great talents and high character I have the fullest confidence—he must for the present console himself with the proud and gratifying conviction that, as remarked by Sir Richmond Shakespeare, he is respected and beloved by the rich and poor of his own country, in which his name will long be known as, *par excellence,* The Dewan, and that he enjoys the high consideration of the British Government, and the esteem and regard of such of its officers as have had the pleasure of knowing him either privately or officially."

All comment on the above quotation is unnecessary; but it should be known by those who take an interest in Indian affairs what rewards the gratitude of England has meted out to this exemplary native statesman; and we think that most who read these pages will admit that these rewards compare somewhat strangely, and not much to the credit of our discernment, with the imperial extravagance of, for instance, the Mysore grant, by which a yearly income of £40,000 was secured in perpetuity to the already wealthy sons and grandchildren of a low-born usurper and oppressor of a peaceful people.

The magnanimity of the Company towards the Maharaja Dhuleep Singh does not rank, in our opinion, as a case in point, for he was the representative of Runjeet Singh, the Lion of the Punjab, who gathered together by his force of character ten millions of the scattered tribes once ruled by Tamerlane; and it should be remembered that nearest to the heart of every Hindostanee proper is the appreciation of hereditary honours, and the continuance of an historic name. Now Dinkur Rao was illustrious by descent; and when it is considered that, with the exception of some unimportant complimentary prefix, the only rank conferred upon him was that of Honourable, as a member of the Viceroy's Council, and that the only solid token of our goodwill he has received is a small confiscated estate in the neighbourhood, not of his home in Gwalior, but of Benares in Bengal, worth £500 per annum, on which, as a crowning proof of our generosity, some trifling taxes are remitted, one cannot help contrasting his services and their reward with those of white men, military and civilian, on whom pensions and estates have been showered in such profusion.

Raja Dinkur Rao was, as has been said, a Hindoo Mahratta of the very highest caste, and it may be therefore argued, a representative man of but one portion of our Indian dominions. Yet that the feelings entertained by him find utterance in other mouths, and prey on other minds of a widely different type, may, we think, be fairly gathered from a final extract, penned by perhaps the ablest Mahomedan of Bengal. Between him, a liberal-minded, self-made man, and the aristocratic and conservative Dinkur Rao, there can exist no bond of sympathy in politics or religion, save the one ambitiou, to promote good government and the welfare of the subject. On December 18, 1865, this Mussulman, writing to one of whose goodwill he felt assured, expressed himself in the following not very hopeful language, of which we must fain confess the fact of Dinkur Rao's career tends somewhat sadly to illustrate the truth:—

" You at least are aware of the humble and precarious tenure on which natives, even the greatest among us, hold our offices. Literally and in fact a breath can unmake us, even as a breath has made. No talents, no integrity, no claims founded on length of service, can avail a day against the active displeasure of our covenanted white superiors. In these cases, and in such a Government as India, justice in a great measure depends upon individuals in power at the time. It is useless to blink at the truth, and I believe it is notorious that in a great many Anglo-Indian minds there lies an undercurrent of hatred towards the natives; but as unfortunately the natives have not one head for convenient decapitation, this feeling finds too often vent against those unhappy natives whom circumstances bring into prominence, and it may be conflict, with the pride of Englishmen. God knows there are many and even numerous exceptions; but the danger is not small to those children of the soil who may act as if the exceptions were the rule."

Now those who would form impressions for themselves on things regarding India, may compare the extracts just quoted, coming as they do unprepared for the public eye fresh from the pen of loyal natives versed in the genius of our rule, whose title to sit in the Councils of their country we have at length approved, with the promises held forth in the gracious Proclamation whereby Her Majesty the Queen assumed

the sovereignty of Hindostan. This document is one
that cannot be too often read by, or too deeply graven
on the hearts of, Anglo-Indian statesmen. It forms the
Magna Charta of 180,000,000 souls belonging to mixed
creeds, and may be studied with advantage by all who
search for landmarks in contemporary history; but it
should not be forgotten that it is a far cry from the
banks of the Ganges to those of the Thames, and
that although the distance is great, even in the case
of wealthy appellants to the Privy Council, it is infinitely more felt by the impoverished, uneducated, and
scantily-fed ryots who constitute nineteen-twentieths of
an Eastern population.

This Proclamation was published by Lord Canning at
Allahabad on 1st November 1858, and was addressed
directly from the Queen to the Princes, Chiefs, and
people of India. Its preamble is devoted to announc-
ing that Her Majesty has, with the advice and consent
of Parliament, taken upon herself the governance of
the territories hitherto vested in the East India Com
pany, and it then proceeds in the following terms:—

" We hereby announce to the native Princes of India,
that all treaties and engagements made with them, by
or under the authority of the Honourable East India
Company, are by us accepted, and will be scrupulously
maintained, and we look for the like observance on
their part. We desire no extension of our present
territorial possessions; and while we will permit no
aggression upon our dominions or our rights to be attempted with impunity, we shall sanction no encroach-
ment on those of others. We shall respect the rights,

dignity, and honour of native princes as our own; and we desire that they, as well as our own subjects, should enjoy that prosperity and social advancement which can only be secured by internal peace and good government. We hold ourselves bound to the natives of our Indian territories by the same obligations of duty which bind us to all our other subjects, and those obligations, by the blessing of God, we shall faithfully and conscientiously fulfil. Firmly relying ourselves on the truth of Christianity, and acknowledging with gratitude the solace of religion, we disclaim alike the right and the desire to impose our convictions on any of our subjects. We declare it to be our royal will and pleasure that none be in any wise favoured, none molested or disquieted by reason of their religious faith or observances, but that all shall alike enjoy the equal and impartial protection of the law; and we do strictly charge and enjoin all those who may be in authority under us, that they abstain from all interference with the religious belief or worship of any of our subjects, on pain of our highest displeasure. And it is our further will that, so far as may be, our subjects, of whatever race or creed, be freely and impartially admitted to offices in our service, the duties of which they may be qualified by their education, ability, and integrity duly to discharge. We know and respect the feelings of attachment with which the natives of India regard the lands inherited by them from their ancestors, and we desire to protect them in all rights connected therewith, subject to the equitable demands of the State; and we will that generally in framing and

administering the law, due regard be paid to the ancient
rights, usages, and customs of India. We deeply lament
the evils and misery which have been brought upon
India by the acts of ambitious men, who have deceived
their countrymen by false reports, and led them into
open rebellion. Our power has been shown by the
suppression of that rebellion in the field; we desire to
show our mercy by pardoning the offences of those
who have been thus misled, but who desire to return
to the path of duty."

The above are truly royal words, admitting of no
cavil or misinterpretation, and they were closely followed by a distinct approval of the clement policy with
which Lord Canning's name will ever be associated, an
approval emanating from the highest terrestrial authority we acknowledge, and from which there happily is
no appeal.

" Our clemency," it was written, " will be extended
to all offenders, save and except those who have been
or shall be convicted of having directly taken part in
the murder of British subjects. With regard to such,
the demands of justice forbid the exercise of mercy.
To those who have willingly given an asylum to murderers, knowing them to be such, their lives alone can
be guaranteed; but in apportioning the penalty due to
such persons, full consideration will be given to any
circumstances under which they have been induced to
throw off their allegiance; and large indulgence will be
shown to those whose crimes may appear to have
originated in too credulous acceptance of the false
reports circulated by designing men. To all others in

arms against the Government we hereby promise unconditional pardon, amnesty and oblivion of all offence against ourselves, our crown, and dignity, on their return to their homes and peaceful pursuits. It is our royal pleasure that these terms of grace and amnesty should be extended to all those who comply with these conditions before the first day of January next. When, by the blessing of Providence, internal tranquillity shall be restored, it is our earnest desire to stimulate the peaceful industry of India, to promote works of public utility and improvement, and to administer its government for the benefit of all our subjects therein. In their prosperity will be our strength, in their contentment our security, and in their gratitude our best reward. And may the God of all power grant to us, and to those in authority under us, strength to carry out these our wishes for the good of our people."

THE END.

PRINTED BY WILLIAM BLACKWOOD AND SONS, EDINBURGH.

———◆———

RALPH DARNELL.

By CAPTAIN MEADOWS TAYLOR, M.R.I.A., Author of 'Tara : a Mahratta Tale,' &c. Three Volumes, post octavo, price £1, 11s. 6d.

"Viewed simply as a contribution to popularised Indian history, we could hardly give it greater commendation than when we say, that its author brings to bear on it the experience of a soldier, the eyes of a patriot, and the hand of an able novelist. None but a writer possessed of all three of these qualifications could have penned the graphic delineations, both of events and of character, which abound, especially through the third volume."—*Athenæum.*

"A very interesting story."—*Pall Mall Gazette.*

"No one acquainted with native life, however hostile to natives, will, we believe, read that sweet sketch (Noor-ool-Nissa) unmoved, or without an inner feeling that the highest life of India, and of Mohammedanism, is there expressed."—*Spectator.*

THE ILIAD OF HOMER.

TRANSLATED INTO ENGLISH VERSE IN THE SPENSERIAN STANZA. By PHILIP STANHOPE WORSLEY, M.A., Fellow of Corpus Christi College, Oxford. Books I.-XII. Post octavo, price 10s. 6d. uniform with the Odyssey, in 2 vols., price 18s.

"No version published in the present century seems at all comparable to his ; and those who feel, as we feel ourselves, that it is an advantage to have great classical works retranslated from time to time in the best manner of particular periods of literature, will read him, as we have read him, with great and real delight."—*Athenæum.*

THE HANDY HORSE-BOOK;

OR, PRACTICAL INSTRUCTIONS IN RIDING, DRIVING, AND THE GENERAL CARE AND MANAGEMENT OF HORSES. By a CAVALRY OFFICER. Second Edition, price 3s. 6d.

"Most certainly the above title is no misnomer, for the 'Handy Horse-book' is a manual of driving, riding, and the general care and management of horses, evidently the work of no un-skilled hand."—*Bell's Life.*

"To find such a book as that whose title I have placed at the head of this paper is really a boon. It is the work of a man who knows his subject and likes it. He tells us, in his few words of preface, that it was from the frequent occasion he was called upon to answer questions and give advice to his friends on horse matters he was induced to commit himself to print. It is not often that the insistance of a man's acquaintance results so profitably for the public. In the present case, we have every reason to be thankful for the persecution. It is all that such a book should be—brief, intelligible, replete with sound sense, and a thorough understanding of what it treats."—*Blackwood's Magazine.*

ETONIANA, ANCIENT AND MODERN·

Being Notes of the HISTORY AND TRADITIONS OF ETON COLLEGE. In fcap. octavo, price 5s.

"The volume before us is just the kind of book to make outsiders acquainted with the living spirit of a great English school as it used to be, and, in fact, as it must always continue to be. It is not a disquisition on Eton education, nor is it a reproduction of the Report of the late Public Schools Commission. It is a collection of illustrations of the history, and what we may call the life, of the school, as distinct from its formal teaching by means of books and lessons." —*Pall Mall Gazette.*

"A most learned and withal readable account of the early records of the school, a full history of the Montem, and a host of anecdotes of bygone Etonians, besides a very reliable notice of its present condition."—*John Bull.*

FAUST : A DRAMATIC POEM.

By GOETHE. Translated into English Verse by THEODORE MARTIN.
In post octavo, price 6s.

"In sound and in sense he has produced a singularly faithful representation of the only considerable German poem since the medieval 'Lay of the Nibelungen.' A good translator must satisfy the double test of comparison with the original, and of the criticism of the unlearned or indigenous reader. Mr Martin's 'Faust' would survive as an interesting and spirited poem if Goethe and his language were, by some unfortunate catastrophe, to disappear."—*Saturday Review.*

"The best translation of 'Faust' in verse we have yet had in England."—*Spectator.*

CORNELIUS O'DOWD UPON MEN AND WOMEN,

AND OTHER THINGS IN GENERAL. Originally published in 'Blackwood's Magazine.' Three vols. crown octavo, price 31s. 6d.

"The flashes of the author's wit must not blind us to the ripeness of his wisdom, nor the general playfulness of his O'Dowderies allow us to forget the ample evidence that underneath them lurks one of the most earnest and observant spirits of the present time."—*Daily Review.*

"In truth one of the most delightful volumes of personal reminiscence it has ever been our fortune to peruse."—*Globe.*

THE DISCOVERY OF THE SOURCE OF THE NILE: A JOURNAL.

By JOHN HANNING SPEKE, Captain H.M. Indian Army. With a Map of Eastern Equatorial Africa by Captain SPEKE; Numerous Illustrations, chiefly from Drawings by Captain GRANT; and Portraits, Engraved on Steel, of Captains SPEKE and GRANT. Octavo, price 21s.

The volume which Captain Speke has presented to the world possesses more than a geographical interest. It is a monument of perseverance, courage, and temper, displayed under difficulties which have perhaps never been equalled."—*Times.*

WHAT LED TO THE DISCOVERY OF THE SOURCE OF THE NILE.

By JOHN HANNING SPEKE, Captain H.M. Indian Army. Octavo, with Maps, &c., price 14s.

"Will be read with peculiar interest, as it makes the record of his travels complete, and, at the same time, heightens, if possible, our admiration of his indomitable perseverance as well as tact."—*Dispatch.*

A WALK ACROSS AFRICA;

Or, DOMESTIC SCENES FROM MY NILE JOURNAL. By JAMES AUGUSTUS GRANT, Captain H.M. Bengal Army, Fellow and Gold-Medallist of the Royal Geographical Society. Octavo, with Map, price 15s.

"Captain Grant's frank, manly, unadorned narrative."—*Daily News.*

"Captain Grant's book will be doubly interesting to those who have read Captain Speke's. He gives, as his special contribution to the story of their three years' walk across Africa, descriptions of birds, beasts, trees, and plants, and all that concerns them, and of domestic scenes throughout the various regions. The book is written in a pleasant, quiet, gentlemanly style, and is characterised by a modest tone. . . . The whole work is delightful reading."—*Globe.*

NARRATIVES OF VOYAGE & ADVENTURE.

By SHERARD OSBORN, C.B., Captain Royal Navy.

CONTENTS.

STRAY LEAVES FROM AN ARCTIC JOURNAL—1850-51.
THE CAREER AND FATE OF SIR JOHN FRANKLIN.
THE DISCOVERY OF A NORTH-WEST PASSAGE by H.M.S. Investigator.
QUEDAH; or, Stray Leaves from a Journal in Malayan Waters.
A CRUISE IN JAPANESE WATERS.
THE FIGHT ON THE PEIHO IN 1859.

In Three Vols., price 17s. 6d.

THE PERPETUAL CURATE.

By the Author of ' Salem Chapel.' Being a New Series of the ' Chronicles of Carlingford.' Three vols. post octavo, price £1, 11s. 6d.

" We can only repeat the expression of our admiration for a work which bears on every page the evidence of close observation and the keenest insight, united to real dramatic feeling and a style of unusual eloquence and power."—*Westminster Review.*
" The ' Perpetual Curate' is nevertheless one of the best pictures of Clerical Life that has ever been drawn, and it is essentially true."—*The Times.*

Illustrated Edition of PROFESSOR AYTOUN'S

LAYS OF THE SCOTTISH CAVALIERS.

The Designs by J. NOEL PATON, R.S.A. Engraved on Wood by JOHN THOMPSON, W. J. LINTON, W. THOMAS, J. W. WHYMPER, J. COOPER, W. T. GREEN, DALZIEL BROTHERS, E. EVANS, J. ADAM, &c. Small quarto, printed on toned paper, bound in gilt cloth, price 21s.

The artists have excelled themselves in the engravings which they have furnished. Seizing the spirit of Mr Aytoun's ' Ballads' as perhaps none but Scotchmen could have seized it, they have thrown their whole strength into the work with a heartiness which others would do well to imitate. Whoever there may be that does not already know these ' Lays,' we recommend at once to make their acquaintance in this edition, wherein author and artist illustrate each other as kindred spirits should."—*Standard.*

CAXTONIANA:

A Series of Essays on LIFE, LITERATURE, and MANNERS. By SIR EDWARD BULWER LYTTON, Bart. Two vols. crown octavo, price 21s.

" It would be very possible to fill many pages with the wise bright things of these volumes."—*Eclectic.*
" Gems of thought, set upon some of the most important subjects that can engage the attention of men."—*Daily News.*

THE CAIRNGORM MOUNTAINS.

By JOHN HILL BURTON. In crown octavo, price 3s. 6d.

" One of the most complete as well as most lively and intelligent bits of reading that the lover of works of travel has seen for many a day."—*Saturday Review.*

ESSAYS ON SOCIAL SUBJECTS.

From the ' Saturday Review.' First and Second Series, crown octavo, 7s. 6d. each.

CONTRIBUTIONS TO NATURAL HISTORY,

CHIEFLY IN RELATION TO THE FOOD OF THE PEOPLE. By a RURAL D.D.
Crown octavo, price 6s.

" What with mussels, oysters, herring, salmon, and the many other fish which can be raised by human care, it seems as if a boundless food-producing province was added to the world ; and the 'Rural D.D.' has certainly done good service in helping to spread information about it amongst his countrymen."—*Saturday Review.*

" The volume contains several able and instructive papers on the abundance of food which is contained in our rivers and seas, and the best means of making it available for our under-fed population."—*Morning Post.*

ADVANCED TEXT-BOOK OF PHYSICAL GEOGRAPHY.

By DAVID PAGE, F.R.S.E. F.G.S., Author of 'Introductory and Advanced Text-Books of Geology,' &c. Crown octavo, with a Glossary of Terms and numerous Illustrations, price 5s.

Mr Page's volume is aptly entitled, and meets the wants of earnest and systematic students."
—*Athenæum.*

" A thoroughly good text-book of Physical Geography."—*Saturday Review.*

THE SCOT ABROAD,

AND THE ANCIENT LEAGUE WITH FRANCE. By JOHN HILL BURTON, Author of the 'Book-Hunter,' &c. Two volumes, crown octavo, in Roxburghe binding, price 15s.

Mr Burton's lively and interesting 'Scot Abroad,' not the least valuable of his contributions to the historical literature of his country."—*Quarterly Review.*

" An excellent book, that will interest Englishmen and fascinate Scotchmen."—*Times.*

" No amount of selections, detached at random, can give an adequate idea of the varied and copious results of reading which are stored up in the compact and pithy pages of 'The Scot Abroad.' "—*Saturday Review.*

" A charming book."—*Spectator.*

THE GREAT GOVERNING FAMILIES OF ENGLAND.

By J. LANGTON SANFORD and MEREDITH TOWNSEND. Two Volumes, octavo, price £1, 8s. in extra binding, with richly gilt cover.

" In the 'Great Governing Families of England' we have a really meritorious compilation. The spirit in which it is conceived, the care expended on the collection and arrangement of the material out of which the various memoirs are fashioned, and the vigorous and sometimes picturesque statement which relieves the drier narrative portions, place it high above the ordinary range of biographical reference books."—*Fortnightly Review.*

" We have here a work which may be considered the foundation of a *Libro d'Oro* for England. Its contents originally appeared in the form of a series of detached papers contributed to the columns of the 'Spectator.' The authors have, however, conferred a signal boon on the public by the issue of their work in this durable form. It is an exceedingly interesting and useful work."—*John Bull.*

BIOGRAPHICAL SKETCHES OF EMINENT

SOLDIERS OF THE LAST FOUR CENTURIES. By the late MAJOR-GENERAL JOHN MITCHELL, Author of 'Life of Wallenstein,' the 'Fall of Napoleon,' &c. Edited, with a Memoir of the Author, by LEONHARD SCHMITZ, LL.D. In post octavo, price 9s.

LIST OF BOOKS

PUBLISHED BY

WILLIAM BLACKWOOD & SONS

EDINBURGH AND LONDON.

THE

HISTORY OF EUROPE,

FROM THE COMMENCEMENT OF THE FRENCH REVOLUTION IN 1789 TO THE BATTLE OF WATERLOO.

By Sir ARCHIBALD ALISON, Bart., D.C.L.

A New Library Edition (being the tenth). In 14 Vols. Demy Octavo, with Portraits, and a copious Index, £10, 10s.

In this Edition, which has been revised and corrected with the utmost diligence, care has been taken to interweave with the original text the new facts which have been brought to light since the last edition was published. It is believed that the Work will be found in all respects brought up to the latest authentic information that has appeared, on the epoch of which it treats.

Crown Octavo Edition, 20 vols., £6. People's Edition, 12 vols., closely printed in double columns, £2, 8s., and Index Volume, 3s.

EXTRACTS FROM REVIEWS OF THIS WORK.

Times, Sept. 7, 1850.

" An extraordinary work, which has earned for itself a lasting place in the literature of the country, and within a few years found innumerable readers in every part of the globe. There is no book extant that treats so well of the period to the illustration of which Mr Alison's labours have been devoted. It exhibits great knowledge, patient research, indefatigable industry, and vast power."

Edinburgh Review.

" There is much in Mr Alison's history of the French Revolution against which we intend to record our decided protest; and there are some parts of it which we shall feel compelled to notice with strong disapprobation. We, therefore, hasten to preface our less favourable remarks by freely acknowledging that the present work is, upon the whole, a valuable addition to European literature, that it is evidently compiled with the utmost care, and that its narration, so far as we can judge, is not perverted by the slightest partiality."

From Preface of the German Translation by D. Ludwig Meyer.

" Alison's *History of Europe*, and the states connected with it, is one of the most important works which literature has produced. Years have elapsed since any historical work has created such an epoch as that of Alison: his sources of information and authorities are of the richest and most comprehensive description. Though his opinions are on the Conservative side, he allows every party to speak for itself, and unfolds with a master's hand how far institutions make nations great, and mighty, and prosperous."

Continuation of the History of Europe, from the Fall of

Napoleon to the Accession of Louis Napoleon. By Sir ARCHIBALD ALISON, Bart., D.C.L. In Nine Vols., £6, 7s. 6d. Uniform with the Library Edition of the Author's "History of Europe, from the Commencement of the French Revolution." People's Edition, Eight Vols. Crown Octavo, 34s. ·

Epitome of Alison's History of Europe. Fourteenth

Edition, 7s. 6d., bound.

Atlas to Alison's History of Europe ; containing 109

Maps and Plans of Countries, Battles, Sieges, and Sea-Fights. Constructed by A. KEITH JOHNSTON, F.R.S.E. With Vocabulary of Military and Marine Terms. Library Edition, £3, 3s. ; People's Edition, £1, 11s. 6d.

Lives of Lord Castlereagh and Sir Charles Stewart,

Second and Third Marquesses of Londonderry. By Sir ARCHIBALD ALISON, Bart., D.C.L. From the Original Papers of the Family, and other sources. In Three Vols. Octavo. £2, 5s.

Life of John Duke of Marlborough. With some Account

of his Contemporaries, and of the War of the Succession. By Sir ARCHIBALD ALISON, Bart., D.C.L. Third Edition, Two Volumes, Octavo, Portraits and Maps, 30s.

Essays ; Historical, Political, and Miscellaneous. By

Sir ARCHIBALD ALISON, Bart. Three Vols. Demy Octavo, 45s.

The Invasion of the Crimea : its Origin, and an Account

OF ITS PROGRESS DOWN TO THE DEATH OF LORD RAGLAN. By ALEXANDER WILLIAM KINGLAKE, M.P. Vols. I. and II., bringing the EVENTS down to the CLOSE of the BATTLE of the ALMA. Price 32s. To be completed in Four Volumes Octavo. Fourth Edition.

The Boscobel Tracts ; Relating to the Escape of Charles

the Second after the Battle of Worcester, and his subsequent Adventures. Edited by J. HUGHES, Esq., A.M. A New Edition, with additional Notes and Illustrations, including Communications from the Rev. R. H. BARHAM, Author of the "Ingoldsby Legends." In Octavo, with Engravings, 16s.

" ' The Boscobel Tracts ' is a very curious book, and about as good an example of single sub-ject historical collections as may be found. Originally undertaken, or at least completed at the suggestion of the late Bishop Copplestone, in 1827, it was carried out with a degree of judgment and taste not always found in works of a similar character. The subject, as the title implies, is the escape of Charles the Second after the battle of Worcester."—*Spectator.*

History of Scotland from the Revolution to the Extinction

of the last Jacobite Insurrection, 1689—1748. By JOHN HILL BURTON, Esq., Advocate. Two Vols. Octavo, 15s.

The Autobiography of the Rev. Dr Alexander Carlyle,

Minister of Inveresk. Containing Memorials of the Men and Events of his Time. Edited by JOHN HILL BURTON. In Octavo. Third Edition, with Portrait, 14s.

" This book contains by far the most vivid picture of Scottish life and manners that has been given to the public since the days of Sir Walter Scott. In bestowing upon it this high praise, we make no exception, not even in favour of Lord Cockburn's *Memorials*—the book which resembles it most, and which ranks next to it in interest."—*Edinburgh Review.*

" A more delightful and graphic picture of the everyday life of our ancestors it has never been our good fortune to meet with. . . . . We do not often pray for autobiographies—for, as a class of literature, they are of very unequal merit—but we shall heartily rejoice to see as many more autobiographies as possible if they are half as well worth reading as *Jupiter* Carlyle's."—*National Review.*

" A more racy vòlume of memoirs was never given to the world—nor one more difficult to set forth—save by the true assertion, that there is scarcely a page which does not contain matter for extract or which would not bear annotation."—*Athenæum.*

Life of the late Rev. James Robertson, D.D., F.R.S.E.,

Professor of Divinity and Ecclesiastical History in the University of Edinburgh. By the Rev. A. H. CHARTERIS, M.A. With a Portrait. Octavo, price 10s. 6d.

Memoir of the Political Life of the Right Honourable

EDMUND BURKE, with Extracts from his Writings. By the Rev. GEORGE CROLY, D.D., Rector of St Stephen's, Walbrook, London. 2 vols. Post Octavo, 18s.

History of Greece under Foreign Domination. By George

FINLAY, LL.D., Athens. Seven Volumes, Octavo—viz. :

Greece under the Romans. B.C. 146 to A.D. 717. A Historical

View of the Condition of the Greek Nation from its Conquest by the Romans until the Extinction of the Roman Power in the East. Second Edition, 16s.

History of the Byzantine Empire. A.D. 716 to 1204; and of

the Greek Empire of Nicæa and Constantinople, A.D. 1204 to 1453. Two Volumes, £1, 7s. 6d.

Mediæval Greece and Trebizond. The History of Greece, from

its Conquest by the Crusaders to its Conquest by the Turks, A.D. 1204 to 1566; and the History of the Empire of Trebizond, A.D. 1204 to 1461. 12s.

Greece under Othoman and Venetian Domination. A.D. 1453

to 1821. 10s. 6d.

History of the Greek Revolution.

Two Volumes, Octavo, £1, 4s.

" His book is worthy to take its place among the remarkable works on Greek history which form one of the chief glories of English scholarship. The history of Greece is but half told without it."—*London Guardian.*

" His work is therefore learned and profound. It throws a flood of light upon an important though obscure portion of Grecian history. . . . In the essential requisites of fidelity, accuracy, and learning, Mr Finlay bears a favourable comparison with any historical writer of our day."—*North American Review.*

Essays in History and Art. By R. H. Patterson.

COLOUR IN NATURE AND ART.	BATTLE OF THE STYLES.
REAL AND IDEAL BEAUTY.	GENIUS AND LIBERTY.
SCULPTURE.	YOUTH AND SUMMER.
ETHNOLOGY OF EUROPE.	RECORDS OF THE PAST; NINEVEH AND
UTOPIAS.	BABYLON.
OUR INDIAN EMPIRE.	INDIA : ITS CASTES AND CREEDS.
THE NATIONAL LIFE OF CHINA.	"CHRISTOPHER NORTH"—IN MEMORIAM.
AN IDEAL ART CONGRESS.	

In One Volume, Octavo. 12s.

The New "Examen ;" or, An Inquiry into the Evidence
of certain Passages in "Macaulay's History of England" concerning

THE DUKE OF MARLBOROUGH.	VISCOUNT DUNDEE.
THE MASSACRE OF GLENCOE.	WILLIAM PENN.
THE HIGHLANDS OF SCOTLAND.	

By JOHN PAGET, Esq., Barrister-at-Law.   In Crown Octavo, 6s.

Curran and his Contemporaries. By Charles Phillips,
Esq., A.B.   A New Edition.   Crown Octavo, 7s. 6d.

"Certainly one of the most extraordinary pieces of biography ever produced.   .   .   .   No library should be without it."—*Lord Brougham.*

"Never, perhaps, was there a more curious collection of portraits crowded before into the same canvass."—*Times.*

Paris after Waterloo.   A Revised Edition of a "Visit to
Flanders and the Field of Waterloo."   By JAMES SIMPSON, Advocate.   With Two Coloured Plans of the Battle.   Crown Octavo, 5s.

Lives of the Queens of Scotland, and English Princesses
connected with the Regal Succession of Great Britain.   By AGNES STRICKLAND. With Portraits and Historical Vignettes.   Post Octavo, £4, 4s.

"Every step in Scotland is historical ; the shades of the dead arise on every side ; the very rocks breathe.   Miss Strickland's talents as a writer, and turn of mind as an individual, in a peculiar manner fit her for painting a historical gallery of the most illustrious or dignified female characters in that land of chivalry and song."—*Blackwood's Magazine.*

Life of Mary Queen of Scots.   By Agnes Strickland.
5 vols. post 8vo, with Portraits and other Illustrations, £2, 12s. 6d.

Studies in Roman Law.   With Comparative Views of the
Laws of France, England, and Scotland.   By LORD MACKENZIE, one of the Judges of the Court of Session in Scotland.   Second Edition, Octavo, 12s.

Letters of Eminent Persons, addressed to David Hume.
Edited by JOHN HILL BURTON, Esq., Advocate.   Octavo, 5s.

Lectures on the History of the Church of Scotland, from
the Reformation to the Revolution Settlement.   By the Very Rev. JOHN LEE, D.D., LL.D., Principal of the University of Edinburgh.   Edited by the Rev. WILLIAM LEE.   Two Vols. Octavo, 21s.

Works of the Rev. Thomas M'Crie, D.D.
A New and Uniform Edition.   Edited by Professor M'CRIE.   Four Volumes, Crown Octavo, 24s.   Sold separately, — viz. :

Life of John Knox.   Containing Illustrations of the History of the Reformation in Scotland.   Crown Octavo, 6s.

Life of Andrew Melville.   Containing Illustrations of the Ecclesiastical and Literary History of Scotland in the Sixteenth and Seventeenth Centuries.   Crown Octavo, 6s.

History of the Progress and Suppression of the Reformation in Italy in the Sixteenth Century.   Crown Octavo, 4s.

History of the Progress and Suppression of the Reformation in Spain in the Sixteenth Century.   Crown Octavo, 3s. 6d.

Sermons, and Review of the "Tales of my Landlord." In One Volume, Crown Octavo, 6s.

The Monks of the West, from St Benedict to St Bernard.
By the COUNT DE MONTALEMBERT.   *Authorised Translation.*   Two Volumes, Octavo, 21s.

"We must, however, say a word of praise for the anonymous translator, who has done his work throughout in a very creditable manner."—*Spectator.*

"If this version had reached us earlier it might have saved us some trouble, as, on a comparison of our own extracts with the corresponding passages, we have found it to be, in general, both faithful and spirited, so that we should have been glad for the most part to make use of the translator's words instead of doing the work for ourselves."—*Quarterly Review.*

The Conquest of Scinde.   A Commentary.   By General Sir
JAMES OUTRAM, C.B.   Octavo, 18s.

An Essay on the National Character of the Athenians.
By JOHN BROWN PATTERSON.   Edited from the Author's revision, by Professor FILLANS, of the University of Edinburgh.   With a Sketch of his Life.   Crown Octavo, 4s. 6d.

The New Revolution ; or, the Napoleonic Policy in Europe.
By R. H. PATTERSON.   Octavo, 4s.

Ten Years of Imperialism in France. Impressions of
a " Flâneur." In Octavo, price 9s.

"There has not been published for many a day a more remarkable book on France than this, which professes to be the impressions of a Flâneur. . . . It has all the liveliness and sparkle of a work written only for amusement ; it has all the solidity and weight of a State paper ; and we expect for it not a little political influence as a fair, full, and masterly statement of the Imperial policy—the first and only good account that has been given to Europe of the Napoleonic system now in force."—*Times*.

Memorials of the Castle of Edinburgh. By James Grant,
Esq. A New Edition: In Crown Octavo, with 12 Engravings, 3s. 6d.

Memoirs and Adventures of Sir William Kirkaldy of
Grange, Governor of the Castle of Edinburgh for Mary Queen of Scots. By JAMES GRANT, Esq. Post Octavo, 10s. 6d.

It is seldom, indeed, that we find history so written, in a style at once vigorous, perspicuous, and picturesque. The author's heart is thoroughly with his subject."—*Blackwood's Magazine*.

Memoirs and Adventures of Sir John Hepburn, Marshal of
France under Louis XIII., &c. By JAMES GRANT, Esq. Post Octavo, 8s.

Annals of the Peninsular Campaigns. By Capt. Thomas
HAMILTON. A New Edition. Edited by F. HARDMAN, Esq. Octavo, 16s. ; and Atlas of Maps to illustrate the Campaigns, 12s.

The Story of the Campaign of Sebastopol. Written in
the Camp. By Lieut.-Col. E. BRUCE HAMLEY. With Illustrations drawn in Camp by the Author. Octavo, 21s.

" We strongly recommend this 'Story of the Campaign' to all who would gain a just comprehension of this tremendous struggle. Of this we are perfectly sure, it is a book unlikely to be ever superseded. Its truth is of that simple and startling character which is sure of an immortal existence ; nor is it paying the gallant author too high a compliment to class this masterpiece of military history with the most precious of those classic records which have been bequeathed to us by the great writers of antiquity who took part in the wars they have described."—*The Press*.

Wellington's Career ; a Military and Political Summary.
By Lieut.-Col. E. BRUCE HAMLEY, Professor of Military History and Art at the Staff College. Crown Octavo, 2s.

Fleets and Navies. By Captain Charles Hamley, R.M.
Originally published in *Blackwood's Magazine*. Crown Octavo, 6s.

Memoir of Mrs Hemans. By her Sister. With a Portrait.
Foolscap Octavo, 5s.

Leaders of the Reformation : Luther, Calvin, Latimer,

and KNOX. By the Rev. JOHN TULLOCH, D.D., Principal, and Primarius Professor of Theology, St Mary's College, St Andrews. Second Edition, Crown Octavo, 6s. 6d.

We are not acquainted with any work in which so much solid information upon the leading aspects of the great Reformation is presented in so well-packed and pleasing a form."-*Witness.*

"The style is admirable in force and in pathos, and the book one to be altogether recommended, both for the merits of those of whom it treats, and for that which the writer unconsciously reveals of his own character."—*Globe.*

English Puritanism and its Leaders: Cromwell, Milton,

BAXTER, and BUNYAN. By the Rev. JOHN TULLOCH, D.D. Uniform with the "Leaders of the Reformation." 7s. 6d.

"His biographic delineations are not collections of vague generalities, but well-selected features combining to a likeness And, while always self-possessed and calm, he is never cold. A steady glow of imaginative fire and radiance follows his pen, and it is evident that he has legitimately acquired the right to interest and move others, by having first been moved himself."-*Dial.*

"It is a book which, from its style—firm and interesting, dispassionate and impartial, but yet warm with admiration—will be hailed for fireside reading in the families of the descendants of those Puritan men and their times."—*Eclectic Review.*

History of the French Protestant Refugees. By Charles

WEISS, Professor of History at the Lycée Buonaparté. Translated by F. HARDMAN, Esq. Octavo, 14s.

The Eighteen Christian Centuries. By the Rev. James

WHITE. Fourth Edition, with Analytical Table of Contents, and a Copious Index. Post Octavo, 7s. 6d.

"He goes to work upon the only true principle, and produces a picture that at once satisfies truth, arrests the memory, and fills the imagination. When they (Index and Analytical Contents) are supplied, it will be difficult to lay hands on any book of the kind more useful and more entertaining."—*Times,* Review of first edition.

"Mr White comes to the assistance of those who would know something of the history of the Eighteen Christian Centuries ; and those who want to know still more than he gives them, will find that he has perfected a plan which catches the attention, and fixes the distinctive feature of each century in the memory."—*Wesleyan Times.*

History of France, from the Earliest Period to the Year

1848. By the Rev. JAMES WHITE, Author of the "Eighteen Christian Centuries." Second Edition. Post Octavo, 9s.

"Mr White's ' History of France,' in a single volume of some 600 pages, contains every leading incident worth the telling, and abounds in word-painting whereof a paragraph has often as much active life in it as one of those inch-square etchings of the great Callot, in which may be clearly seen the whole armies contending in bloody arbitrament, and as many incidents of battle as may be gazed at in the miles of canvass in the military picture-galleries at Versailles."—*Athenæum.*

"An excellent and comprehensive compendium of French history, quite above the standard of a school-book, and particularly well adapted for the libraries of literary institutions."—*National Review.*

Lays of the Scottish Cavaliers, and other Poems. By

W. EDMONDSTOUNE AYTOUN, D.C.L , Professor of Rhetoric and Belles-Lettres in the University of Edinburgh. Fourteenth Edition, Foolscap Octavo, 7s. 6d.

" Mr Aytoun's 'Lays' are truly beautiful, and are perfect poems of their class, pregnant with fire, with patriotic ardour, with loyal zeal, with exquisite pathos, with noble passion. Who can hear the opening lines descriptive of Edinburgh after the great battle of Flodden, and not feel that the minstrel's soul has caught the genuine inspiration?"—*Morning Post.*
" Professor Aytoun's ' Lays of the Scottish Cavaliers '—a volume of verse which shows that Scotland has yet a poet. Full of the true fire, it now stirs and swells like a trumpet-note—now sinks in cadences sad and wild as the wail of a Highland dirge."—*Quarterly Review.*

Aytoun's Lays of the Scottish Cavaliers. An Illustrated

Edition. From Designs by J. NOEL PATON and W. H. PATON, A.R.S.A. En-graved by John Thompson, W. J. Linton, W. Thomas, Whymper, Cooper, Green, Dalziels, Evans, &c. In Small Quarto, printed on Toned Paper, bound in gilt cloth, 21s.

" The artists have excelled themselves in the engravings which they have furnished. Seizing the spirit of Mr Aytoun's ' Ballads ' as perhaps none but Scotchmen could have seized it, they have thrown their whole strength into the work with a heartiness which others would do well to imitate Whoever there may be that does not already know these ' Lays ' we recommend at once to make their acquaintance in this edition, wherein author and artist illustrate each other as kindred spirits should."—*Standard.*

Bothwell: A Poem. By W. Edmondstoune Aytoun, D.C.L.,

Professor of Rhetoric and Belles-Lettres in the University of Edinburgh. Third Edition. Foolscap Octavo, 7s. 6d.

" A noble poem, healthy in tone and purely English in language, and closely linked to the historical traditions of his native country."—*John Bull.*
" Professor Aytoun has produced a fine poem and an able argument, and ' Bothwell ' will assuredly take its stand among the classics of Scottish literature."—*The Press.*

The Ballads of Scotland. Edited by Professor Aytoun.

Second Edition. Two Volumes, Foolscap Octavo, 12s.

" No country can boast of a richer collection of Ballads than Scotland, and no Editor for these Ballads could be found more accomplished than Professor Aytoun. He has sent forth two beautiful volumes which range with Percy's 'Reliques'—which, for completeness and accuracy, leave little to be desired—which must henceforth be considered as the standard edition of the Scottish Ballads, and which we commend as a model to any among ourselves who may think of doing like service to the English Ballads."—*The Times.*

Poems and Ballads of Goethe. Translated by Professor

AYTOUN and THEODORE MARTIN. Second Edition, Foolscap Octavo, 6s.

" There is no doubt that these are the best translations of Goethe's marvellously-cut gems which have yet been published."—*The Times.*

The Book of Ballads. Edited by Bon Gaultier. Eighth

Edition, with numerous Illustrations, by DOYLE, LEECH, and CROWQUILL. Gilt Edges, Post Octavo, 8s. 6d.

Firmilian, or the Student of Badajoz. A Spasmodic

Tragedy. By T. PERCY JONES. In Small Octavo, 5s.

" Humour of a kind most rare at all times, and especially in the pesent day, runs through every page, and passages of true poetry and delicious versification prevent the continual play of sarcasm from becoming tedious "—*Literary Gazette.*

Poetical Works of Thomas Aird. Complete Edition, in
One Volume, Foolscap Octavo, 6s.

"Mr Aird is a poet of a very high class, and in that class he occupies no mean or middling place. His imagination is lofty, his invention fertile, his sentiments heroic, and his language generally clear and forcible."—*Scotsman.*

Poems. By the Lady Flora Hastings. Edited by her
SISTER. Second Edition, with a Portrait. Foolscap, 7s. 6d.

The Poems of Felicia Hemans. Complete in one Volume,
Royal Octavo, with Portrait by Finden, Cheap Edition, 12s. 6d. *Another Edition,* with MEMOIR by her SISTER, Seven Volumes, Foolscap, 35s. *Another Edition,* in Six Volumes, cloth, gilt edges, 24s.

"Of no modern writer can it be affirmed with less hesitation, that she has become an English classic; nor, until human nature becomes very different from what it now is, can we imagine the least probability that the music of her lays will cease to soothe the ear, or the beauty of her sentiment to charm the gentle heart.—*Blackwood's Magazine.*

The following Works of Mrs HEMANS are sold separately, bound in cloth, gilt edges, 4s. each:—

RECORDS OF WOMAN.	DRAMATIC WORKS.
FOREST SANCTUARY.	TALES AND HISTORIC SCENES.
SONGS OF THE AFFECTIONS.	MORAL AND RELIGIOUS POEMS.

The Odyssey of Homer. Translated into English Verse in
the Spenserian Stanza. By PHILIP STANHOPE WORSLEY, M.A., Scholar of Corpus Christi College. Two Volumes, Crown Octavo, 18s.

Poems and Translations. By P. S. Worsley, M.A.,
Scholar of Corpus Christi College, Oxford. Foolscap Octavo, 5s.

Poetical Works of D. M. Moir (Delta). With Portrait, and
Memoir by THOMAS AIRD. Second Edition. Two Volumes, Foolscap Octavo, 12s.

Translations by Theodore Martin:

Goethe's Faust. Second Edition, Crown Octavo, 6s.

The Odes of Horace. With Life and Notes. Second Edition, Post 8vo, 9s.

Catullus. With Life and Notes. Post 8vo, 6s. 6d.

The Vita Nuova of Dante. With an Introduction and Notes. Square 8vo, 7s. 6d.

Aladdin: A Dramatic Poem. By Adam Oehlenschlaeger. Foolscap Octavo, 5s.

Correggio: A Tragedy. By Oehlenschlaeger. With Notes. Foolscap Octavo, 3s.

King Rene's Daughter: A Danish Lyrical Drama. By HENRIK HERTZ. Second Edition, Foolscap, 2s. 6d.

The Course of Time: A Poem. In Ten Books. By Robert
POLLOK, A.M. Twenty-third Edition, Foolscap Octavo, 5s.

"Of deep and hallowed impress, full of noble thoughts and graphic conceptions—the production of a mind alive to the great relations of being, and the sublime simplicity of our religion."
—*Blackwood's Magazine.*

An Illustrated Edition of the Course of Time. In Large
Octavo, bound in cloth, richly gilt, 21

"There has been no modern poem in the English language, of the class to which the 'Course of Time' belongs, since Milton wrote, that can be compared to it. In the present instance the artistic talents of Messrs FOSTER, CLAYTON, TENNIEL, EVANS, DALZIEL, GREEN, and WOODS, have been employed in giving expression to the sublimity of the language, by equally exquisite illustrations, all of which are of the highest class."—*Bell's Messenger.*

Poems and Ballads of Schiller. Translated by Sir Edward
BULWER LYTTON, Bart. Second Edition, Octavo, 10s. 6d.

"The translations are executed with consummate ability. The technical difficulties attending a task so great and intricate have been mastered or eluded with a power and patience quite extraordinary; and the public is put in possession of perhaps the best translation of a foreign poet which exists in our language. Indeed, we know of none so complete and faithful."—*Morning Chronicle.*

St Stephens; Or, Illustrations of Parliamentary Oratory.
A Poem. *Comprising*—Pym—Vane—Strafford—Halifax—Shaftesbury—St John—Sir R. Walpole—Chesterfield—Carteret—Chatham—Pitt—Fox—Burke—Sheridan—Wilberforce—Wyndham—Conway—Castlereagh—William Lamb (Lord Melbourne)—Tierney—Lord Grey—O'Connell—Plunkett—Shiel—Follett—Macaulay—Peel. Second Edition. Crown Octavo, 5s.

Illustrations of the Lyric Poetry and Music of Scotland.
By WILLIAM STENHOUSE. Originally compiled to accompany the "Scots Musical Museum," and now published separately, with Additional Notes and Illustrations. Octavo, 7s. 6d.

The Birthday, and other Poems. By Mrs Southey. Second
Edition, 5s.

Professor Wilson's Poems. Containing the "Isle of
Palms," the "City of the Plague," "Unimore," and other Poems. Complete Edition, Crown Octavo, 6s.

Poems and Songs. By David Wingate. In Fcap. Octavo.
5s.

"It contains genuine poetic ore, poems which win for their author a place among Scotland's true sons of song, and such as any man in any country might rejoice to have written."-*London Review.*
"We are delighted to welcome into the brotherhood of real poets a countryman of Burns, and whose verse will go far to render the rougher Border Scottish a classic dialect in our literature."
—*John Bull.*

Tales from "Blackwood." Complete in Twelve Volumes,

Bound in cloth, 18s. The Volumes are sold separately, 1s. 6d., and may be had of most Booksellers, in Six Volumes, handsomely half-bound in red morocco.

CONTENTS.

VOL. I. The Glenmutchkin Railway.—Vanderdecken's Message Home.—The Floating Beacon.—Colonna the Painter.—Napoleon.—A Legend of Gibraltar.—The Iron Shroud.

VOL. II. Lazaro's Legacy.—A Story without a Tail.—Faustus and Queen Elizabeth.—How I became a Yeoman.—Devereux Hall.—The Metempsychosis —College Theatricals.

VOL. III. A Reading Party in the Long Vacation.—Father Tom and the Pope.—La Petite Madelaine. — Bob Burke's Duel with Ensign Brady. — The Headsman: A Tale of Doom.—The Wearyful Woman.

VOL. IV. How I stood for the Dreepdaily Burghs.—First and Last.—The Duke's Dilemma : A Chronicle of Niesenstein.—The Old Gentleman's Teetotum.—"Woe to us when we lose the Watery Wall."—My College Friends : Charles Russell, the Gentleman Commoner.—The Magic Lay of the One-Horse Chay.

VOL. V. Adventures in Texas.—How we got possession of the Tuileries.—Captain Paton's Lament.—The Village Doctor.—A Singular Letter from Southern Africa.

VOL. VI. My Friend the Dutchman.—My College Friends—No. II. : Horace Leicester.—The Emerald Studs.—My College Friends—No. III. : Mr W. Wellington Hurst.—Christine : A Dutch Story.—The Man in the Bell.

VOL. VII. My English Acquaintance. — The Murderer's Last Night.—Narration of Certain Uncommon Things that did formerly happen to Me, Herbert Willis, B.D.—The Wags.—The Wet Wooing : A Narrative of '98.—Ben-na-Groich.

VOL. VIII. The Surveyor's Tale. By Professor Aytoun.—The Forrest-Race Romance.—Di Vasari : A Tale of Florence.—Sigismund Fatello.—The Boxes.

VOL. IX. Rosaura : A Tale of Madrid.—Adventure in the North-West Territory.—Harry Bolton's Curacy.—The Florida Pirate.—The Pandour and his Princess.—The Beauty Draught.

VOL. X. Antonio di Carara.—The Fatal Repast.—The Vision of Cagliostro.—The First and Last Kiss.—The Smuggler's Leap.—The Haunted and the Haunters.—The Duellists.

VOL. XI. The Natolian Story-Teller.—The First and Last Crime.—John Rintoul.—Major Moss.—The Premier and his Wife.

VOL. XII. Tickler among the Thieves !—The Bridegroom of Barna.—The Involuntary Experimentalist—Lebrun's Lawsuit.—The Snowing-up of Strath Lugas.—A Few Words on Social Philosophy.

Jessie Cameron : A Highland Story. By the Lady Rachel

BUTLER. Second Edition. Small Octavo, with a Frontispiece, 2s. 6d.

The Old Bachelor in the Old Scottish Village. By Thomas

AIRD. Foolscap Octavo, 4s.

"It is simply a series of village sketches of character, manners, and scenery, but the book is full of a quiet sustained humour, genuine pathos, simple unaffected poetry, and displays not only fine imaginative power, but a hearty sympathy with nature in all her aspects, and with the simple tastes and pleasures of rustic life. A more delightful book we cannot imagine."—*Manchester Advertiser.*

Tara : A Mahratta Tale. By Captain Meadows Taylor.

3 vols., Post Octavo, £1, 11s. 6d.

"A picture of Indian life which it is impossible not to admire. We have no hesitation in saying, that a more perfect knowledge of India is to be acquired from an attentive perusal and study of this work, than could be gleaned from a whole library."—*Press.*

Tom Cringle's Log. A New Edition, with Illustrations
Crown Octavo, 6s.

Cheap Editions of Popular Works

Lights and Shadows of Scottish Life. Foolscap 8vo, 3s. cloth.

The Trials of Margaret Lyndsay. By the Author of "Lights and Shadows of Scottish Life." Foolscap 8vo, 3s. cloth.

The Foresters. By the Author of "Lights and Shadows of Scottish Life." Foolscap 8vo, 3s. cloth.

Tom Cringle's Log. Complete in One Volume, Foolscap 8vo, 4s. cloth.

The Cruise of the Midge. By the Author of "Tom Cringle's Log." In One Volume, Foolscap 8vo, 4s. cloth.

The Life of Mansie Wauch, Tailor in Dalkeith. Foolcap 8vo, 3s. cloth.

The Subaltern. By the Author of "The Chelsea Pensioners." Foolscap 8vo, 3s. cloth.

Peninsular Scenes and Sketches. By the Author of "The Student of Salamanca." Foolscap 8vo, 3s. cloth.

Nights at Mess, Sir Frizzle Pumpkin, and other Tales. Foolscap 8vo, 3s. cloth.

The Youth and Manhood of Cyril Thornton. By the Author of "Men and Manners in America." Foolscap 8vo, 4s. cloth.

Valerius: A Roman Story. Foolscap 8vo, 3s. cloth.

Reginald Dalton. By the Author of "Valerius." Foolscap 8vo, 4s. cloth.

Some Passages in the Life of Adam Blair, and History of Matthew Wald. By the Author of "Valerius." Foolscap 8vo, 4s. cloth.

Annals of the Parish, and Ayrshire Legatees. By John Galt. Foolscap 8vo, 4s. cloth.

Sir Andrew Wylie. By JOHN GALT. Foolscap 8vo, 4s. cloth.

The Provost, and other Tales. By JOHN GALT. Foolscap 8vo, 4s. cloth.

The Entail. By JOHN GALT. Foolscap 8vo, 4s. cloth.

Life in the Far West. By G. F. RUXTON. A New Edition. Foolscap 8vo, 4s. cloth.

Works of George Eliot. Library Edition ·

Adam Bede. Two Vols., Foolscap Octavo, 12s.

The Mill on the Floss. Two Vols., Foolscap Octavo 12s.

Scenes of Clerical Life. Two Vols., Foolscap Octavo 12s.

Silas Marner. Foolscap Octavo, 6s.

The Same. Cheap Edition, each Complete in One Vol.,
price 6s.

Adam Bede.

The Mill on the Floss.

Scenes of Clerical Life, and Silas Marner.

PUBLISHED BY W. BLACKWOOD AND SONS,

Works of Professor Wilson. Edited by his Son-in-Law,
PROFESSOR FERRIER. In Twelve Vols., Crown Octavo, £3, 12s.

Recreations of Christopher North. By Professor Wilson.
In Two Vols. New Edition, with Portrait, 8s.

'Welcome, right welcome, Christopher North; we cordially greet thee in thy new dress, thou genial and hearty old man, whose 'Ambrosian nights' have so often in imagination transported us from solitude to the social circle, and whose vivid pictures of flood and fell, of loch and glen, have carried us in thought from the smoke, din, and pent-up opulence of London, to the rushing stream or tranquil tarn of those mountain ranges," &c.—*Times.*

The Noctes Ambrosianæ. By Professor Wilson. With
NOTES and a GLOSSARY. In Four Vols., Crown Octavo, 16s.

Tales. By Professor Wilson. Comprising "The Lights
and Shadows of Scottish Life;" "The Trials of Margaret Lyndsay;" and "The Foresters." In One Vol., Crown Octavo, 4s., cloth.

Essays, Critical and Imaginative. By Professor Wilson.
Four Vols., Crown Octavo, 24s.

Lady Lee's Widowhood. By Lieut.-Col. E. B. Hamley.
Crown Octavo, with 13 Illustrations by the Author. 6s.

"A quiet humour, an easy, graceful style, a deep, thorough confident knowledge of human nature in its better and more degrading aspects, a delicate and exquisite appreciation of womanly character, an admirable faculty of description, and great tact, are the qualities that command the reader's interest and respect from beginning to end of 'Lady Lee's Widowhood.'"
—*The Times.*

Chronicles of Carlingford ·
Salem Chapel. A New Edition, in one Vol., 5s.

The Rector, and The Doctor's Family. Do., 4s.

The Perpetual Curate. Do., 6s.

"We must pronounce this Carlingford series the best contribution to fiction of recent years lively, pregnant and rich in imagination, feeling, and eloquence. They will irresistibly carry to the end every reader who ventures upon them."—*Spectator.*

The Novels of John Galt—viz. :
Annals of the Parish.

The Steam Boat.

Sir Andrew Wylie.

The Entail, or the Lairds of Grippy.

Four Volumes, Foolscap Octavo, 4s. each.

Complete Library Edition of Sir Edward Bulwer Lytton's

Novels. In Volumes of a convenient and handsome form. Printed from a large and readable type. Forty-one Vols. Foolscap Octavo, 5s. each.

"It is of the handiest of sizes; the paper is good; and the type, which seems to be new, is very clear and beautiful. There are no pictures. The whole charm of the presentment of the volume consists in its handiness, and the tempting clearness and beauty of the type, which almost converts into a pleasure the mere act of following the printer's lines, and leaves the author's mind free to exert its unobstructed force upon the reader."—*Examiner.*

"Nothing could be better as to size, type, paper, and general getting-up."—*Athenæum.*

Caxtoniana : A Series of Essays on Life, Literature, and

Manners. By SIR EDWARD BULWER LYTTON. Two Vols. Post Octavo, £1, 1s.

"Gems of thought set upon some of the most important subjects that can engage the attention of men. Except in one or two instances, they are so short that they will not tax the application of even lazy readers, yet there is not one of them that does not contain a lesson worthy of an abiding place on the handiest shelf of memory."—*Daily News.*

Katie Stewart: A True Story. By Mrs Oliphant. Fcap.

Octavo, with Frontispiece and Vignette, 4s.

"A singularly characteristic Scottish story, most agreeable to read and pleasant to recollect. The charm lies in the faithful and lifelike pictures it presents of Scottish character and customs, and manners and modes of life."—*Tait's Magazine.*

Chapters on Churchyards. By Mrs Southey. Second

Edition, Foolscap Octavo, 7s. 6d.

The Wonder Seeker, or the History of Charles Douglas.

By M. FRASER TYTLER, Author of 'Tales of the Great and Brave,' &c. A New Edition, Foolscap, 3s. 6d.

Works of Samuel Warren, D.C.L. Uniform Edition, Five

Volumes, Crown Octavo, 24s. :

The Diary of a late Physician. One Vol., Crown Octavo, 5s. 6d. *Another Edition*, in Two Vols., Foolscap, 12s. Also an *Illustrated Edition*, in Crown 8vo, handsomely printed, 7s. 6d.

Ten Thousand A-Year. Two Volumes, Crown Octavo, 9s. *Another Edition*, in Three Volumes, Foolscap, 18s.

Now and Then. Crown Octavo, 2s. 6d. *Another Edition*, Foolscap, 6s.

Miscellanies. Crown Octavo, 5s.

The Lily and the Bee. Crown 8vo, 2s. *Another Edition*, Foolscap, 5s.

Journal of the Discovery of the Source of the Nile. By

J. H. SPEKE, Captain H.M. Indian Army. Octavo, price 21s. With a Map of
Eastern Equatorial Africa by CAPTAIN SPEKE; numerous Illustrations, chiefly
from Drawings by CAPTAIN GRANT; and Portraits, engraved on Steel, of CAPTAINS
SPEKE and GRANT.

"The volume which Captain Speke has presented to the world possesses more than a geographical interest. It is a monument of perseverance, courage, and temper displayed under
difficulties which have perhaps never been equalled."—*Times*.

"Captain Speke has not written a noble book so much as he has done a noble deed. The
volume which records his vast achievement is but the minor fact—the history of his discovery,
not the discovery itself: yet even as a literary performance it is worthy of very high praise. It
is wholly free from the traces of book manufacture. . . . It is, however, a great story that
is thus plainly told ; a story of which nearly all the interest lies in the strange facts related, and,
more than all, in the crowning fact that it frees us in a large degree from a geographical puzzle
which had excited the curiosity of mankind—of the most illustrious emperors and communities
—from very early times."—*Athenæum*.

Narrative of the Earl of Elgin's Mission to China and

Japan. By LAURENCE OLIPHANT, Private Secretary to Lord Elgin. Illustrated
with numerous Engravings in Chromo-Lithography, Maps, and Engravings on
Wood, from Original Drawings and Photographs. Second Edition. In Two
Volumes Octavo, 21s.

"The volumes in which Mr Oliphant has related these transactions will be read with the
strongest interest now, and deserve to retain a permanent place in the literary and historical
annals of our time."—*Edinburgh Review*.

Russian Shores of the Black Sea in the Autumn of 1852,

with a Voyage down the Volga and a Tour through the Country of the Don
Cossacks. By LAURENCE OLIPHANT, Esq. Octavo, with Map and other Illustrations. Fourth Edition, 14s.

Minnesota and the Far West. By Laurence Oliphant.

Octavo, Illustrated with Engravings, 12s. 6d.

"It affords us increased knowledge of the extraordinary resources which await the emigrant
at the head of the Great American Waters, and is a lively forecast of the prosperity of the States
just emerging into existence in the Heart of the Wilderness. Mr Oliphant has foreseen great
future events with a clear eye."—*The Times*.

The Transcaucasian Campaign of the Turkish Army under

Omer Pasha : A Personal Narrative. By LAURENCE OLIPHANT, Esq. With Map
and Illustrations. Post Octavo, 10s. 6d.

Egypt, the Soudan, and Central Africa : With Explorations

from Khartoum on the White Nile to the Regions of the Equator. By JOHN
PETHERICK, F.R.G.S., Her Britannic Majesty's Consul for the Soudan. In Octavo,
with a Map, 16s.

Three Months in the Southern States. April—June 1863.

By LIEUT.-COL. FREMANTLE. With Portraits of PRESIDENT DAVIS, GENERALS
POLK, LEE, LONGSTREET, BEAUREGARD, AND JOHNSTON. Crown Octavo, 7s. 6d.

"The whole of the book is as well worth reading as that published extract. It conveys a very
fair idea of what manner of men they are who are now fighting in the South for their independence ; and being written in a very unpretending style, it is both an agreeable and valuable
glimpse of the interior of the Confederacy."—*Spectator*.

The Punjab and Delhi in 1857 : Being a Narrative of

the Measures by which the Punjab was saved and Delhi recovered during the Indian Mutiny. By the Rev. J. CAVE-BROWNE, Chaplain of the Punjab Movable Column. With Plans of the Chief Stations and of the different Engagements, and Portraits of Sir J. Lawrence, Bart., Sir H. Edwardes, Sir R. Montgomery, and Brig. Gen. J. Nicholson. Two Volumes, Post Octavo, 21s.

" To those who wish to possess a condensed narrative of the siege of Delhi, but especially of the heroic doings of the handful of Englishmen scattered throughout the Punjab, these volumes recommend themselves by their scrupulous accuracy, while to the future historian of the India of 1857 they will prove invaluable."—*Allen's Indian Mail.*

" This is a work which will well repay the trouble of perusal. Written by one who was himself present at many of the scenes he narrates, and who has had free access to the papers of Sir J. Lawrence, Sir R. Montgomery, and Sir H. Edwardes, it comes with all the weight of official authority, and all the vividness of personal narrative."—*Press.*

The Campaign of Garibaldi in the Two Sicilies : A Per-

sonal Narrative. By CHARLES STUART FORBES, Commander, R.N. Post Octavo, with Portraits, 12s.

"A volume which contains the best sketch hitherto published of the campaign which put an end to Bourbon rule in the Two Sicilies. It is accompanied with plans of the chief battles ; and its honest unexaggerated record contrasts very favourably with the strained and showy account of the Garibaldians just published by M. Dumas."—*Examiner.*

Men and Manners in America. By Capt. Thos. Hamilton,

With Portrait of the Author. Foolscap, 7s. 6d.

Notes on North America : Agricultural, Economical, and

Social. By Professor J. F. W. JOHNSTON. Two Volumes, Post Octavo, 21s.

"Professor Johnston's admirable Notes. . . . The very best manual for intelligent emigrants, whilst to the British agriculturist and general reader it conveys a most complete conception of the condition of these prosperous region than all that has hitherto been written."—*Economist.*

Journal of a Tour in Greece and the Ionian Islands.

By WILLIAM MURE of Caldwell. Two Volumes, Post Octavo, Maps and Plates, 24s.

A Cruise in Japanese Waters. By Capt. Sherard Osborn, C.B.

Third Edition. Crown Octavo, 5s.

Life in the Far West. By G. F. Ruxton, Esq.

Second Edition. Foolscap Octavo, 4s.

" One of the most daring and resolute of travellers. . A volume fuller of excitement is seldom submitted to the public."—*Athenæum.*

Narrative of a Journey through Syria and Palestine.

By Lieut. VAN DE VELDE. Two Volumes Octavo, with Maps, &c., £1, 10s.

" He has contributed much to knowledge of the country, and the unction with which he speaks of the holy places which he has visited, will commend the book to the notice of all religious readers. His illustrations of Scripture are numerous and admirable."—*Daily News.*

Lightning Source UK Ltd.
Milton Keynes UK
UKOW04f1858050716

277774UK00017B/434/P